EFFECTIVE

LABOUR

RELATIONS

Effective Management
Series Editor: Alan H. Anderson

Effective Personnel Management
Alan H. Anderson

Effective Business Policy
Alan H. Anderson and Dennis Barker

Effective General Management
Alan H. Anderson

Effective Organizational Behaviour
Alan H. Anderson and Anna Kyprianou

Effective Labour Relations
Alan H. Anderson

Effective Marketing
Alan H. Anderson and Thelma Dobson

Effective International Marketing
Alan H. Anderson, Thelma Dobson and James Patterson

Effective Marketing Communications
Alan H. Anderson and David Kleiner

Effective Entrepreneurship
Alan H. Anderson and Peter Woodcock

Effective Enterprise Management
Alan H. Anderson and Dennis Barker

Effective Accounting Management
Alan H. Anderson and Eileen Nix

Effective Financial Management
Alan H. Anderson and Richard Ciechan

EFFECTIVE LABOUR RELATIONS

a skills and activity-based approach

ALAN H. ANDERSON

First published 1994

Blackwell Publishers, the publishing imprint of
Basil Blackwell Ltd.
108 Cowley Road
Oxford OX4 1JF
UK

Basil Blackwell Inc.
238 Main Street
Cambridge, Massachusetts 02142
USA

British Library Cataloguing in Publication Data

A CIP catalogue record for this book is available from the British Library.

Library of Congress Cataloging-in-Publication Data

Anderson, Alan H., 1950–
    Effective labour relations: a skills and activity-based approach/ Alan H. Anderson.
       p. cm.– (Effective management)
    Includes bibliographical references and index.
    ISBN 0-631-19122-4 (pbk.: acid-free paper)
       1. Industrial relations. I. Title. II. Series: Effective management (Oxford, England)
    HD6971. A65 1994
    658.3'15–dc20

                        94–13284
                           CIP

Designed and typeset by VAP Group Ltd., Kidlington, Oxfordshire

Printed in Great Britain by TJ Press Ltd., Padstow, Cornwall

This book is printed on acid-free paper

I would like to dedicate this book to my wife Maureen, my son Ross and my daughter Kerry.

Thank you

Contents

Figures

Boxes

Activities

Introduction to the Series

The Concept

In this series 'effective' means getting results. By taking an action approach to management, or the stewardship of an organization, the whole series allows people to create and develop their skills of effectiveness. This interrelated series gives the underpinning knowledge base and the application of functional and generic skills of the effective manager who gets results.

Key qualities of the effective manager include:

- **functional expertise** in the various disciplines of management;
- an understanding of the **organizational context**;
- an appreciation of the **external environment**;
- **self-awareness** and the power of **self-development**.

These qualities must fuse in a climate of **enterprise**.

Management is results-oriented so action is at a premium. The basis of this activity is **skills** underpinned by our qualities. In turn these skills can be based on a discipline or a function, and be universal or generic.

The Approach of the Series

These key qualities of effective management are the core of the current twelve books of the series. The areas covered by the series at present are:

People	*Effective Personnel Management*
	Effective Labour Relations
	Effective Organizational Behaviour
Finance	*Effective Financial Management*
	Effective Accounting Management
Marketing and sales	*Effective Marketing*
	Effective International Marketing
	Effective Marketing Communications
Operations/Enterprise	*Effective Enterprise Management*
	Effective Entrepreneurship
Policy/General	*Effective Business Policy*
	Effective General Management

The key attributes of the effective manager are all dealt with in the series, and we will pinpoint where they are emphasized:

- *Functional expertise.* The four main disciplines of management – finance, marketing, operations and personnel management – make up nine books. These meet the needs of specialist disciplines and allow a wider appreciation of other functions.
- *Organizational context.* All the 'people' books – the specialist one on *Effective Organizational Behaviour,* and also *Effective Personnel Management* and *Effective Labour Relations* – cover this area. The resourcing/control issues are met in the 'finance' texts, *Effective Financial Management* and *Effective Accounting Management.* Every case activity is given some organizational context.
- *External environment.* One book, *Effective Business Policy,* is dedicated to this subject. Environmental contexts apply in every book of the series: especially in *Effective Entrepreneurship, Effective General Management,* and in all of the 'marketing' texts – *Effective Marketing, Effective International Marketing* and *Effective Marketing Communications.*
- *Self-awareness/self-development.* To a great extent management development is manager development, so we have one generic skill (see later) devoted to this topic running through each book. The subject is examined in detail in *Effective General Management.*
- *Enterprise.* The *Effective Entrepreneurship* text is allied to *Effective Enterprise Management* to give insights into this whole area through all the developing phases of the firm. The marketing and policy books also revolve around this theme.

Skills

The functional skills are inherent within the discipline-based texts. In addition, running through the series are the following generic skills:
- self-development
- teamwork
- communications
- numeracy/IT
- decisions

These generic skills are universal managerial skills which occur to some degree in every manager's job.

Format/Structure of Each Book

Each book is subdivided into six units. These are self-contained, in order to facilitate learning, but interrelated, in order to give an effective holistic view. Each book also has an introduction with an outline of the book's particular theme.

Each unit has *learning objectives* with an overview/summary of the unit.

Boxes appear in every unit of every book. They allow a different perspective from the main narrative and analysis. Research points, examples, controversy and theory are all expanded upon in these boxes. They are numbered by unit in each book, e.g. 'Box PM1.1' for the first box in Unit One of *Effective Personnel Management*.

Activities, numbered in the same way, permeate the series. These action-oriented forms of learning cover cases, questionnaires, survey results, financial data, market research information, etc. The skills which can be assessed in each one are noted in the code at the top right of the activity by having the square next to them ticked. That is, if we are assuming numeracy then the square beside Numeracy would be ticked (✓), and so on. The weighting given to these skills will depend on the activity, the tutors'/learners' needs, and the overall weighting of the skills as noted in the appendix on 'Generic Skills', with problem solving dominating in most cases.

Common cases run through the series. Functional approaches are added to these core cases to show the same organization from different perspectives. This simulates the complexity of reality.

Workbook

The activities can be written up in the *workbook* which accompanies each book in the series.

Handbook

For each book in the series, there is a *handbook*. This is not quite the 'answers' to the activities, but it does contain some indicative ideas for them (coded accordingly), which will help to stimulate discussion and thought.

Test bank

We are developing a bank of tests in question-and-answer format to accompany the series. This will be geared to the knowledge inputs of the books.

The Audience

The series is for all those who wish to be effective managers. As such, it is a series for management development on an international scale, and embraces both management education and management training. In management education, the emphasis still tends to be on cognitive or knowledge inputs; in management training, it still tends to be on skills and techniques. We need both theory and practice, with the facility to try out these functions and skills through a range of scenarios in a 'safe' learning environment. This series is unique in encompassing these perspectives and bridging the gulf between the academic and vocational sides of business management.

Academically the series is pitched at the DMS/DBA types of qualification, which often lead on to an MA/MBA after the second year. Undergraduates following business degrees or management studies will benefit from the series in their final years. Distance learners will also find the series useful, as will those studying managerial subjects for professional examinations. The competency approach and the movement towards Accredited Prior Learning and National Vocational Qualifications are underpinned by the knowledge inputs, while the activities will provide useful simulations for these approaches to management learning.

This developmental series gives an opportunity for self-improvement. Individuals may wish to enhance their managerial potential by developing themselves without institutional backing by working through the whole series. It can also be used to underpin corporate training programmes, and acts as a useful design vehicle for specialist inputs from organizations. We are happy to pursue these various options with institutions or corporations.

The approach throughout the series combines skills, knowledge and application to create and develop the effective manager. Any comments or thoughts from participants in this interactive process will be welcomed.

Alan H. Anderson
Melbourn, Cambridge

The Series: Learning, Activities, Skills and Compatibility

The emphasis on skills and activities as vehicles of learning makes this series unique. Behavioural change, or learning, is developed through a two-pronged approach.

First, there is the **knowledge-based (cognitive)** approach to learning. This is found in the main text and in the boxes. These cognitive inputs form the traditional method of learning based on the principle of receiving and understanding information. In this series, there are four main knowledge inputs covering the four main managerial functions: marketing/sales, operations/enterprise, people, and accounting/finance. In addition, these disciplines are augmented by a strategic overview covering policy making and general management. An example of this first approach may be illustrative. In the case of marketing, the learner is confronted with a model of the internal and external environments. Thereafter the learner must digest, reflect, and understand the importance of this model to the whole of the subject.

Second, there is the **activity-based** approach to learning, which emphasizes the application of knowledge and skill through techniques. This approach is vital in developing effectiveness. It is seen from two levels of learning:

1 The use and application of *specific skills*. This is the utilization of your cognitive knowledge in a practical manner. These skills emanate from the cognitive aspect of learning, so they are functional skills, specific to the discipline.

   For example, the learner needs to understand the concept of job analysis before he or she tackles an activity that requires the drawing up of a specific job evaluation programme. So knowledge is not seen for its own sake, but is applied and becomes a specific functional skill.

2 The use and application of *generic skills*. These are universal skills which every manager uses irrespective of the wider external environment, the organization, the function and the job. This is seen, for example, in the ability to make clear decisions on the merits of a case. This skill of decision making is found in most of the activities.

There is a relationship between the specific functional skills and the generic skills. The specific functional skills stand alone, but the generic skills cut across them. See figure SK.1.

In this series we use activities to cover both the specific functional and the generic skills. There are five generic skills. We shall examine each of them in turn.

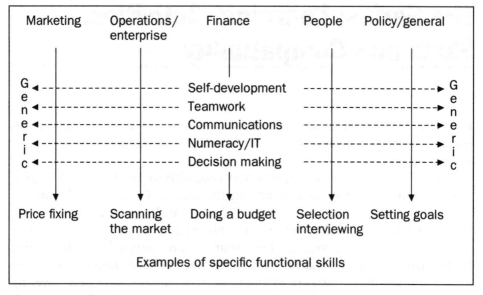

Figure SK.1 Series skills matrix: functional and generic skills.

Self-development

The learner must take responsibility for his or her learning as well as 'learning how to learn'. Time management, work scheduling and organizing the work are involved in the procedural sense. From a learning perspective, sound aspects of learning, from motivation to reward, need to be clarified and understood. The physical process of learning, including changing knowledge, skills and attitudes, may be involved. Individual goals and aspirations need to be recognized alongside the task goals. The ultimate aim of this skill is to facilitate learning transfer to new situations and environments.

Examples of this skill include:

- establishing and clarifying work goals;
- developing procedures and methods of work;
- building key learning characteristics into the process;
- using procedural learning;
- applying insightful learning;
- creating personal developmental plans;
- integrating these personal developmental plans with work goals.

Teamwork

Much of our working lives is concerned with groups. Effective teamwork is thus at a premium. This involves meeting both the task objectives and the socio-emotional processes within the group. This skill can be used for groups in a training or educational context. It can be a bridge between decision making and an awareness of self-development.

Examples of this skill include:

- clarifying the task need of the group;
- receiving, collating, ordering and rendering information;
- discussing, chairing and teamwork within the group;
- identifying the socio-emotional needs and group processes;
- linking these needs and processes to the task goals of the group.

Communications

This covers information and attitude processing within and between individuals. Oral and written communications are important because of the gamut of 'information and attitudinal' processing within the individual. At one level communication may mean writing a report, at another it could involve complex interpersonal relationships.

Examples of this skill include:

- understanding the media, aids, the message and methods;
- overcoming blockages;
- listening;
- presenting a case or commenting on the views of others;
- writing;
- designing material and systems for others to understand your communications.

Numeracy/IT

Managers need a core mastery of numbers and their application. This mastery is critical for planning, control, co-ordination, organization and, above all else, for decision making. Numeracy/IT are not seen as skills for their own sake. Here, they are regarded as the means to an end. These skills enable information and data to be utilized by the effective manager. In particular these skills are seen as an adjunct to decision making.

Examples of this skill include:

- gathering information;
- processing and testing information;

- using measures of accuracy, reliability, probability etc.;
- applying appropriate software packages;
- extrapolating information and trends for problem solving.

Decision making

Management is very much concerned with solving problems and making decisions. As group decisions are covered under teamwork, the emphasis in this decision-making skill is placed on the individual.

Decision making can involve a structured approach to problem solving with appropriate aims and methods. Apart from the 'scientific' approach, we can employ also an imaginative vision towards decision making. One is rational, the other is more like brainstorming.

Examples of this skill include:
- setting objectives and establishing criteria;
- seeking, gathering and processing information;
- deriving alternatives;
- using creative decision making;
- action planning and implementation.

This is *the* skill of management and is given primary importance in the generic skills within the activities as a reflection of everyday reality.

Before we go about learning how to develop into effective managers, it is important to understand the general principles of learning. Both the knowledge-based and the activity-based approaches are set within the environment of these principles. The series has been written to relate to Anderson's sound principles of learning which were developed in *Successful Training Practice*.

- *Motivation* – intrinsic motivation is stimulated by the range and depth of the subject matter and assisted by an action orientation.
- *Knowledge of results* – ongoing feedback is given through the handbook for each book in the series.
- *Scale learning* – each text is divided into six units, which facilitates part learning.
- *Self-pacing* – a map of the unit with objectives, content and an overview helps learners to pace their own progress.
- *Transfer* – realism is enhanced through lifelike simulations which assist learning transfer.
- *Discovery learning* – the series is geared to the learner using self-insight to stimulate learning.
- *Self-development* – self-improvement and an awareness of how we go about learning underpin the series.

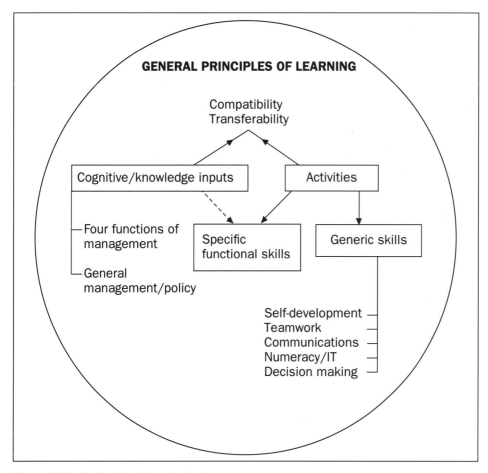

GENERAL PRINCIPLES OF LEARNING

Compatibility
Transferability

Cognitive/knowledge inputs

Activities

— Four functions of management

Specific functional skills

Generic skills

— General management/policy

Self-development
Teamwork
Communications
Numeracy/IT
Decision making

Figure SK.2 Series learning strategy.

- *Active learning* – every activity is based upon this critical component of successful learning.

From what has been said so far, the learning strategy of the series can be outlined in diagrammatic form. (See figure SK.2.)

In figure SK.2, 'compatibility and transferability' are prominent because the learning approach of the series is extremely compatible with the learning approaches of current initiatives in management development. This series is related to a range of learning classification being used in education and training. Consequently it meets the needs of other leading training systems and learning taxonomies. See figures SK.3–SK.6.

Functional knowledge and skills	An educational classification
People:	
Personnel management	—— People
Labour relations	
Organizational behaviour	
Marketing/sales:	
Marketing	—— Marketing
Marketing communications	
International marketing	
Operations/enterprise:	
Entrepreneurship	—— Operations/enterprise
Enterprise	
Finance:	
Accounting management	—— Finance
Finance	
Policy/management:	
Policy	—— Business environment/
General management	business administration

Generic skills

Self-development ———————— Managing and developing self

Teamwork ———————— Working with and relating to others

Communications ———————— Communications

———————— Applying design and creativity

Decisions ———————— Managing tasks and solving problems

Numeracy/IT ———————— Applying technology

———————— Applying numeracy

———————— direct relationship

- - - - - - - indirect relationship

Figure SK.3 Series knowledge and skills related to an educational classification.

Source: Adapted from Business Technician and Education Council, 'Common skills and experience of BTEC programmes'.

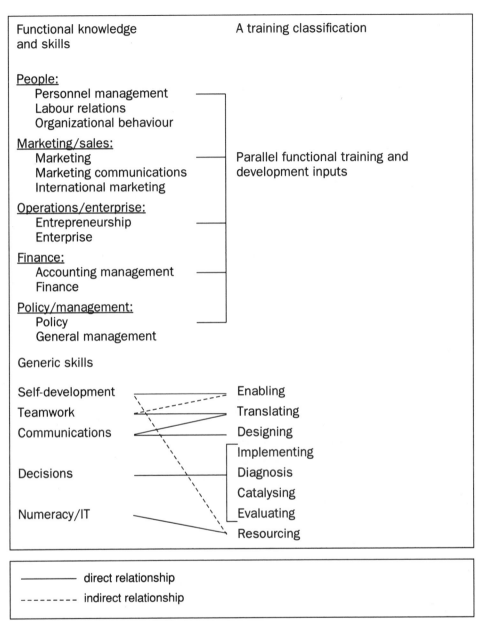

Figure SK.4 Series knowledge and skills related to a training classification.

Source: Adapted from J.A.G. Jones, 'Training intervention strategies' and experience of development programmes.

Functional knowledge and skills	MCI competency
People:	Managing people
Personnel management	
Labour relations	
Organizational behaviour	
Marketing/sales:	
Marketing	Managing operations and managing information (plus new texts pending)
Marketing communications	
International marketing	
Operations/enterprise:	
Entrepreneurship	
Enterprise	
Finance:	Managing finance
Accounting management	
Finance	
Policy/management:	Managing context
Policy	
General management	
Generic skills	
Self-development	Managing oneself
Teamwork	Managing others
Communications	Using intellect
Decisions	Planning
Numeracy/IT	

——————— direct relationship

- - - - - - - - indirect relationship

Figure SK.5 Series knowledge and skills related to Management Charter Initiative (MCI) competencies.

Source: Adapted from MCI diploma guidelines.

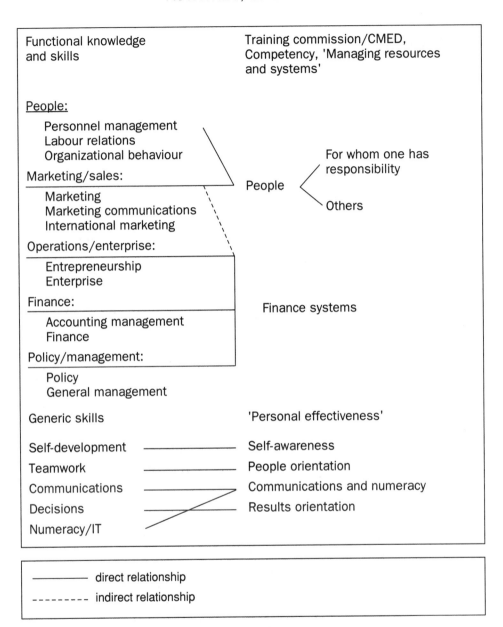

Figure SK.6 Series knowledge and skills related to Training Commission/Council for Management Education (CMED) competencies.

Source: Adapted from Training Commission/CMED, 'Classifying the components of management competencies'.

Preface

❝ We don't want more bread, we want the bakery. ❞

P. Dubois[1]

Outline Themes

Labour relations concern the 'frontier of control' between capital and labour and between management and trade unions. This control aspect gives a perspective to the objectives, methods and machinations of the two primary parties, employers/managers and employees/trade unions. It can also be applied to the State or third party in this relationship. We shall find a constant vying for position, and hence the 'frontier' idea between the prerogatives of management and labour is a useful way of looking at the subject.

Consequently, labour relations concern not only job and workplace regulation, but conflict with all its manifestations to gain some control over the job, terms and conditions, the nature of work itself and the decisions which affect the working lives of employees. Ultimately this can result in a questioning of 'who runs the bakery?' and 'who owns it?'

Labour relations must be one of the most complex and difficult areas in which a manager will find himself or herself. Unlike most managerial functions, not only does the effective manager take account of the internal dynamics of an organization, but the subject matter is often dictated by the external environmental context. In particular, conflict is never far from the surface and this level of conflict and how it is managed can make or break the organization. The role of the State is often writ large in the relationship as well, and again this can be difficult to 'manage'.

Labour relations demand an understanding of the dynamics of the wider society because work organization is merely a microcosm of that wider society. We need to build this understanding into our approach to the subject.

This vying for control between labour and management can be seen in the role of trade unions. Here we find a dual loyalty system in unionized organizations: the employee is part of the work organization but at the same time a member of another organization which may not (probably will not) have the same objectives and principles as that work organization. Non-labour managers can focus their attention on organizational objectives and/or personal aims. The labour specialist and manager of employees is unionized environments must do more: he or she must have a wider understanding of the following:

- this dual loyalty theme;
- the various participants within labour relations;
- the institutions and rules;
- the dynamics of conflict;
- power;
- conflict/power resolution processes;
- the impact of the external environment;
- key issues currently facing management;
- the nature of control and its limitations.

So to summarize the themes of this book:

- Control is critical to the whole approach.
- Job/work regulation is included in this approach but a 'rules orientation' is only part of the story.
- The subject can be quite mundane – discussions on subpara 2 of an agreement – to esoteric, such as ownership of the means of production and distribution.
- Conflict is an important aspect of the whole dynamic of labour relations.
- The subject matter can be difficult to 'manage'.
- A wider understanding of the nature of the external environment pressures is required by all who manage the subject.
- The discipline is very demanding and is a constant challenge to practitioners.
- Change is continual.

Learning Aims

- To provide an analytical framework for understanding the subject.
- To create a dynamic labour relations system.
- To develop key labour relations skills of problem solving.
- To understand the roles and objectives of the parties (actors) to this framework/system.
- To analyse the nature of conflict within labour relations.
- To apply mechanisms, institutions and skills of conflict resolution within labour relations.
- To introduce and apply fair and equitable policies and practices in labour relations.
- To consider current issues in labour relations.
- To develop a 'quality' approach to the subject.

Format and Content

We have covered the generic skills and the activity-based format, so we shall focus on the knowledge input. There is a main 'plot' which excludes the 'boxes'. The function of the boxes has been covered in the series introduction.

The series aims to be international in its approach. This is evident here but the UK with its first venture into industrialization (and possibly its current position of post-industrialization) is used as an illustrative example throughout. This is particularly so in Unit Two concerning trade unions. However, the transferability of Units One, Two, Three, Four and Five should be universal. Unit Six with its focus on current issues should be relevant to any developed state.

The actual framework of the book revolves around a systems approach to the subject which is seen as a replication of everyday reality. We develop this framework later in Unit One and again in Unit Four, so we shall give only the indicative content of the book at this stage without the underpinnings of the system.

The indicative content is as follows.

Unit topic	*Sub-themes*
1 Concept and context	Definitions of the subject are difficult because different philosophies and intellectual paradigms are used. We examine 'theories of' and frames of reference/philosophies of labour relations. A predictive model is applied. Power and its manifestations are seen as writ large. A working frame of reference is put forward.
2 Trade unions	A much maligned party, trade unions are critical to an understanding of labour relations from a manager's perspective. Their origins, aims, development, government and relative decline are all covered.
3 The State, management and the media	These three items are not placed together as some form of tripartite conspiracy but they are the main 'actors' which complete the picture before we look at the processes of conflict and rule making. Their respective roles, objectives and philosophies are all covered.
4 Conflict	Conflict is seen as very important to this subject, so a whole unit is devoted to this area. It covers the nature of, schools of

Unit topic	*Sub-themes*
	thought, models of, the consequences of, and focuses in on two types – strikes and disputes. A conflict approach is linked to our earlier frame of reference.
5 Rules and conflict resolution	Rule making is the traditional 'liberal' approach to the subject. It is important and must be seen in the context of conflict and not just for the sake of efficiency or whatever. We look at the institutionalizing of conflict. Collective bargaining in its various guises is covered. A 'bounded rationality' viewpoint of negotiations is then examined. Bargaining structures are looked at. Rule making is reiterated and procedures are applied.
6 Some current issues	We revert back to our 'frontier of control' here. Some key issues of the 1990s are examined:

- participation
- equality (sex)
- productivity/efficiency
- flexibility
- pay (performance-related pay)
- quality of labour relations

We use the term labour relations to signify that primary, secondary and tertiary sectors are included and it bypasses problems of post-industrial or industrialized societies. However, the terms labour relations and industrial relations are really synonymous but we shall use labour relations rather than industrial relations to cover more sectors of the economy.

An Outline of the Units

To conclude this introduction, the summary overleaf gives an outline of the six units of the book.

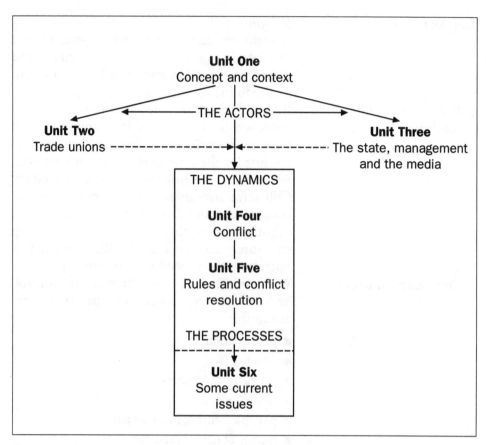

Figure 0.1 Outline of the units.

Unit One

Concept and Context

Learning Objectives

After completing this unit you should be able to:

- understand the concept of labour relations;
- relate theory to practice;
- note the importance of the subject;
- apply diverse perspectives;
- test a predictive approach to the subject;
- review the suggested approach;
- apply the generic skills.

Contents

Overview

The Subject – Towards a Definition

Towards a Theory?

The Importance of Labour Relations

Frames of Reference

A Predictive Model?

Labour Relations – A Working Framework

▶ The external environment

▶ The actors

▶ The focus

▶ The outcomes

▶ The relationship

▶ The concept of power

Unit One

❝ People have become more individual in their approach and often want to be treated as such. Collectivism is no longer flavour of the month and personal recognition is now important.❞

J. Foulds, Director of Employment Affairs, Chemical Industries Association[1]

Overview

We need a working definition of the subject that we feel represents reality. As such, it must take account of both rule making and rule breaking.

The examination of theory is not for its own sake. Labour relations is a political and yet a 'sensitive' area. To understand practice we need to examine the principles and underlying concepts which can be brought to the subject. Theory and practice are very much intertwined and the distinction is probably artificial anyhow.

In spite of the lack of academic chairs on the subject compared with other disciplines, labour relations is important in any concept of effective management. Of all the human/personnel aspects, it can break the organization or, if effectively managed, enhance the quality of both the organization and its employees.

The ideological issues raised by the theoretical underpinnings of the subject continue through the debate on the philosophy or frame of reference used by practitioners and commentators.

We then turn to the issue of prediction. Is it possible to have a working model which allows us to predict possible events in labour relations? The unit is concluded by a description of propositions which can give us a working framework for the study of the subject. This is developed in subsequent units – particularly Unit Four.

Figure 1.1 shows the unit in diagrammatic form.

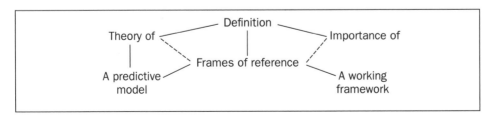

Figure 1.1 Overview of the unit.

The Subject – Towards a Definition

Not only do labour relations cause disagreements amongst practitioners, but the diversity of ideas, concepts and approaches causes an almost equal conflict between students of the subject. Collective bargaining was once described as the 'institutionalisation of conflict'.[2] I feel that this definition goes to the core of labour relations as a whole. We have potentially a sea of conflict between the main parties with rules and regulations, laws, customs, practices and agreements being drawn up to prevent total anarchy at the place of work. Goodrich[3] described the area as the 'frontier of control' between the managed and managers, a fluid area, a moving mass, depending upon the impact of the power equation between the primary parties (employer/employees and their agents) both vying for control over working conditions, if not over work itself.

The subject is an ideological quagmire and definitions and frames of references all reflect the approach of the writer. Here a balance between conflict and rules is made. The subject is not all about rule making as many would have us believe, for this misses the point that the rules exist because of the conflict and the potential for untold anarchy. Equally, conflict is not necessarily endemic at all times for there are common interests between labour and management and the survival of the enterprise itself must give some shared vision.

The subject can be seen at various levels as well – department, plant, division, company, national and international. It is very much part of a given society and is a microcosm of society with its changing influences at any time. Finally, the subject is not a 'pure' discipline in the sense of, say, physics, as it draws upon a range of disciplines from economics to politics and from organizational behaviour to history. This lack of 'purity' may mean that the various disciplines, far from making it a multidisciplinary subject, actually approach the matter from too narrow a perspective.

Towards a Theory?

It may be an ideological mess but we should still look for the theoretical underpinnings of the subject before we start. Any study of the theoretical underpinnings should help us to:

- clarify our thinking;
- refine our analysis;
- improve our understanding of the roles and views of others;
- take a broader perspective on the dynamics of a given situation;
- expose hypocrisy and ideological slants which may prevail amongst governments and the media as well as amongst writers on the subject.

Somers[4] argues the case for the importance of theory to labour relations: theory impacts on the definition, the models used and ultimately the analysis itself. From a different political slant, Allen[5] put the issue succinctly: 'the theory simplifies the situations, signifies what should be data, and what should not be and how the data should be arranged. It does this through its own structure, through the analytical tools, the concepts and definitions it employs.'

Dunlop[6] is seen as the father of the discipline of industrial or labour relations. In this book the term labour relations is used to cover both a manufacturing and a service orientation whereas the expression industrial relations is linked more to a manufacturing-only economic base. The work of Dunlop was particularly innovative in giving us a wide frame of reference, while Barbash gives a more individualistic perspective of the 'actors'.[7] Please refer to Boxes LR1.1 and LR1.2.

BOX LR1.1

A theory of industrial relations

Theory is important as 'practice' does not exist as a self-standing entity: everyday usage has some theoretical (if unstated) concepts and assumptions. Theory may also allow us to predict or forecast everyday events. So theory and practice are very much interrelated.

J.T. Dunlop,[1] the 'father' of industrial relations, aimed and aims to present a general theory of industrial relations. Writing way back in the 1950s, he really put industrial relations on the map as a coherent discipline. His theory seeks to interpret and to gain a wider understanding of a range of industrial relations facts and practices. It did not set out to be a predictive approach *per se* – more a tool and framework for understanding the complexity of the subject.

The framework can be applied to three levels:

- to an enterprise, industry or segment of a country and to like-minded comparisons between these levels;
- to industrial relations in a country as a whole and to comparisons between countries;
- to understanding industrial relations in the course of economic development.

The concepts of work relationships are best understood, according to Dunlop, by analysing certain common properties as well as noting the wider contexts of the subject. The common properties are the actors:

- workers and their organizations;
- managers and their organizations;
- government and its agencies.

To Dunlop another common theme is that of rule making. A 'web of rules', complex arrangements to govern the workplace and the work community, is the functional core of labour relations. The rules are there to

■ define the status of the actors, e.g. union recognition;
■ govern conduct of the actors in both procedural and substantive terms.

So the actors combine to form these rules and this system is bound together by some ideology. The functional explanation of this ideology involves a shared understanding between the parties.

This system is not static as the actors must come to terms with three interrelated contexts:

■ technology;
■ market and budgetary issues;
■ power relations in the wider community and the derived statuses of the actors.

The main task of labour relations, according to this American professor, is to explain the 'why' and the 'how' of rules and their response to changes in the industrial relations system.

Source:
1   Adapted from Dunlop, *Industrial Relations Systems*

BOX LR1.2

Understanding labour relations

Barbash[1] aims to get near the 'spirit' of labour relations. His fundamental premise is that to come to terms with the subject the reader must first understand the topic or issue, 'in the participants' own terms'.

The detached academic or student of the subject should in theory be able to 'cross sides'. This ability to see all sides allows us to 'hover' above the subject.

It is difficult to get into someone's shoes at any time and it may be more difficult for adversaries to do that, particularly in times of strained relationships.

Yet perhaps if the actors can think themselves into the position of others it may broaden understanding. If this occurs perhaps the scope for conflict resolution would be enhanced.

Barbash does focus on the activities of the actors perhaps at the expense of the wider dynamics of the labour relations system, but seeing things through the eyes of the other protagonists may be a useful way forward for the actors involved in labour relations. It may also give more objectivity to the commentators on the subject.

Source:
1   Barbash, *The Elements of Industrial Relations*

The Importance of Labour Relations

Before we develop the various approaches to the subject and the specific frame of reference being used here, we need some discussion on the subject matter and its relevance to the 'actors' in any system. It has significance to individual employees, trade unions, the State and its agencies and management. Given the rationale behind this series, we shall emphasize the managerial aspect without being managerialist.

In a sense the importance of labour relations is often seen in negative terms. 'Good' labour relations have been seen as conflict free or a situation in which strikes and other overt forms of conflict are fewer than those of our competitors at home or abroad or fewer than last year's figures. But good labour relations are about more than this: for the employee they are about good earning capacity for individuals; a voice for employees in the 'government' of the enterprise; a decent working environment; a safe place of work; sound job design and a stake in the firm. For the employer, they are about resource mobilization; getting the best out of people; higher productivity; efficiency; getting a competitive edge and effective management. For the State, with its economic role of housekeeping, sound labour relations, fair legislation on employment, the ability to solve disputes in an even handed fashion, a 'value neutrality' in dealing with the interested parties and a tolerance of trade unions not only help towards better economic management but also go to the heart of the democratic political system. Under Nazism and Stalinism, the unions were seen to become whipping boys – before they vanished underground (literally in many cases). A tolerant, pluralistic State must take account of many interests and not act in a selfish group capacity for either big business or organized labour. However, we shall focus on the importance to management. One way is to accept this relevance and look at the basic aspects of what management needs to know about the subject matter to perform more effectively. Before we do this, Activity LR1.1 may be illustrative.

ACTIVITY LR1.1

DOMSEC AND THE HARSH WORDS

Activity code

- ☑ Self-development
- ☑ Teamwork
- ☑ Communications
- ☐ Numeracy/IT
- ☑ Decisions

Ted 'Plodder' Harvey was a shrewd businessman who co-ordinated the work of Domsec, a company in the safety and security sector covering both the domestic and industrial sectors.

In a sense, there were really two operating units: the security firm with its emphasis on the domestic market and the safety firm with its orientation on the business-to-business or industrial market. The domestic security market to date could be termed 'low tech'. There were no closed circuit TVs or access controls, no video entry systems or security grilles or doors. They would put in window bars if the customer demanded it but 'Boots' was against the concept on safety grounds. So it was not a state-of-the-art electronic detection. Nor did it involve highly trained 'officers' or dog handlers to protect property or people. It was on a basic level: door spy-holes, intercoms, bolts, snibs and digital locking systems whereby the homeowners could punch in their number. But even this digitial system has been quite a recent innovation. The industrial security market had demanded greater technical specialization and manpower, so the company to date had majored on the new building, refurbishment and security-conscious owner market segments.

The health and safety part of the business was co-ordinated by 'Boots'. The firm provided 'any safety piece of equipment', or so it boasted. It manufactured nothing as a deliberate policy but it provided safety shoes, goggles, gloves, breathing apparatus, protective uniforms and suits, and so on. In addition, the firm provided guidance on safety to the industrial users and con-sultancy-cum-training skills for representatives. It also crossed over to the other 'division' in giving advice on such things as fire alarms to domestic users but this advice had largely become routine apart from at the initial sales pitch for large construction contracts.

The company was unionized. The manual workers belonged almost as a group to union A. The supervisors belonged in the main to union B.

The relationship between the owners and the unions was quite reasonable but there had been friction and tension between the two unions. Sloppy workmanship particularly over electrical installation had been a running battle between the supervisors and the manual workers. The top managers/owners did not condone sloppy work but they were keen to keep the men working to tight time schedules and asked the supervisors to give electrical work its final check. This caused some misgivings amongst the supervisors.

An apprentice, Garry Marshall, who was quite new to the job and to London sparked a major row. He was installing an electrical security device and he mixed up the colour codes. His supervisor, Harry Davidson, a short-tempered fellow, 'caught' him. Davidson told Marshall that he was 'a contradiction in terms' . . . 'we are supposed to be security/safety advisors not demolition experts!' The debate was slightly heated and Marshall claimed that Davidson shouted and swore at him.

Later that day, Marshall spoke to the shop steward and told him his account of the story. The shop steward made an appointment to see 'Boots', the other owner. He was nicknamed as such for his lack of sensitivity.

'Boots' said that he was sure that the supervisor was just being his normal self and that Marshall should not be so sensitive. When asked he said that he would not transfer the supervisor to another post. The relationship between the steward and the supervisor was not too good anyway and he resented the comments of 'Boots'. 'Look, he is a young trainee and he will not put up with verbal battering from an old waster like Davidson.' He left the room.

Next day, he called a meeting of the men at the depot. An all-out strike would not be on but an overtime ban would show the depth of their feelings. The ban would coincide with the lucrative commercial contract job just received by Domsec and its time penalties for missing deadlines would be a small revenge for the attitude of management. Overtime would have to be 'switched on' at the weekend at more lucrative rates when the 'dispute' stopped. Not that it was a dispute – but the men would not work additional non-contracted hours if asked.

The overtime ban began to bite. Harvey, the other owner, felt that if the supervisor could apologize it would all blow over. 'Boots' thought otherwise but the job demands were such that the operation had to go on.

The supervisor was asked to apologize. He declined and said that it was a mere 'fabrication' anyway as he had not sworn at the apprentice. He went to his union. He claimed victimization. The full-time officer appeared on the scene some three days later saying that his members should not be victimized for trying to manage, and management should back up its junior/front-line managers. The overtime ban was solid now amongst the manual workers.

Task

'Boots' and Harvey need a way out of this labour relations dilemma. Recommend a plan of action for them to follow.

Frames of Reference

Before we develop the frame of reference being used here, we must scan the various, often contradictory, approaches used by academics and by practitioners in labour relations.

The first approach is **pragmatism**. This may be particularly evident amongst managers rather than academics. The basis here is that the organization exists for profit/service maximization and labour plays a key role in meeting these objectives. So whatever it takes to keep labour 'in line' with the corporate objectives can be rationalized on this viewpoint. Of course this may lead to swings in policy and to changes of style, from co-habiting with unions and compromise policies to banning unions and adopting a paternalistic or autocratic approach to labour. This pragmatism is based on the fundamental *power relationship* between labour and management and compromise may occur more often when labour is stronger, as in times of full employment say. When times favour management, pragmatism may reflect the underlying philosophy of **unitarism**.

Fox[8] delineates the views and approaches of the actors (and their observers) in an industrial relations situation. The unitarist perspective sees the organization as an integrated body with a single authority system (management). Common goals, aspirations and interests are assumed to prevail across the organization.

The organization is a harmonious whole. Conflict may exist but it is blamed on misunderstandings, ignorance and wilfulness. Whatever its cause, conflict is an aberration, a spot on the rosy complexion of the institution which will soon disappear through good management.

This approach is really a managerial manifesto. It reinforces the role of the key (sole?) decision maker and it legitimizes the authority of management's 'right to manage'. Leadership and good communications, reminiscent of the **human relations** approach,[9] should prevail in organizations with this frame of reference. An ambivalent, if not overtly hostile, view is taken of trade unions. They are regarded with a sense of distaste if they exist, and most unitarists would prefer not to recognize them in the first place as trade unions are perceived as divisive, conflict-oriented and against managerial prerogatives. Unions are often seen as something outside of the organization, interlopers who can disrupt the idyllic family atmosphere of the firm. Loyalty is king and loyal servants should not be in someone else's camp. When allied to pragmatism, the unitarists may tolerate if not suffer existing trade unions, but their natural inclination would be to have no unions or legal restraints on collective bargaining and union organization, or to pursue a policy of union derecognition.

The managerial outcry at participative experiments and proposed legislation in the UK in the 1970s, for example, illustrates the depth of feeling and support amongst managers for such a unitarist perspective.[10]

The unitarist vision is embedded in many family firms, American multinationals and Japanese organizations. It is often accompanied by progressive (high) payment and incentive schemes, employee briefing groups and quality circles allied to trappings of paternalism.[11] The mood can swing, though, like the drunken father who returns from a drinking spree and abandons his paternalistic attitude for a more authoritarian or pugnacious stance. The unitarist perspective may be a 'natural' position for most managers but anecdotal experience of some twenty-five years shows that some managers, senior ones in particular, do not necessarily believe in this philosophy at all; nevertheless it is a useful device for managerial control. Few writers or academics on the subject go down this unitary route but there is a link to **functionalism**. (See Box LR1.3.)

BOX LR1.3

Functionalism

The Functionalists see society as an interrelated system. One part, a sub-society, must be seen in the context of the whole. Functionalists look to the 'how' of structures and their impact on the maintenance and survival of any social system. They look to the goals or aims and focus their attention on how that given society or subsociety goes about meeting those aims.

In the context of labour relations, the system dominates and the aim tends to be harmonious relations, so rules are writ large.

The basis of the system of labour relations concerns some 'value consensus' or shared agreement on the values within that system. The emphasis is very much an institutional orientation and an examination of how the consensus is maintained. Control is exercised through 'rules'. In turn the rules of the system help make for 'value consensus'.

It is very easy to criticize this school of thought as it fails to take account of the dynamics of conflict and values may not be shared – quite the reverse in fact. Its attempt to understand by asking 'how' needs to take account of the actors as well as their interaction with the institutions. Yet the systems idea and the objectives/functions perspective does contribute to our understanding of labour relations. However, the 'why' of labour relations seems to be unanswered.

Most academics take a **pluralistic** view, a **Marxist** perspective or adhere to a **social action** approach. Increasingly there seems to be a move towards a **labour process** perspective amongst academics. Some practitioners from the trade union perspective would share some of these frames of reference, while more 'liberal' managers may go down a pluralistic route.

Unlike the unitarists, the pluralists can come to terms with conflict and handle it far better. To them society and the work organization is made up of interest groups. One interest group may not coincide with another. Objectives differ and how we achieve these goals will differ as well. However, it is not a nihilistic vision for there is room for compromise here. Indeed, the pluralists are in the market of 'continuous compromise' between the various interest groups in society and the firm. 'Tensions' must be managed in this 'competitive' environment and managers sensitive to events and aware of the power dynamics need to be able negotiators.[12]

Trade unions are seen as less hostile than in the unitarist view. Perhaps being seen as more legitimate to some pluralists and being accepted as an interest group to others, trade unions are seen to exist to represent the employees. Management has a role as well, but authority is not decreed from above as in some sort of absolute monarchy; it has to be earned and worked on by management itself. The perspective lends itself more to management by consent. This is not some soft liberal or libertarian view though, for cynics would argue that it is management tinkering with the system to allow the continuation of that system. Undoubtedly there is a conservative thread here for the status quo does not fundamentally alter: some 'equilibrium' is perceived as being the aim of the ongoing compromises. By letting the steam out of the kettle, it does not challenge why the kettle is being boiled in the first place.

Please refer now to Box LR1.4 on the Marxist vision which does challenge the status quo.

BOX LR1.4

Industrial relations – a Marxist vision

Hyman[1] seeks to sketch an alternative approach to labour relations. The subject is rooted in a 'totality of the social relations of production'.

The rule-bound definition of industrial relations is too restrictive. Stability and maintenance are not an accurate reflection of everyday labour management reality. Equally, the wider society and its environment provide a dynamo of industrial relations and the rule-oriented approach takes little of this perspective. In many ways the issue is about **control**, a shifting relationship, a 'moving frontier' between management and managed. Conflict is seen as endemic to this vision, for such conflict to a Marxist is inevitable in capitalism and labour relations provides the coalface of that economy.

Unlike Taylor and his corporatism the unions to Hyman should be challenging the existing economic order. He points out the irony: when the aims and actions of unions do not challenge the 'natural' order they are more likely to be accorded legitimacy by management and government. So by becoming 'accepted' (more difficult in the 1990s) the unions are in essence compromising and repressing their 'natural' aims and objectives. The price of recognition is therefore a compromise on aims and objectives.

Increasingly he sees capitalism drifting from crisis to crisis and this growing instability manifesting itself in changing power relationships, constraints on worker incomes, intensive work pressures and more managerial controls over the workforce.

The State is not value neutral either for it is an extension of the interests of capital and it increasingly becomes a mediator (not in the 1980s/1990s) as conflict becomes more prevalent between managers and managed.

His analysis of the dynamics of a wider definition of industrial relations looks quite sound but he tends to idealize over union aims and objectives and he does not fully come to terms with the conservative nature of 'the revolutionary vanguard'. His recognition/legitimacy/compromise view is relevant of course. Managers seem to be part of a master plot aided by a hostile government. Although written in the mid-1970s it could well be an historical overview of labour relations of the 1980s and early 1990s. The role of the State looks logical enough but it has not really developed this mediation role since the 1970s. The upward role of control over one's working life and the downward pressures from managerial control are the essence of the labour process theories which have dominated much of the literature.

Source:
1 Adapted from Hyman, *Industrial Relations: a Marxist introduction*

The status quo is not really challenged by the pluralist frame of reference and collective bargaining becomes important as the mechanism of compromise and adjustment. Inherent in the pluralist view is that the interest groups have some equal allocation of power (in crude terms only), for if power were all on one side real compromise would not occur and the 'equilibrium' would be always weighted on one side.

The **Marxists** or **radicals** would reject such an 'equilibrium': the workplace is the coalface of the prevalent economic order and reflects the power dynamics of the wider society. We can appreciate the gross inequalities of resources and power, we can distinguish the principal disparity between owning capital and supplying labour if we can take an historical perspective, seeing societal change as the dynamic of changing economic phases. The radicals are strong on analysis but weaker on prognosis.

Conflict is the dynamic of change. Class conflict is seen as an inevitable outcome of the disparities in a given economic system. It assumes a class consciousness of course.

Conflict is more than just a feature of organizational life – it is inherent in every society from feudal to capitalist. (We could also add that it was inherent in the then Eastern bloc and the dissolving Soviet Union.)

Trade unions take on a differing perspective if we follow the radical perspective. To some the unions become part of the working-class consciousness, some mechanism of class solidarity. To others in this camp, they prop up the very system by their compromises and negotiation. These pundits would rather see some revolutionary change.

A socio-economic flux has occurred through the following: enhanced social mobility, a more 'open' education system, political parties 'representing' groups, some diffusion of power, an increase in property (home) ownership allied to a consumption mentality. Skilled and unskilled workers (often unemployed) repeatedly vote for 'parties of capitalism'. Taken together these socio-economic factors dent the revolutionary perspective. We cannot put all this down to 'false consciousness'. Equally conflict may have a multitude of causes at the workplace. Yet the understanding of the dynamics of historical societies in a longer time-frame looks more realistic in this school of thought. Marsden[13] argues, though, that Marxist industrial relations are a contradiction in terms (see Boxes LR1.5 and LR1.4[14] for contrasting perspectives).

BOX LR1.5

Industrial relations – methods of study and approaches

Marsden[1] looks at the nature of industrial relations and argues that 'it is trapped theoretically within the confines of empiricism'. Not only is the methodology flawed but Marsden sees the subject as that of 'objectified ideologies or rules'.

Empiricism is experiment based, a process that rests on trials and tests, a method which rejects all *a priori* knowledge and rests on experience and induction. Marsden is right to point out the dilemma between the subjectivity of the researcher and the so-called objectivity of the subject matter. Further, the ideological orientation of the researcher pre-selects information and constructs a world view of events before studying them. As Marsden says:

the object which empiricists claim to discover among the facts is really a knowledge of their theoretical object so they do have a thought-object but they do so unconsciously, without being aware of it. It is an object constituted prior to theory by ideology.

So the *'a priori* knowledge' is not rejected at all; quite the reverse, as it lays the foundation of the visualization of the whole subject before the study takes place.

How do we get over this? With great difficulty, for any study of the social sciences starts with some ideological viewpoint of the research,[2] particularly in the area of labour relations, which is politically emotive. We need to be aware of our views and bias before we embark on serious study. I am reminded of a former professor of mine who always started off his lecture on Soviet history with a statement of his own prejudices and views. Awareness of self and bias will not remove Marsden's argument but it will dilute it.

Next Marsden turns to the subject matter of labour relations. He traces the history from the Marxist dialect to the neoclassical economists. The division between these two camps is discussed and the shortcomings of marginalist economists are noted, particularly with respect to the labour supply. The subject of industrial relations was thus an extension of labour economics to Marsden for labour economics had failed to explain the 'supply and sale of labour power'. The systems theory identified with Dunlop[3] was born.

Yet Marsden argues that the Dunlopian system is a 'vulgarized version of Parson's social system', an ideal type and not a theory *per se*. Any ideal type is a social construct, an aid to researchers and a frame of reference to come to terms with the subject. So we have a model, not a theory, of industrial relations if we use the systems approach.

Next the Marxists are put under the microscope. The concept of industrial relations is alien to the real Marxists according to Marsden as the conflict is between capital and labour – a revolutionary dynamic – while industrial relations smack of class compromise and a conservative ideology. As Marsden puts it:

> The position of industrial relations is analogous to that of nineteenth century classical political economy in that both assume as facts what has to be explained. And just as Marx reproached Proudhon with having criticized political economy from the standpoint of political economy so we should be wary of criticizing industrial relations from the standpoint of industrial relations. To share its standpoint is to think in its terms and to be unable to work out the means of its supersession. There is no such thing as a 'Marxist introduction to industrial relations', the project is a contradiction in terms. However there is a Marxist theory of relations of production and it is precisely this that is the object of *Capital*.

Yet conflict is seen by many to be self-evident at the place of work and indeed this perspective is taken here. This absence of harmony does not make for a Marxist interpretation of course, and we can have a **conflict** school of thought rather than a Marxist view of industrial relations. Alternatively, the Marxists could argue that the macro dynamic of historical events is on their side anyway while the micro study of labour and management at the place of work under a smaller time-frame is justified as a microcosm of the wider society at that particular time. However, for our purposes we will term this approach the **conflict school** and we will term the **systems** approach, not as a theory *per se*, but as a **frame of reference** or a **school of thought**.

Sources:
1   Adapted from Marsden, 'Industrial relations: a critique of empiricism'
2   See also Albrow, 'The study of organisations – objectivity or bias'
3   Dunlop, *Industrial Relations Systems*

The radical cum Marxist view, however, is unlikely to find much favour amongst most managers as it challenges their whole being. The workers may take this perspective and some of their leaders, shop stewards and full-time officials may definitely adopt this position. Many academics flirt with the concept. The real problem starts when Marxist union officials come against a unitarist management.

If the radicals/Marxists emphasize the macro dynamics of socio-economic change, the **social action** theorists take a micro personal approach. The actor in any situation is dominant. The individual response is critical; the subjective feelings, the social (and personal) construction of reality, the individual experience and expectation dominate this perspective.

Freer choice exists for individuals but we are still constrained by our construction of our social reality. The philosophy of social action assumes that individuals are aware of the inputs and the construction of their 'reality'. Of course these inputs are manifestations of, and caused by, the social reality itself, so it may be a chicken–egg syndrome.

This perspective does put the individual centre stage, unlike most of the other views which tend to abstract from the individual, and it turns our attention to overall norms and behavioural expectations. Both co-operation and collaboration are as inevitable as conflict. The perspective is very good on the diversity of interactions between the 'actors' but is less convincing in its explanation for the diversities and the power dynamics of the whole relationship. So it is an important perspective as it focuses on the world view of the actors but it needs more context and depth to be a self-standing approach. On this basis it has some value for practitioners and academics of the subject. Please refer to Box LR1.6, 'A perspective on employment relationships – the labour process approach'. Then tackle Activity LR1.2 which is concerned with frames of reference.

BOX LR1.6

A perspective on employment relationships – the labour process approach

---

Writing from a sociological perspective Brown[1] looks at four aspects of industrial sociology:

1 systems thinking;
2 context, contingency and choice;
3 orientation and action;
4 labour power and process.

We have covered the systems view in depth while the contingency approach may be more reflective of organizational behaviour than labour relations. We have noted the social action view as well, so we shall concentrate on 'labour power and process'.

The 'father' of the 'labour process approach' is Braverman[2] who wrote *Labor and Monopoly Capital* in 1974 (see later). Drawing upon a Marxist view of the labour process the concept is as follows:

1 purposeful activity, that is, work itself;
2 the object on which that work is performed; and
3 the instruments of that work.

Brown usefully summarizes the capitalist labour process as 'one in which the purpose of the activity is laid down by the capitalist, and the means of production, both the objects on which work is to be carried out and the instruments to be used in performing the work, are the property of the capitalist'.

To Braverman the issue of control over the labour process goes to the heart of the worker–capitalist relationship: 'what the worker sells, and what the capitalist buys, is not an agreed amount of labor, but the power to labor over an agreed period of time'.

The technology, the managerial style, the nature of scientific management, machine pacing and the 'bureaucratization of work' all lend themselves to control mechanisms over this labour process. Littler,[3] for example, emphasizes the bureaucratic controls imposed by management which can influence the total employment relationship and support the job design/division of labour and task performance controls.

To Braverman the workers look somewhat passive in their response to these control processes but overt conflict, rate busting, informal controls and regulation of working conditions through trade unions would all have to be taken into account.

So the issue is one of *control* and an inevitable *deskilling* of work according to Braverman, if not an inevitable degradation of work as well. The deskilling/degradation views will be discussed later (Unit Six). Suffice to say that the issue to the labour theorists is one of control.

Sources:
1 Brown, *Understanding Industrial Organisations – Theoretical Perspectives in Industrial Sociology*
2 Braverman, *Labor and Monopoly Capital*
3 Littler, *The Development of the Labour Process in Capitalist Societies*

ACTIVITY LR1.2

THE QUALITY FOOD STORE

Activity code
☑ Self-development
☑ Teamwork
☑ Communications
☐ Numeracy/IT
☑ Decisions

The food side of this huge company was divided up into three segments: the shops, the processing/distribution side and headquarters. Its name was something of a misnomer as it had developed into many non-food, non-retail areas, but retailing food was still the core business. The shops were non-unionized and the headquarters staff, excluding cleaners, maintenance porters and drivers, were non-union.

The labour relations history of the distribution/processing side had been troubled: dispute after dispute over what management perceived as trivia with the workers exploiting the perishability of the product. To the workers, management were task oriented and fond of breaking agreements to push on with the tight timescales of the process. Specialist labour advisors existed in each of the six plants with a co-ordinated force of researchers and specialists at headquarters.

Consultation and negotiation were both well established on this side of the business. The earnings were double if not treble those of the shop/retail side.

There was consultation with the employees at headquarters and in the retail side of the business but no real negotiation occurred. A procedural agreement existed with the unionized workers at headquarters so that they could invoke the help of the full-time union official but no substantive agreements occurred.

The retail side had traditionally been well paid in the context of a poorly paid sector. However, the wages were beginning to fall away with bonus/overtime difficulties concerned with Sunday working. The full-time officials of the unions within the distribution/processing side, always keen to encourage more members, were delighted when they were approached by the staff of the London region. The staff were keen on having trade union recognition.

Management at headquarters shuddered at the prospect. The Personnel Director noted to his board: 'it is bad enough being held to ransom by these distribution people – if the retail side goes to the union, so does the business'. The Managing Director wished to preserve the friendly atmosphere of the firm. The consensus of the board was to resist any more 'encroachment by the unions.'

A plan was drawn up. A staff association would be formed; pay rates would be reviewed; new communication/staff briefings would be installed; leadership training would be compulsory for all supervisors/managers; and welfare officers would be appointed at regional level to discuss any staff problems of a personal nature.

The unions withdrew to consider their position once they had heard the company plans.

Task

1 Discuss the philosophies of management towards the labour force.
2 How would you analyse the response of management to union 'encroachment'? To what extent do you feel that it will be successful?

A Predictive Model?

We are not going to fuse these frames of reference and come up with some hybrid formula as these theories have different intellectual origins and paradigms. The idea of a system as a frame of reference has some attraction as it can encapsulate the main actors and processes in some context – environmental or organizational. The idea of rule making at the 'hub' of the system is too static – if not too conservative – so we need a wider dimension. Before we develop our framework we should look at a predictive model of labour relations in the innovative work of Parker and Scott.[15] The use of any frame of reference gives us a map of the land, but if we can isolate the clusters of variables making up the map it may facilitate prediction of future events, and this seems to be the rationale behind Parker and Scott's model.

To these writers the 'quality of industrial relations' is the key. This is not seen in terms of 'conflict reduction' but quality is expressed really through the eyes of the actors and their level of satisfaction with the system. Their attitudes and behaviour are seen to impact on this 'quality' issue. External influences, particularly the product and labour markets, are seen as important. Further, the system of labour relations and the nature of the organization and its technology all impact on the 'quality' issue. Please refer to Box LR1.7, 'A predictive labour relations model'.

BOX LR1.7

A predictive labour relations model

The variables	Examples
(a) Organization/production	Industry type
	Levels of management
	Technology, etc.
(b) Outside influences	Local labour market
	Product market
	Prosperity of area, etc.
(c) System of labour relations	Degree of formality
	History
	National procedure, etc.
(d) Attitudes/behaviour of actors	Militancy
	Attachment to the job
	Autonomy at work, etc.
(e) Quality of labour relations	Degree of satisfaction of the actors

Source: Adapted from Parker and Scott, 'Developing models of workplace industrial relations'

From this model, we can see that the writers hypothesize causal relationships between the variables which can be empirically tested. Now we do not have the facility of testing these relationships but we have the device of a questionnaire developed from the variables. You should turn to the activity on this issue and answer the questions in the context of your existing firm or organization. For those not working or in full-time study, we have used the questionnaire to examine an organization which I know quite well. The task is to take a view on the value of this predictive model. Please refer to Activities LR1.3 and LR1.4 on the application of predictive models.

ACTIVITY LR1.3

PREDICTIVE MODEL I

Activity code

- ✓ Self-development
- ✓ Teamwork
- ✓ Communications
- ✓ Numeracy/IT
- ✓ Decisions

Apply the questionnaire below to your current organization or an organization of your choice. The organization should be unionized. If not, please refer to Activity LR1.4.

The scale/ranking is self-explanatory.

	Always	Sometimes	Usually	Never
The local labour market fails to get the best people into our firm	1	2	3	4

	Very poor	Poor	Rich	Very rich
Our catchment area for employees is prosperous	1	2	3	4

	Never	Sometimes	Usually	Always
Our products are highly successful	1	2	3	4

	Hostile	Don't care	Favourable	Very favourable
Describe the traditional attitudes of labour to your organization	1	2	3	4

	Never	Sometimes	Usually	Always
We are an efficient firm	1	2	3	4
Our firm uses the highest technology possible	1	2	3	4
We have too many levels of management	1	2	3	4

	No	Leads in some products	Leads in most products	Yes
We work for an industry leader	4	3	2	1

	Full agreement	Some agreement	Mostly disagree	Totally disagree
The negotiating machinery with unions is well established	4	3	2	1
There are formal procedures, e.g. discipline in the organization	4	3	2	1
The industrial relations are too formal	1	2	3	4
We don't belong to any National Procedure/Agreement	4	3	2	1
There is a lot of union militancy	1	2	3	4
The workers are committed to the organization	1	2	3	4
The shop stewards and managers could easily reverse roles	4	3	2	1
We have a lot of autonomy to do our work	4	3	2	1
The level of strikes is marginal in our organization	1	2	3	4
When conflict arises it is well managed	1	2	3	4
The workers are satisfied with the industrial relations	1	2	3	4
The managers are satisfied with the industrial reations	1	2	3	4

Source: The five clusters or groups, not the questionnaire, are adapted from Parker and Scott, 'Developing models of workplace industrial relations'

ACTIVITY LR1.4

PREDICTIVE MODEL II

Activity code
- ✓ Self-development
- ✓ Teamwork
- ✓ Communications
- ✓ Numeracy/IT
- ✓ Decisions

Refer to the numbering scale in Activity LR1.3 by question, and answer according to the facts outlined below.

1 ■ The labour market is such that the firm has its pick of staff.
It pays very well indeed although it is 'localized' and sometimes
skill shortages are evident.

Number

■ The catchment areas are not too prosperous as the plants
and other outlets are often in industrial and run-down areas.

Number

■ The products are extremely successful.

Number

■ The labour force is either hostile or does not really care
about the firm. It varies of course but absence, injury and
disputes are quite high while labour turnover was particularly
acute before the recession.

Number
Subtotal _____

2 ■ The firm is quite efficient on methods/products/techniques and
delivery but there is a fair bit of waste and excessive overtime.

Number

■ It is a low technology industry sector but it uses the latest
computers and sorting arrangements.

Number

■ It is very large and structured with many levels of
management (excessive levels).

Number

■ It is an industry leader – no doubt.

Number
Subtotal _____

3 ■ The negotiating machinery is very well established in part
of the company and almost non-existent in other divisions.

Number

■ Formal (very bureaucratic) procedures exist throughout the firm.

Number

■ The relationships are not too formalized although annual
rituals of negotiation and more frequent 'consultation' occur.

Number
Subtotal _____

4 ■ There is no National Agreement.

Number

■ Union militancy is a byword in part of the company.

Number

■ Workers' commitment is mixed.

Number

■ Many shop stewards actually become managers.

Number

■ The large company has many little jobs with little room for autonomy.

Number
Subtotal _____

5 ■ A very high level of strikes occur.

Number

■ Conflict is quite damaging and is not handled particularly well (panic).

Number

■ Pretty mixed/negative view of overall relationships.

Number

Subtotal _____

Now let us use the model (for your own score for your company and/or for 'your' score using this example).

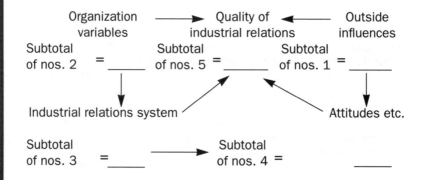

Let us turn to causation now. Do you have any thoughts on the relationship in your case and/or this case between

2 to 5,   1 to 5,   2 to 3,   3 to 5,   1 to 4,   4 to 5   and   3 to 4?

Labour Relations – A Working Framework

The external environment

The external environment clearly impacts on the organization and vice versa. A PEST type of analysis sums up these external forces. *Political* (P) aspects include the law in labour relations for the law is not value free (quite the reverse) and can range from legislation for trade union recognition to 'Combination Acts' preventing the formation and existence of unions. The legal framework and statutes on labour clearly differ from country to country. While not neglecting this important legal context (we must never forget it), to facilitate transferability of this series of books we have deliberately tried to avoid UK-only precedents, and labour laws in Britain must come under this category.

Economic (E) factors, such as balance of payments crises, inflation levels and rates of unemployment, will all impact on the labour relations within the firm. For example a pool of the dispossessed unemployed will impact on union strength, numbers and perhaps its negotiating strategy.

Social (S) trends are important as well. A feeling of citizenship outside of work linked to higher aspirations of work people may not tally with the disenfranchisement at the place of work and with autocratic managerial styles.

We live in a period of rapid *technological* (T) advance with robotics and automation, for example, in the car industry replacing the need for, and arguably deskilling, labour. We shall return to this technological change and deskilling issue in the last unit.

The actors

The primary parties are management representing the power of capitalism and trade unions representing the power of organized labour. Arguably if we have 'unorganized' labour we still have labour relations. In this book, labour is seen to be 'organized', and collective (not individualized) relationships are emphasized.

The State and its agencies, the third party, only provide part of the external environment but they can be very much leading players in the drama. The recent coal and steel disputes in the UK give testimony to this point. Likewise Reagan's administration in the USA and its attitude towards air traffic controllers supports the viewpoint that the Federal State can be omnipresent. Other 'interested' parties would include the media and labour relations commentators from students to academics specializing in the subject. The latter group may become involved via arbitration on a case by commenting upon the subject but they tend to be passive (if critical) spectators more than performers.

The focus

We started by saying that labour relations concerned the institutional-ization of conflict. The crux of the framework is seen as conflict, not rules. The issue of rules and their importance comes into play through the regulation of this conflict. These rules involve bargaining structures and institutions from consultation and conciliation to negotiation and arbitration. At a less formal level the rules include the processes of interaction on a day to day basis. The levels of informality or formality will differ but these processes will cover such items as discussion, involvement and participation in decisions and co-determination of issues through collective bargaining or some other mechanism. The informality will also spread to the customs and practices established by the work group and usually tolerated by management depending upon its 'indulgency pattern'.

The focus will also include latent and manifest conflict. For example, we can have a grudging acceptance of working conditions at one end of the spectrum allied to 'indulgency' through to the withdrawal of goodwill by the workers and victimization by managers, to outright strikes and lock-outs. This idea of 'indulgency' is important to effective labour relations and is developed in Box LR1.8.

BOX LR1.8

Indulgency patterns

This classic study at a plant owned by the General Gypsum Company in Oscar Center concerns the so-called indulgency pattern.[1]

The worker–management relationships rested on a set of shared expectations. One group have specific rights and privileges while the other group conformed to these expectations in its daily work.

A series of 'expectations' was seen to exist by the researcher.

- *Leniency* – this was very important to the workers for they looked upon themselves as producers, and this was their role obligation (rather than some obedience thing to managerial authority). Too close a control by supervision meant resentment and apathy from the workforce.

- *Second chance* – the men praised the firm for rehiring those who had left or for warning men before taking disciplinary action. The men and managers had a 'flexible' approach to the interpretation of work rules.

- *Job shifting* – more worker discretion cum weakening of managerial control occurred through the facility of job changes – although it was resented by some foremen.

- *Protection* – a welfarist expectation occurred with the workers expecting to be 'taken care of', particularly in the event of injury at work.

- *Discount/use of equipment* – the workers expected discount off the final product and the right to use company equipment at home for home repairs, etc.

Together these expectations formed the indulgency pattern. This set of expectations helped motivate the workers and generated a form of loyalty to the firm.

A new management headed by Peele replaced the old indulgencies with a strict approach to discipline which curbed the freedoms held by the employees. Tension and hostility mounted and new grievances surfaced. The issue of 'who rules' seemed to dominate management thinking. These 'difficulties' culminated in a strike.

So this study is important to the understanding of the concept of labour relations:

- whether the strike was spontaneous is more debatable (see Unit Four);
- there is a fluid 'frontier of control' between the parties;

- this frontier can be 'bedded down' and based on reciprocal understandings over a longer period;
- perhaps one party's 'indulgence' means a loss of control for the other side;
- the views of the workers towards their job and the authority of management are quite interesting for they were there to do a job, not to be 'controlled' *per se*;
- changes made by either party, particularly management, can upset the established 'social order' at the workplace.

Source:
1   Adapted from Gouldner, *Wildcat Strike – A Study in Worker–Management Relationships*

The outcomes

The result of all this interaction is not necessarily rules at all. Of course, substantive agreements on terms and conditions linked to procedural agreements on 'how we govern our relationship' will prevail in most organizations. Laws passed by the State will impact on labour relations at the level of the firm as well. The informal customs and practices will co-exist with these formal regulations. But conflict will continue and new battles may be grafted onto hitherto 'settled' issues. In harsher economic times with trade unions in relative decline there may be more of a grudging acceptance of the situation. The conflict may manifest itself in more individualized outbreaks such as withdrawal from work from absence to lower performance/output levels. Conflict and rules co-exist in the system of labour relations.

The relationship

The fundamental motor of the whole system is **power**. Like conflict, this power can be manifest or latent. Perhaps it is not so much an equilibrium in some power equation but more of a balance of fear between the parties. Power is seen as critical to the whole framework. We shall develop this idea.

The concept of power

To Parsons[16] power is almost infinite with its division and distribution almost akin to the miracle of the loaves and fishes. To Dahrendorf,[17] the distribution of power is the key: if A wins it is at the expense of B. The picture may be more complex than Dahrendorf suggests for 'influence' needs to be taken into account.

This idea of A winning over B does give a 'zero sum' perspective. It is complicated, though, for issues may come and go while the residual power bases will still apply. This leads us on to the connection between manifest/open power and latent/dormant power. Bierstedt[18] argues that the 'potential to' rather than the 'actual of' may be adequate. Power becomes: 'the predisposition or prior capacity which makes the application of force possible . . . the ability to employ force not its actual employment, the ability to apply sanctions, not their actual application'. There is a lot of sense in this latent concept. However, if called upon to exercise manifest power it must be exercised in order that the latent power retains some credibility. Examples in international relations can be cited. The inaction of the League of Nations in the 1930s and the parallel inaction of the United Nations in Bosnia illustrate this point.

Ultimately, whether it is manifest or latent, the power base in labour relations comes down to coercion. Weber[19] sums up this coercive dimension of power as 'the probability that one actor within a social relationship (labour relationship) will be in a position to carry out his will despite resistance, regardless of the basis on which that probability rests'. Dahl[20] put it very succinctly: A has power over B to the extent that he can get B to do something that B would not otherwise do. Further, a game plan can be present in labour relations. Power can become a two-way process whereby one actor attempts to anticipate the decision or reaction of the other, in almost a game (a serious one at that) of 'anticipated reaction'. So some form of reciprocity may also occur.

Can we measure this power? Tannenbaum[21] attempts to gauge the role of power within an organization via 'control graphs' but this assumes more of a distributive vision of power than a zero plus frame of reference.

There are winners and there are losers in this zero plus frame of reference. The crux of the matter is not the measurement of power, but who has it and who uses it or alludes to it in issues of labour relations. The importance of power is seen in Activity LR1.5 and differing dimensions of power are noted, including coercive and non-coercive elements. The latter perspective would move us away from the zero plus vision but it is important to gauge the range of power dimensions within an organization. Having said this, the coercive power is still seen to be paramount. Please see Activity LR1.5.

Another perspective where power is perhaps less concentrated can be seen in Activity LR1.6 which examines a different perspective of labour relations with the example of Japan.

ACTIVITY LR1.5

POWER AND LABOUR RELATIONS

Activity code

☑ Self-development
☑ Teamwork
☐ Communications
☐ Numeracy/IT
☑ Decisions

Some years ago I was interviewed for a senior position in labour relations. The interviewer asked me to define the subject matter in one word. 'Rules', 'conflict', 'interests', etc. came to mind before I settled for *power*. I got the job which turned out to be quite dreadful with some power-mad individuals and obnoxious people – so be careful. Either way we cannot escape from the concept of power in labour relations.

Task

Your task is to review a classical piece of work on power and apply these concepts to the actions of the three main parties in labour relations.

Five main bases of power have been identified.[1] We shall apply them to a work scenario.

Reward   A form of subtle bribery where compensation is given to some for attending work. It goes to the core of the work relationship between managed and managers.

Coercive   A naked form of power. No holds are barred and it is punitive with one side holding the upper hand at any one time.

Legitimate   A perception of what is right and accepted, of what prerogatives exist, and of what behavioural codes and standards apply can be seen in this power base.

Referent   This also involves acceptance but it is more concerned with group norms and involvement with, say, a peer group.

Expert   Where X perceives Y to have great specialist proficiency or knowledge/skill, etc.

However, the power bases of French and Raven do not look behind *what actually determines these manifestations of power*. We could argue that this determination of power in the labour relations system is a reflection of the determination of the power relations outside of that system.

To Marxists the concept of power reduces to the ability to control the social and physical environment. So influence and power would be intertwined and not separate as outlined by French and Raven. For example, the ability to overcome opposition is a visible sign of power but latent power may preclude that opposition arising as the legitimacy of the power is never questioned in the first place.

Apply each of these power bases/manifestations of power to labour relations. You may wish to consider the various actors, to derive some examples and to weigh these five bases in importance.

Power base	Application
Reward	
Coercive	
Legitimate	
Referent	
Expert	

Source:
1 Adapted from French and Raven, 'The bases of social power'

ACTIVITY LR1.6

THE JAPANESE EXAMPLE

Activity code
✓ Self-development
✓ Teamwork
✓ Communications
☐ Numeracy/IT
✓ Decisions

Task

First read the briefing below on Japanese labour relations. You should then extrapolate these themes to a national labour relations system of your choice (non-Japanese) to discern the degree of transferability to your chosen labour relations system.

The Japanese experience has proved a constant source of fascination to observers in the West. By contrast to other developed economies, Japan's postwar achievement seems both paradoxical and unique. It is the uniqueness of Japan's position which seems at first sight to be most striking . . .

Above all, within 30 (40) years, Japan has built the second largest economy in the world from the ruins of a disastrous war, and now boasts the highest average GNP per square mile that any country has ever achieved in history.[1]

The Japanese experience in labour relations has certainly contributed to this phenomenal success story. We can determine some themes of that labour relations system.

Lifetime commitment

In the large organizations we can see a cradle-to-grave philosophy which results in labour costs being more fixed and external poaching of staff being minimized. Training costs can be more justified by the employer as the worker is less likely to leave. There is a hint of an army cum prison type of institution about these large firms according to the journalist Satoshi Kamata:[2]

> There are so many ranks that I can't memorize them all at once. It's as if we've joined the army (i.e. Toyota). . . . The Company informs me that this number (8818639) will be used instead of my name for all official business.

Flexibility

The 'flexible firm' (see Unit Six) is certainly here with forms of early retirement of its core staff and a host of peripheral workers, subcontracting or on temporary contracts.

Reward systems

The incremental pay scales reward age and loyalty of service. The reward system consolidates the cradle-to-grave vision of the core workers and allows flexibility as pay and status are not linked to existing skills. So we have a flexible 'internal labour market', paid as such.

Harmony

Conflict is pathological and the normal state of affairs is seen as a harmonious whole. As Wickens[3] says, 'companies do seek employee loyalty and they do want to develop an environment where industrial action is inconceivable'. This impacts on the decision-making process and the high involvement of the workers in issues that affect their working lives. This gives greater commitment to the decision as the agreement tends to be made before the event.

Trade unions

They tend to be termed 'Enterprise Unions' and are geared to a specific company, so their full 'independence' may be debatable. They are affiliated to federations which may give some more independence from the company perspective.

State

Corporatism rules (see Unit Three), and the State is very closely involved with industry.

Labour practices

No strike agreements with binding arbitration on the parties allied to single union deals cement the concept of harmony and conflict avoidance. Negotiation or collective bargaining does occur but a mixture of bargaining and consultation go on in the Company Advisory Boards usually before formal union bargaining occurs – if it occurs.

The unions apart from their 'annual offensive' over terms and conditions seem to adhere to the bureaucratic paternalism of this unitarist culture.

Sources:
1 Teasdale, 'The paradoxes of Japanese success'
2 Kamata, 'Diary of a human robot'
3 Wickens, *The Road to Nissan, Flexibility, Quality, Teamwork*

We have spent a lot of time in this unit on the concept and the context of labour relations. The system and its dynamics, particularly power and conflict, have been noted. We will pick up the actors now for they can rise above the context and may make a new system of labour relations. Please turn to Activity LR1.7 on actors – roles and training needs, which usefully leads us in to the next unit on the trade union actors in the labour relations system. This unit concludes with a summary of a working framework of labour relations (see figure 1.2).

ACTIVITY LR1.7

ACTORS – ROLES AND TRAINING NEEDS

Activity code
- ✓ Self-development
- ✓ Teamwork
- ✓ Communications
- ✓ Numeracy/IT
- ✓ Decisions

Anderson Associates, Personnel and Management Advisors (AApma), had been asked in to the heavily unionized firm, London Brewery, to discuss the training needs of the whole company in the areas of labour relations. The Personnel Director was very progressive and he believed strongly that good communications and a sound knowledge of labour relations allied to associated skills would enhance the competitive advantage of the whole firm. The training needs analysis would cover every group in the organization. 'Global' group needs would be identified and acted upon.

Task

The groups will be noted below with a brief mention of their respective roles in labour relations. Your role is to pull together the content of this unit, to examine the information below and to extrapolate what you would regard as minimum levels of proficiency in labour relations for each of the groups. This could involve knowledge/information, skills/activities and attitudes/belief systems. A report should be constructed around the needs of each group.

Groups	Needs
All non-managerial personnel	E.g. awareness of the grievance and disciplinary procedures
A trade union representative within the Company	E.g. representational skills
Management specialist in labour relations	E.g. legal knowledge of labour law concerning individual and collective issues
Supervisor/first-line manager – a line manager who has a daily interaction with the workgroup	E.g. an understanding of how their daily personnel decisions impact on labour relations
Middle manager – a line manager with people responsibility as part of his or her job in marketing/ distribution, etc. They 'execute' policy	E.g. negotiating skills
Senior/top managers at or around board level responsible for policy	E.g. the national/company employee relations systems need to be known and understood

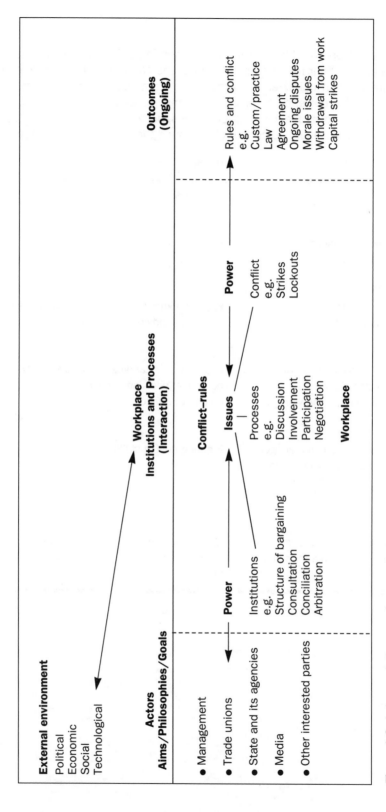

Figure 1.2 Labour relations – a framework.

Notes

1 *Personnel Management Plus*, January 1993 quoting Foulds.

2 Dubin, 'Constructive aspects of conflict'.

3 Goodrich, *The Frontier of Control.*

4 Somers, *Essays in Industrial Relations Theory.*

5 See Allen, 'Marxism and the personnel manager' and Allen, *The Sociology of Industrial Relations: studies in method.*

6 Dunlop, *Industrial Relations Systems.*

7 Barbash, *The Elements of Industrial Relations.*

8 Fox, 'Industrial sociology and industrial relations'.

9 We develop this theme in Anderson and Kyprianou, *Effective Organizational Behaviour.*

10 Poole makes this point with his 'pronounced hostility to the power of trade unions, antipathy to forms of participation that circumscribed managerial powers'. See Poole, *Workers' Participation in Industry.*

11 This is developed in Anderson, *Effective Personnel Management.*

12 This pluralist idea of competition, perhaps more than Marxist conflict, is developed by Clegg, *The Changing System of Industrial Relations in Great Britain.*

13 Marsden, 'Industrial relations: a critique of empiricism'.

14 Hyman, *Industrial Relations: a Marxist introduction.*

15 Parker and Scott, 'Developing models of workplace industrial relations'.

16 Parsons, see *The Social System* and *Essays in Sociological Theory.*

17 Dahrendorf, *Class and Class Conflict in Industrial Society.*

18 Bierstedt, 'An analysis of social power'.

19 Weber, *The Theory of Social and Economic Organisation.*

20 Dahl, 'The concept of power'.

21 Tannenbaum, *Control in Organisations.*

Unit Two

Trade Unions

Learning Objectives

After completing this unit you should be able to:

- understand the concept of trade unionism;
- derive and update trade union aims;
- place these aims in an historical context of union development;
- apply a model of union government to trade union structures;
- examine the reasons for decline and look at potential remedies;
- develop the concept of union effectiveness;
- apply the generic skills.

Contents

Unit Two

> ❝ The growing competition among the bourgeois, and the result-
> ing commercial crises, make the wages of the workers ever
> more fluctuating. The increasing improvement of machinery,
> ever more rapidly developing, makes their [the workers']
> liveli-hood more and more precarious; the collisions between indi-
> vidual workmen and individual bourgeois take more and more
> the character of collisions between the two classes.
> Thereupon the workers begin to form combinations (Trade
> Unions) against the bourgeois . . .❞

*Marx and Engels, 'Bourgeois and proletarians', Manifesto of the
Communist Party*[1]

Overview

This whole unit is dedicated to trade unions as they form one of the main
'actors' on the stage of labour relations. The other actors follow in the next
unit. This unit examines what unions aim to be and what they are in
practice. A comparison with professional associations is made. The
development and growth of unions is traced. The government of unions
and their structures are examined as examples of 'democratic institutions'
(unlike most managerial hierarchies). The relative decline of trade unions
is examined and growth potential concludes the unit. Figure 2.1 shows the
unit in diagrammatic form.

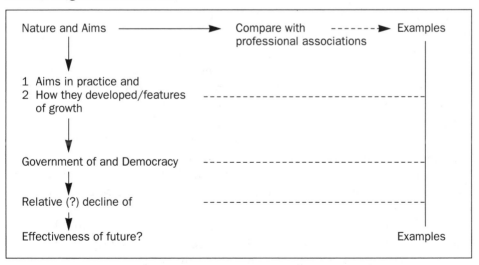

Figure 2.1 Unit outline.

Many non-trade-unionists seem to have a very jaundiced outlook towards trade unions. Perhaps media distortions (see Unit Three) and 'suffering' owing to the results of industrial action account for this perspective. Again some of the actions of unions and their leaders would make a public relations advisor cringe, so there could well be an image problem that unions have to face. The imagery is compounded by harsh reality for, as Adams[2] points out, unions are in relative (if not absolute) decline in many countries of the Western world. We shall develop this theme later. But first we need to examine what unions are all about and the pressures upon them. In addition to this we have randomly selected a cross-section of trade unions so that we will be able to go deeper into their aims, objectives, government, etc.

Trade Unions – Concept and Objectives

To paraphrase the Webbs,[3] a trade union is a continuous association of working people coming together to maintain or improve the conditions of their working lives. The Webbs used the term 'wage earners' but times have moved on and we have used working people to cover salaried personnel as well as wage earners.

Continuity is important. The early unions, not protected in law, often suffered from treasurers absconding with funds, and some other attempts at wholesale unionism in, say, the 1830s failed to pass this continuity test. The so-called 'model unions' in the UK of the 1850s established the model of continuity with a permanent constitution, a union structure and government/leadership.

To the Webbs, the collective vision is perhaps the key. The approach used is essentially economic: left to individual bargaining, workers, the semi-skilled and unskilled in particular, will become involved in suicidal competition which will even lower the going rate. Their only strength lies in their collectivity, or their banding together to promote their group interests. Indeed the Webbs envisaged individual bargaining giving way almost in entirety to this collective bargaining. Clearly this has not happened and the skill mix and the labour supply can actually further individualism which will inhibit 100 per cent unionism.

The interests of the membership are ongoing. This can be defensive, holding onto what they have, or a more offensive strategy of attempting to better terms and conditions of employment. Yet the unions are not just concerned about monetary matters. They are concerned with wider issues to improve the working lives of their members.

This means a concern with wider social issues, welfare and Friendly Society benefits. Issues from housing to education all impact on union membership and unions will take on board some of these non-employment matters. Although the Webbs' concept of trade unionism has held over the years, the labour relations systems are forever changing and the weighting and importance of union aims may alter accordingly. However, there is a view that unions constantly seek some sort of monopoly in the marketplace akin to an employers' cartel. (See Box LR2.1.)

BOX LR2.1

Trade union aims and objectives – towards a monopoly situation?

Unions exist to regulate relations primarily between managed and managers; to provide benefits to their members; and to impose restrictive conditions on the conduct of trade.

To what extent do they set out to form a 'labour cartel'? Certainly unions attempt to control the supply of labour and this has been particularly evident amongst craft unions. Controls on entry with apprenticeship quotas and fixed amounts of trainees backed up by rigid demarcation lines, the closed shop and seniority principles in, say, times of redundancy attempt to consolidate this supply side of the equation.

Controls over inputs and effort restrictions can safeguard job security and maintain earnings (e.g. through more overtime) while custom and practice can artificially regulate all output which in turn has a knock-on effect for more labour supply.

Union sanctions, particularly strike action, can deter the free supply of labour or cut it off completely in the short term. These sanctions in turn can give a competitive situation over limited areas in collective bargaining which can further strengthen the union.

So do unions strive for monopoly? Barriers to entry can clearly be raised; output can be withheld to maximize wages; production being withheld means a misallocation of resources relative to the perfect competition system; and under some conditions they may attempt to be the single producer of goods with no close substitute.

Shortcomings exist on these aspirations though. Not all employees are union members so there is no monopoly of this resource; technology can also be a substitute for labour; barriers to entry and input controls and sanctions can be curbed by legislation, e.g. against the closed shop; the State and its regulations may provide 'competition' via legislation on pay or health and safety. Much of collective bargaining seems to be a competitive struggle between unions rather than between employers and unions, and trade unions, albeit in relative decline, never formed a homogeneous body.

> So some unions may wish to act as a monopolist particularly in times of full(er) employment, but mass unionism out of control forming a monopoly, like some oil cartel, seems to be more of a horror story of the press than an economic reality even in times of economic growth and expansion.

The continuity and change within unions on what they really stand for can be seen in the specific examples of unions below. Before we examine these we should remain with a more 'macro' view. In its evidence to the Royal Commission on Trade Unions and Employer Associations,[4] the Trades Union Congress noted the following aims of trade unions which seem to be universal.

- *Improved terms of employment* – This covers higher wages/salaries, shorter working hours and longer holidays.
- *Improved conditions of employment* – Maximum standards of health and safety at work and jobs which have an improved job content design are sought.
- *Full employment* – This aim is linked to national prosperity and full employment and an increasing real national output.
- *Security, work* – Essentially this covers job and income security concerning redundancy and unfair dismissal.
- *Security, social* – The unions looked to financial security for members in times of injury, unemployment, sickness and old age.
- *Fair shares in national income and wealth* – This is a radical aim of a new society with wealth redistribution in the country.
- *Democracy at work* – Workers should have more say in the decision-making apparatus at the place of work.
- *Government* – The unions were not advocating corporatism or a sharing of government with the State but were seeking a voice in government, perhaps more of a lobbying role.
- *Improved public and social services* – Health to education to housing were included in the shopping list.
- *State control of certain industries* – Some organizations should be run for the sake of the community and not for the accumulation of private wealth.

Before we consider specific examples we should focus our attention on these objectives. The impact of continuity/change can be demonstrated by Activity LR2.1.

ACTIVITY LR2.1

TRADE UNION AIMS

Activity code
☑ Self-development
☑ Teamwork
☑ Communications
☐ Numeracy/IT
☑ Decisions

Task

The general aims below are for UK unions in the late 1960s. Your task is to update these aims to the 1990s noting whether you feel that they are still as relevant today. For non-UK readers, first discern whether these objectives are in line with those of unions in your own country. Note any changes. Thereafter update the objectives to the 1990s.

1960s objectives	**Comment/weighting of importance to the 1990s and reasons for change (if any)**
Improved terms of employment, e.g. higher wages	
Improved conditions of employment, e.g. health/safety	
Full employment	
Security (work)	
Security (social)	
Fair shares in national income and wealth	

1960s objectives	Comment/weighting of importance to the 1990s and reasons for change (if any)
Democracy at work	
Voice in government	
Improved public and social services	
State control of certain industries	

Before we go to the 'micro' aims and objectives of some unions we should not forget the wider democratic vision. Trade unions are interest groups in a democratic society, and tolerance of unions is indicative of a wider tolerance of a democratic state (see Box LR2.2). Once this is examined the specific examples of what unions aim to do can be seen in Box LR2.3. We shall pick up Flanders'[5] point (Box LR2.2) about 'what is' rather than 'what ought to be' in Box LR2.3. To conclude this aspect of union aims and objectives we shall compare and contrast trade unions with professional associations. (See Activity LR2.2, 'Trade unions and professional associations'.)

BOX LR2.2

Trade unions – aims and democracy

Flanders[1] looks at the role of unions in society. The first and overriding responsibility of unions is the welfare of their members. He takes an 'action' type of approach, preferring to infer what they are (and what they stand for) by what they do (not necessarily what they say they do).

Collective bargaining is centre stage in these activities. This process of negotiation is fundamental to job regulation and control (perhaps we should use the wider term of work regulation and control). Unions have created a 'code of industrial rights' based on the grounds of social justice.

Clegg[2] in another essay in this series compares trade unions to the parliamentary opposition. Both oppose the administration/management in power and hope to modify their policies accordingly. However, the analogy breaks down as unions would be in 'permanent opposition' with no chance of ever being the government in power. Perhaps his analogy is too constitutional in its approach as well, for unions will seek extra 'parliamentary/debating' action as part of their tactics. Clegg does, however, touch upon democracy at the place of work which is important. He sees real democracy as a management which accepts and comes to terms with trade unionism. The option is perhaps welfarism[3] but such an approach gives no independent barrier against management degenerating into autocracy. He is correct. Further, unions in society as a whole have an important role to play as a lobbying group in a pluralist society and as an integral part of democracy where the rights of workers are given some say in that social system. Interestingly under totalitarian regimes of the Right and Left, union opposition is one of the first things to be outlawed.

Sources:
1 Flanders, *Trade Unions*
2 Clegg, 'Trade Unions in Industrial Democracy' both in McCarthy, *Trade Unions*
3 See Anderson, *Effective Personnel Management*

BOX LR2.3

Trade union aims – specific

We will cite several examples of the stated aims of some trade unions.

FDA (Association of First Division Civil Servants) was initially concerned with the pay of its members and the promotion of public service. Currently, as a trade union, it aims to regulate relationships, to represent/further its members' interests and to promote the efficiency of the public service.

A summary of the aims of **USDAW** (Union of Shop, Distributive and Allied Workers) is as follows:

- to improve conditions and protect the interests of its members;
- to obtain and maintain reasonable hours of labour, proper rates of pay and general conditions of service for members;
- to provide legal aid or assistance to any member in matters of employment or secure compensation following injury by accidents at work;
- to aid and join with any other union or group of unions whose primary objective is to promote the interests of employees in the workplace;
- to settle disputes between its members and their employees, and to regulate relations with them by withholding labour if necessary;
- to further the interests of its members by representation in Parliament, in Assemblies and on local governing bodies;
- to aid employees who have become unemployed through no fault of their own.

The aims of **UNISON** (an amalgamation of COHSE, NUPE and NALGO) are based on three guiding principles:

- the need for a revival of collective public provision;
- a commitment to a democratic, pluralist and decentralized approach;
- equal opportunities and fair representation.

ACTIVITY LR2.2

TRADE UNIONS AND PROFESSIONAL ASSOCIATIONS

Activity code
- ☑ Self-development
- ☑ Teamwork
- ☑ Communications
- ☐ Numeracy/IT
- ☑ Decisions

This activity is suitable for a debate, a group discussion or a self-developmental exercise.

Task

Discuss or debate the issue that professional associations such as lawyers groups or architects etc. are trade unions in all but name.

More information is available on the pros and cons of this debate in Box LR2.4. You may not agree with the argument being put forward.

Format	Professional associations	Trade unions
CONCEPT		
Similar points		
Dissimilar points		
AIMS/OBJECTIVES		
Similar points		
Dissimilar points		
ACTIVITIES/ACTIONS TO REALIZE THEIR OBJECTIVES		
Similar points		
Dissimilar points		
CONCLUSION		
(Compare with that of Box LR2.4)		

Trade Union Aims in Practice – Trade Union Development

Using the frame of reference that was suggested in Unit One (figure 1.2) the dynamic of the system means that the unions' aims in practice cannot be seen just to be the prerogative of the unions themselves. For example, the external environment impacts on union activities. Take economics as an instance, high unemployment may mean greater resistance to unionization and the level of strike activity tends to go down. Other actions are relevant. The State, for example, may believe in taking the union movement into some form of partnership as happened in the Second World War in the UK, so the trade union aims become highly political – but in a constitutional fashion. Parliamentary lobbying should be a key role for unions. The media can be quite hostile to unions but in turn public opinion can be influenced by the media, so sound public relations skills are called for in this interaction with the media representatives. Membership may become increasingly alienated through the growth of union bureaucracy if not oligarchy and the rise of the shop steward movement can be seen as giving union activities a new direction with a greater emphasis on local bargaining, custom/practice and 'wildcat' action. Management's actions from its philosophy to its style, from its attitudes towards the legitimacy of unions to its skill in handling labour relations issues, will all impact on union aims in practice.

An historical dimension gives a context to these aims and practices, highlights the developmental forces in unionization and may offer some solace in the union decline argument. The UK, the first country to industrialize with unions, will be our example.

The origins of trade unions are a little obscure.[6] We know that in Tudor times the State regulated terms and conditions and we know that local justices of the peace fixed wages and prohibited 'combinations' of workers. We know also that craft skills existed in the Middle Ages particularly in urban areas, but these combinations are not trade unions *per se*. The craft skills were not usually continuous and, more importantly, the guilds included the 'master' (i.e. the owner) and the workers, so the guilds were not trade unions – but they were examples of some organized collective activity.

Trade unionism is a phenomenon identified with industrialization. The trade unions are a product of the factory system which itself is linked to increasing urbanization. Skilled artisans such as hatters, brush makers, spinners and printers formed embryonic trade unions through their eighteenth-century 'trade clubs'. These clubs did negotiate on behalf of a favoured few although it was hardly a negotiation as we understand it – for it was a 'take it or leave it' approach often by the artisans towards their employing organizations.

The main thrust of their actions seems to have been the provision of benefits as these clubs or combinations were primarily 'friendly societies' at a time of *laissez-faire* economic policy by the state and employers alike. This may in part explain why unions developed.

BOX LR2.4

Trade unions and professional associations – the same wine (but different vintage) in different bottles?

Trade unions exist to maintain and improve the working lives of their members. Professional associations offer their members a 'club', some form of training/competence and a sense of collective responsibility and attempt to regulate competence standards and discipline. They also seek to maintain and improve the working lives of their members.

Similarities exist in particular between the more skilled unions and these associations:

- both attempt to carve out their 'job territories';
- both employ 'restrictive practices' to maintain their distinctive job territory;
- entry points are controlled through agreements or by some examination;
- attempts are made (successfully by many professional associations) to form a near monopoly;
- both lobby government.

Differences exist as well:

- unions depend on collective strength while professional associations are less reliant on such solidarity;
- unions will use more blatant sanctions, e.g. strikes, while the professionals will tend to use more subtle routes, e.g. refusal by doctors to accept contracts;
- unions tend to have a greater social and political awareness;
- membership is more controlled by the association and expulsion of deviants is more acceptable;
- professionals may have a legal monopoly, e.g. medicine;
- unions strive for collective agreements while associations focus on fee-earning arrangements more on an industrial level;
- unions may be an expression of working-class consciousness while professional associations are more 'middle-class social clubs'.

So there are similarities but the economic power and relationships with the user or client differentiate professional associations from trade unions. Perhaps the social divide and the political consciousness of both groups are more fundamentally different and they are more like beer and gin than different vintages of wine.

A radical view would be that trade unions started as a reaction to industrialization and urbanization as working class consciousness was being cemented by these immense upheavals to an agrarian-based society.

Another view is to see the breakdown of the semi-feudal relationship in the countryside with enclosures and people moving off the land into towns as a breakdown of the 'protection' from the local lord of the manor. Left to their own devices with Parliament oblivious to their desperate fate in the new factories and slums, workers had to rely upon their own collective help – hence trade unions. Yet it was not all workers – it was very much the 'aristocracy of labour' who were involved with the early trade unionism.

The negative role of government is illustrated by the period of repression during the wars with France. Fearful of a revolution by the 'lower orders', the Combination Acts (1799–1800) were passed to prohibit 'combinations' of workmen. After many years of agitation, with a 'safer' regime prevailing in France and, some would argue, because of the bumbling of MPs, the Act was repealed in 1824–5 and unions were no longer illegal bodies.

The hardship of the factory system went on unabated. Localized, small units of financially weak unions emerged but they tended to be ineffective. The supply of labour seemed to be the key in the power relationship: where it could be manipulated, unions stood some chance of imposing 'settlements'; where it could not be manipulated, as in many trades (with transient/travelling labour) the unions were ineffective. There could be no real coercive action or 'molestation'/'obstruction'.

An attempt was made to form a massive trade union for workers, irrespective of their level of skill. Owen and Doherty led the General National Consolidated Trade Union (GNCTU) in a spirited, if not considered, fashion. Yet the 1830s were a troubled time with heavy unemployment; only a third of the alleged half a million members paid (or managed to pay) their subscriptions. Hundreds of small unions were determined not to lose their identity either and so the GNCTU slipped away into bankruptcy. Much of the labour agitation moved now into Chartism to secure universal manhood suffrage. Unions continued on a small scale of course, and we find the beginnings of 'industrial unionism' particularly in mining and textiles. The 'revolutionary period' of radical trade unionism seems to have died before the Year of Revolutions (1848) in Europe.

Realism rather than the idealism of the 'utopian socialists', organization, discipline, financial stability and leadership from the top characterized the next 'phase'. The 'New Model Unionism' came upon the scene. These unions were into benefits rather than strike action – although this weapon would be used as a last resort. Able leadership in the Engineering Union and organizational ability meant that other crafts followed their example. The governments of the unions became very important as stabilizing and organizing factors. The craft unions grew in spite of hostility from employers and their attempts to smash the Amalgamated Society of Engineers.

An embryonic national movement was established in 1868 with the first annual Trades Union Congress. Self-help was given a boost by the government passing the 1871 Act, which meant that unions could now protect their funds, and the 1875 Act, which protected unions from 'criminal conspiracy' through strike actions. Lobbying of Parliament also occurred via two ex-miners who became MPs for the Liberal Party. The unskilled and semi-skilled were still outside of the normal union catchment area.

Socialist leaders in the main, a more militant stance (the membership could not afford protracted conflicts or Friendly Society benefits) and a mobilization of the masses pushed unions for the less skilled on the scene from the 1880s to the period up to the First War. There was also a spin-off to the more established unions as they were forced to broaden their base.

It was not all coercion though, for collective bargaining was taking off in a big way, in part stimulated by the Conciliation Act of 1896 whereby unions were fully acknowledged in disputes agreements. Again, legislation helped unions in the Trades Disputes Act by giving greater immunity to unions and members for actions in tort. The parliamentary pressure and lobbying tactic can be seen in the reversal of the earlier Taff Vale decision which had threatened union funds for damages caused by strikes. Prior to the war, union growth continued, which may be a reflection of the economic expansion of the time as well of the spin-off from gains emanating from strike action.

Employer opposition and harsh economic times in the 1920s had the opposite effect: embittered relationships, wage cuts and strikes. This culminated in the General Strike of 1926.

The State is fickle and it can be punitive as well. The Trade Disputes Act (1927) after the General Strike meant that trade unionists had to 'contract in' to a political fund, that sympathetic strikes were now illegal and that the civil service unions could not be affiliated to the Trades Union Congress. Perhaps unions became more 'industrial' in their activity and less 'political' after 1926 but the 1970s tell us otherwise.

Corporatism certainly occurred during and immediately after World War II with the unions increasingly being absorbed into the decision-making apparatus of government. By 1945 membership had got back to approximately its early 1920 figure of around the 8 million mark.

The government's interventionist role in labour relations continued on an *ad hoc* basis with incomes policies and with legislation, particularly in the 1970s. The 1950s and 1960s more so led to plant bargaining and a growth of the shop steward movement negotiating locally with management. Union members increased in this period of so-called full employment. The industrial action tended to be localized and short but snappy. Overall a post-war consensus seemed to prevail – although strike incidence climbed higher and higher. Meanwhile many of the administrative and professional classes were slowly moving into trade unions.

By the early 1970s national strikes had re-emerged, unemployment was rising and a recession was hitting the labour force. Prices and incomes policies alienated many trade unionists by the end of the period and a new administration overtly hostile to unions took office in 1979 determined to break the trade union movement though monetarist policies, public spending squeezes, legislative curbs and by the creation of a permanent pool of unemployed. Perhaps even more damaging to the collective vision of trade unions, the new government deliberately created and stimulated a self-help rugged individualism which seems to have taken root at the time of writing.

We have deliberately spent considerable time on this development for it gives a context to the whole labour relations system. It gives us a feel for the external environments, the actors, the processes and the power dynamics. Now complete the brief Activity LR2.3 ('Trade union development'). Thereafter we turn to the government/structure of trade unions.

ACTIVITY LR2.3

TRADE UNION DEVELOPMENT

Activity code

✓ Self-development
✓ Teamwork
☐ Communications
☐ Numeracy/IT
✓ Decisions

A cynic once remarked that history does not repeat itself – only historians do. While accepting that every period is unique we can extrapolate themes which may help us cope with the present and save us from repeating the same errors in the future.

Task
Please read the preceding section 'Trade union aims in practice – trade union development', and then extrapolate key themes causing the 'growth' and the 'decline' of trade unions in the UK. An example is given.

Trends: e.g. the ability to organize selves into a disciplined unit is important. Contrast the 1850s with the 1830s for example.

Organization, Structure and Government

As we have seen, the ability to organize and sustain itself particularly in hard times must be a critical component of any trade union's development. The 'government' of the unions is an important aspect of the movement. From an organizational behaviourist's perspective it is also interesting as a bottom-up non-hierarchical organization (in theory at least). We shall look at the government of the unions in this section.

Each union will have its own rules, structure and form of government. We shall again look at 'our' selected unions in this context. But we need a core understanding and this can be provided by the model (see figure 2.2). Generalizations will be made as a consequence.

The **branch** is the hub of the union where members meet. Branches can be found at the place of work or they can be organized on a geographical basis. The officials at branch level may include a membership advisor and a secretary. They are usually elected, assuming that people want to stand, and are usually shop stewards in their own right. The branch acts as a forum for discussion; it communicates up and down the union 'hierarchy' and can advise members on social security issues, etc. Most importantly of all, the policies which 'guide' the union should emanate from the branch as all the branches usually have the right to originate resolutions for Conference. Of course, there will be a tremendous shake-out of resolutions and few will actually make it to Conference – let alone become 'policy' for the union.

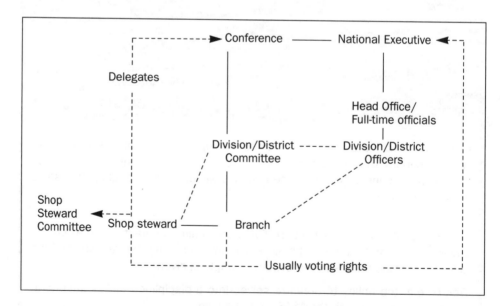

Figure 2.2 Trade union government.

The **shop steward** is the 'lay representative' of the members. In a sense he or she is an informal group leader, voted or cajoled into office (many members do not want to stand for office). The steward takes up grievances, communicates between the union and management, extends union membership and acts as a negotiator cum representative from bargaining to accompanying members in disciplinary hearings and appeals over grading, etc.

The steward can have an uphill battle maintaining membership interest in union affairs for apathy tends to rule at branch level amongst the rank and file membership. Consequently, the unions are often accused of being run by a majority of 'militants' or 'activists' depending on your perspective, with the offices falling to these individuals who are not really representative of their members. Stewards often belong to an informal committee of fellow shop stewards representing different unions in an organization with several unions. The committee exchanges information and establishes a common line towards management. Historically, when legislation allowed it, they could organize sympathetic industrial action. The shop steward phenomenon is important to labour relations and we shall discuss this later.

At **district level**, usually a geographical area but it can be geared to one or two large companies, the membership and its lay representatives come in contact with the paid full-time officers. Normally stewards are not paid although some full-time paid stewards do exist (I used to deal with *de facto* four full-time stewards in one plant and sixteen for the company as a whole).

The **full-time officers** usually cover an area and can be subject to some form of periodic re-selection. A 'lay' committee from the branches (often stewards) assist the full-time officials. These paid officials of the union are responsible for carrying out union policy and act as a channel for grievances and disputes which go 'upwards'. For example, when a dispute is not settled 'locally' by management and stewards, the full-time officer at this level will normally become involved in this procedure. Thereafter national officers may get involved if the dispute escalates to the next levels of procedure.

At **Head Office** we find national full-time officers and a secretariat covering issues such as education and training, membership development, communications, legal services and negotiations, etc. The secretariat is normally responsible to the Executive of the union.

The **Executive** of a union carries out union policy at national level. It normally has a **General Secretary** appointed by some periodic vote usually by the members. The Executive is voted in by the members and a rotation system is used so that some core Executive is always there while perhaps one-third retire on a given basis. This helps continuity of policy.

The Executive is a powerful creature, with control of the union purse strings (although reports may have to go to Conference), the ability to interpret often vague Conference resolutions and the ability to move for an official strike (subject to ballots/agreement). The Executive is indeed a powerful unit of 'government'.

The policy in theory is made at **Conference** – usually an annual event. On paper, Conference acts as a form of legislature with new policies emanating from this body. Delegates from branches all around the country attend the Conference. Rules of the union can be changed, the Executive's actions of the past year are scrutinized, and policy resolutions will be debated and 'hammered out' to guide the union for the next year.

(Please refer to Box LR2.5 for more details on specific union organization and to Box LR2.6 on the shop steward.)

BOX LR2.5

Examples of trade union government and organizational structures

FDA (Association of First Division Civil Servants)

The membership is an elite of the public service so it is not a mass organization depending on weight of numbers.

- Lay officials negotiate on behalf of its members across some 170 departments and agencies.
- The sovereign body is the Annual Delegate Conference attended by 350 representatives.
- The Executive Committee is responsible for policy organization/implementation.
- The Executive Committee serves for two years and is rotated.
- A President is elected by the membership and a Vice President and Treasurer are elected by the Executive Committee.
- Day to day administration falls to the General Secretary and to a small team of full-time officials.

USDAW (Union of Shop, Distributive and Allied Workers)

- The union has some 102 full-time officials based throughout the country. They can be regionally or company based.
- The Annual Delegate Meeting is the policy-making forum of the union.
- It has an Executive Committee of some sixteen members – two from each of the eight regional divisions.
- A Divisional Council acts in an advisory role ensuring that the policy/rules are adhered to.

UNISON (amalgamation of COHSE, NUPE and NALGO)

It is a large general union with a decentralized structure. The three traditional partner unions had a geographical government and much of this will remain in the new thirteen regions/service groups.

The union is made up of autonomous service groups covering health, electricity, water, gas, transport, higher education and local government. Each group elects leaders and is responsible for pay and occupational issues. Further, each group will contain service sectors to represent professions and occupations within their group. These sectors can develop policies within their own right.

Conference is held by each service group. In addition there is a National Delegate Conference which becomes the policy forum of the union with representatives from each Council, service group, sectional and self-organized group. Hence this new union is more like a spider's web than the normal inverted pyramid.

A regional office network co-ordinates union communications. The service groups each have a Service Group Executive elected by secret ballot. The real government of the union is controlled by the National Delegate Conference although the National Executive Council (the existing three union executives of the partner unions for a two-year period) is all-important – secret ballots will elect these executive council members in due course. There are three joint Presidents in this interim period of government.

BOX LR2.6

The shop steward

A shop steward is a lay official of the trade union. To the Commission on Industrial Relations[1] 'he' is 'a representative accredited by a union who acts on behalf of union membership in an establishment where "he" is employed'.

We shall not trace the development of the shop steward, but his or her 'governmental' role in the trade union has traditionally centred on:

- recruiting new members;
- handling queries/grievances;
- collecting subscriptions;
- being a communication point between the members and the trade union 'hierarchy'.

As Salamon[2] advises us, there is almost a role ambiguity about shop stewards deriving their power from both formal and informal expectations from the interaction of the rule book, union policy and the relationship with the full-time official. His or her personal interpretation and interaction with management will also impact on this ill-defined role.

To McCarthy and Parker[3] a range of factors influences his or her role:

- the labour market;
- the level of decision making;
- wage structures/payment;
- the scope of collective agreements;
- the socio-technical system;
- attitudes of the employer, union and workgroup.

The typology put forward by Batstone[4] is quite interesting in demonstrating how the role of the steward works out in practice. There is a clear leadership–group dependency dimension whereby at one extreme the steward determines or influences the group and at the other end of the spectrum he or she is a mouthpiece for the views of the group. The steward can follow union principles on the one hand or pursue narrow membership interests on the other. We end up with real leaders, nascent leaders, cowboys or populists cum populists depending on the combination of these four forces. For example, the real leader pursues trade union principles and determines decisions and so on.

So here we have a unique role, employed by one organization and yet acting as an official of another. To a great extent the shop steward may be the unofficial group leader. This may relate to the group dynamics and it may also be the result of an increasing alienation of the membership from the official 'hierarchy' of the trade union 'officialdom'.

The drive to 'localize' collective bargaining, payments by results, productivity schemes and a desire by management particularly in the 1960s to discuss local issues with shop stewards certainly increased their power in the government of the union. Increasingly from being in part a reaction against the union 'hierarchy' of officialdom they have been absorbed into the trade union government by the rulebook and by the activities of the full-time officials. Perhaps the 'unofficial leaders' have become increasingly institutionalized at a time when the labour relations context has been particularly harsh towards the trade union movement.

Sources:
1   CIR 'Facilities afforded to shop stewards'
2   Salamon, *Industrial Relations – Theory and Practice*
3   McCarthy and Parker, Shop stewards and workshop relations
4   Batstone et al., *Shop Stewards in Action*

Before we end this section on union government and structure we must mention the Trades Union Congress (the TUC). Reference to Box LR2.7 gives some historical insight. Here we focus on its current role and its government/structure.

The TUC has certain key roles.

■ *A voice of its affiliated members*   For example, it attempts to lobby government and to influence governmental policies on labour issues. It also *attempts* to present a united front with common policies for its affiliated union members. An international presence through the International Labour Organization and European Trade Union Confederation (ETUC) is also evident.

■ *Regulating inter-union conflict*   Rules exist (the Bridlington Agreement) to regulate difficulties in recruitment and transfer of union members. For example, the 'deviant' Electricians Union was expelled for failing to honour these principles in 1988.

■ *Servicing its members*   Support from legal advice to training, from dealing with intractable disputes to advice on bargaining, through to supplying employment information can be provided.

The 'government' of the TUC lies with Congress and the General Council. Policy making occurs at Annual Congress with some 1,000 delegates representing affiliated unions in attendance. The delegates are usually mandated to support the policies of their own unions. Congress appoints the new General Council, discusses motions, and considers the work done by the outgoing General Council.

The General Council transacts business between each Annual Congress. This involves monitoring legislation, adjudication of disputes between member unions and general support for fellow trade unionists. The Council normally meets monthly. The Council has some fifty-three members allocated by union size with an additional proviso for women membership if a union of 200,000+ has at least 100,000 female members. The Council considers reports from the Standing Committees (nine) on economic issues to training to equal rights.

In addition there is a Special Review Body to improve union organization and to promote trade unionism. There is an Environmental Action Group for wider environmental issues. The industry-based co-ordination of collective bargaining occurs through a range of committees representing construction to printing. The TUC works closely with the Scottish TUC and the Northern Ireland Committee of the Irish Congress of Trade Unions. The TUC has a regional network covering England and Wales with full-time secretaries.

Regional Councils also exist to deal with such things as economic development. At local level some 400 trade councils act as local 'agents' for the TUC. These councils meet annually as a group.

A further discussion of the TUC and its co-ordinating role in trade union government is worth examining before we tackle Activity LR2.4 on union democracy. Please refer to Box LR2.7 entitled 'The TUC'.

BOX LR2.7

The TUC

The development of the Trades Union Congress from 1868 at the Mechanics Institute in Manchester to 1968 is covered by Lovell and Roberts.[1] Some historical 'highlights' may be illustrative of overall trade union development:

- the craft guilds and Friendly Societies formed Trade Councils which stimulated the trade union movement;
- powerful leaders such as Potter and Howell were critical in this growth period;
- the role of lobbying the State proved important in 1871 when a parliamentary committee was established to give a political voice to the TUC;
- the growth of the movement in the 1880s reflected the dilution of the New Model Unions by the unskilled masses;
- the hostility of employers and of the judiciary in the Taff Vale case in part led to the formation of the Labour Party;
- the flirtation with Syndicalism advocated by Mann was short lived and the conservative forces in the TUC predominated in 1912;
- the 'betrayal' of 1926 or the 'expediency', depending on your views of the TUC and its role in the General Strike, was a watershed of the movement;
- continued employer hostility via federations plus the weakened union position in the period made the TUC a less powerful player;
- wartime involvement in mobilizing labour with Bevin at the Ministry of Labour is an example of 'corporatism' (see Unit Three) as is the programme of reconstruction after the war;
- nationalization of coal, etc., led to prominent labour leaders taking more 'managerial roles in these industries; the example of Citrine can be noted;
- the TUC wielded membership influence in the late 1950s which was perhaps sapped by the growth of plant bargaining and the shop steward movement in the 1960s;
- corporatism again appeared through Labour administrations;
- the hardship and relative decline of the UK trade union movement in the late 1970s and 1980s is mirrored by the increased marginalization of the TUC as a lobbying interest on the Government;
- Lovell and Roberts sum up the core change when it is argued that union power (TUC power) only occurred in times of high employment; the decline of unions' bargaining power must, in part, be related as in the 1930s to the rise in unemployment in the 1980s and the 1990s.

Source:
1   Adapted from Lovell and Roberts, *A Short History of the TUC*

ACTIVITY LR2.4

DEMOCRACY AND UNION GOVERNMENT

Activity code

- ☑ Self-development
- ☑ Teamwork
- ☐ Communications
- ☐ Numeracy/IT
- ☑ Decisions

Task

From your general knowledge of union government and the specific examples shown, determine how democratic the government of a 'typical' union is.

You may wish to consider and develop some of these points.

- Is the structure democratic?
- Compare it to a typical managerial structure.
- Is it bureaucratic?
- What do we mean by democracy?
- Where does policy really come from?
- Apathy
- Fraud and 'rigged' voting
- Complex rules which few understand
- Few candidates for office
- 'Activists'/'Militants'

Trade Union Decline?

Tight organization, democratic institutions and a structured approach by the TUC or some other co-ordinating body are not enough to sustain growth and development. The numbers of trade unionists seem to be falling in most developed economies.[7] In the USA some 15 per cent or fewer workers are unionized, in France the number is less than 10 per cent and in Spain also the unions are sustaining losses. Germany with Sweden seem to buck the trend and Japan's 'safer' company unions are also quite stable. Lloyd[8] writing in 1987 even posed the question: 'can the unions survive?' Their radical demise or drop in numbers can be seen in Activity LR2.5, 'The numbers game'.

ACTIVITY LR2.5

THE NUMBERS GAME

Activity code
☑ Self-development
☐ Teamwork
☑ Communications
☑ Numeracy/IT
☑ Decisions

Task

1 Analyse the statistics in table 2.1.
2 What conclusions do you draw from these figures derived from the Department of Employment and the TUC?

Table 2.1 Change in membership of major trade unions affiliated to the TUC from 1979 to 1986

	Trade union		Number of members		increase or decrease	Increase or decrease (%)
			1979	1986	1979–86	1979–86
1	Transport & General Workers' Union	TGWU	2,086,281	1,377,944	−708,337	−34.00
2	Amalgamated Engineering Union	AEU	1,298,580	857,559	−441,021	−34.00
3	General, Municipal, Boilermakers & Allied Trades Union[a]	GMB	967,153	814,084	−153,069	−15.8
4	National & Local Government Officers' Association	NALGO	753,226	750,430	−2,796	−0.37
5	National Union of Public Employees	NUPE	691,770	657,633	−34,137	−4.9
6	Association of Scientific, Technical & Managerial Staffs	ASTMS	491,000	390,000	−101,000	−20.6
7	Union of Shop, Distributive & Allied Workers	USDAW	470,017	381,984	−88,033	−18.7
8	Electrical, Electronic, Telecommunication & Plumbing Union	EETPU	420,000	336,155	−83,845	−20.0
9	Union of Construction, Allied Trades & Technicians	UCATT	347,777	249,485	−98,292	−28.3

	Trade union		Number of members		increase or decrease	Increase or decrease (%)
			1979	1986	1979–86	1979–86
10	Technical, Administrative & Supervisory Section	TASS	200,954	241,000	+40,046	+19.9
11	Confederation of Health Service Employees	COHSE	212,930	212,312	−618	−0.3
12	Society of Graphical & Allied Trades '82	SOGAT 82	205,784	199,594	−6,190	−3.0
13	Union of Communication Workers[b]	UCW	203,452	191,959	−11,493	−5.6
14	National Union of Teachers	NUT	248,896	184,455	−64,441	−25.9
15	Banking, Insurance & Finance Union	BIFU	131,774	158,746	+26,972	+20.5
16	National Communications Union[c]	NCU	125,723	155,643	+29,920	+23.8
17	Civil & Public Services Association	CPSA	223,884	150,514	−73,370	−32.8
18	National Graphical Association (1982)	NGA	111,541	125,587	+14,046	+12.6
19	National Union of Railwaymen	NUR	180,000	125,000	−55,000	−30.6
20	National Association of Schoolmasters/Union of Women Teachers	NAS/UWT	122,058	123,945	+1,887	+1.5
	Total TUC membership		12,172,508	9,243,297	−2,929,211	−24.1
	Number of TUC affiliates		109	87		

[a] GMBATU restyled as GMB in June 1987
[b] Formerly Union of Post Office Works (UPW).
[c] Formerly Post Office Engineering Union (POEU).

Source: Trades Union Congress, 1987, and the Department of Employment

We need to address Lloyd's question and determine whether the decline is absolute or relative. For if it is absolute the whole concept of labour relations will shift from collectivity to greater individuality and to human resource management.[9]

Can we explain this decline? Various answers come to mind in the case of the UK.

■ The union strongholds (steel, coal, etc.) are in decline with a resultant 'shake-out' of labour and union loss.

■ Recession, particularly in manufacturing (again a traditional strength of unions), means more unemployment and redundancy amongst trade unionists.

■ The growth sectors of the economy, from banking and financial services to computing, have not got a strong unionized base.

- The public sector, traditionally a strong base of union support, is being denuded through de-nationalization, privatization and work being put out to tender.
- Managerial practices, particularly human resource management, are attempting to usurp the collective union base and emphasize individualism.
- Statutory restraints on unions through legislative curbs mean that the climate of derecognition is being fostered by the State.
- The fragmentation of work through 'flexible' work arrangements means that part-timers, subcontractors, etc. have lost their basic contractual rights as employees, let alone as trade unionists.
- The unions focus on their strengths and attempt to 'top up' their members in 'developed' areas while neglecting the more difficult job of recruiting in the hostile areas of smaller firms in the growth sectors.

Bain and Price[10] give us a more detailed rationale on growth factors, the absence of which may mean stability or relative decline. (See Box LR2.8, 'Union development or decline?')

Box LR2.8

Union development or decline?

Bain and Price[1] cite six main factors which impact on union growth (or decline):

- composition of potential union membership;
- the business cycle;
- employers' policies and government action concerning union recognition (derecognition);
- personnel and job-related characteristics;
- industrial structure;
- union leadership.

The 'mix' of membership is examined under composition (white-collar/blue-collar, male/female, etc.) and suggests that this is a contributing factor, not a major determinant. Perhaps in the 1990s this is more of an issue, particularly for potential growth.

High unemployment levels and the threat of job loss in these difficult times for those in employment is seen to be an area of the business cycle which relates to the decline of membership.

Union growth and recognition are seen as 'mutually dependent'.

Under a Labour administration we find stimulants to recognition of unions from the State, and a reversal of this policy under the Tories. The role of employers in union recognition is more ambivalent, but Bain and Price note that 'additional' recognition under a supportive State occurs in areas which are already unionized. This suggests that the push needs to come from both a union power base and the State, as well as suggesting that employer hostility still exists in the less unionized areas.

Industry sector seems to be correlated with union membership rather than specific job characteristics *per se*. Women, though, are under-represented in membership. These two factors are worth developing. The 'old' unionized sectors are gradually dying or being strangled, e.g. coal, and the growth sectors, such as financial services and computing, have less union density. Women are making up more of the labour force, often in part-time jobs, and a potential growth area looks difficult to tap, particularly amongst the part-timers.

High labour turnover means a more unstable 'permanent' labour force and union recruitment and retention becomes more difficult. We could add with hindsight that redundancy and a semi-permanent pool of 3–4 million unemployed adds to this impermanence. This is furthered by the 'flexible' working and subcontracting of the 1980s and early 1990s.[2]

Occupational structure is another item. They note the blue-collar union strength and the white-collar weakness. The changes in occupational structure in the 1980s and the 'shake-out' from firms and the public sector would emphasize this area as an important aspect of research. The prevalent ideologies of the workers and their attitudes to unions would be a fruitful area of research. The 'market' for unions and their 'marketing' policies both need to be understood.

Concentration of workers in large groups seems to raise the union consciousness and so industrial structure is important. Of course decentralization of bargaining and the break-up of larger business units, as occurred in the 1980s and early 1990s, would inhibit such growth.

Union leadership is not seen by Bain and Price to be a key determinant of union development. Leadership is another factor in the equation, though, and perhaps the inability to respond meaningfully to events such as new technology in the newspaper industry or to settle at a more timely period as in the coal strikes of the late 1980s can be put down to ineffective leadership. Without effective leadership, the unions become a floating cork on troubled waters, as a result of economic forces and a 'hostile conspiracy' between employers and government. This seems to have been the case in the UK in the 1980s and the early 1990s.

Sources:
1 Adapted from Bain and Price, 'Union growth: dimensions, determinants and destiny'
2 See the innovative work of Pollert, *Farewell to Flexibility*

Falling numbers are bad enough for the unions but density problems also exist. Indeed, density is perhaps more of an 'acid test' of decline or growth. (Density is the actual numbers divided by the potential numbers in that sector.) The public sector density has always been high, as has the manual workers density in manufacturing. White-collar manufacturing workers, private sector services and agriculture, forestry and fishing have always been low. But even in the density strongholds the numbers have been withering away. Is it absolute?

Lloyd's thesis[11] is that, even under 'friends' in the Labour Party, market socialism means greater individual rights and fewer collective rights. The State and the marketplace dominate under this scenario and the individual citizen turns increasingly away from the collective umbrella of trade unions. This is a leftwing perspective by Lloyd: the rightwing's views on individualism mean no place whatsoever for collective organizations like unions.

There is no doubt that the union movement is taking a beating at the moment. Structural changes in the economy and employers' hostility allied to an economic blizzard make life difficult to say the least. This does not mean that unions will disappear though; unions are inextricably linked to industrialization and the prevalent economic mode of capitalism. Communist variants have existed[12] but there is some debate whether these countries were ever really Communist – they were more akin to regimes of State capitalism. If we move to a post-capitalist or post-industrial society the unions may not make such an adjustment, but the post-capitalist society is meaningless for even in a service-dominated economy (post-industrial) rampant capitalism is still as work. As such, I feel that unions will still survive owing to the fundamental inequalities of that mode of production and distribution.

So I would suggest that the decline is relative rather than absolute. A key player in this game is the State. The 1980s witnessed a move to the Right in many of the Western democracies (and France has recently gone this way as well). The trend has been reversed in the USA and the Democratic party, the old friend of organized labour, may come to its assistance again. The State is the key; it was the blend of Thatcher's so-called 'popular capitalism' and Major's 'citizenship' for 'Essex Man' that pushed individualism. With allies in a predominantly rightwing press, this anti-collectivism has taken a firm hold. Attitudes have been fused with legislation hostile to trade unions. There has been a deliberate dismantling of trade unions through legislative curbs. For example, these have included balloting for strike action, outlawing the closed shop, inhibiting types of picketing and abolishing the constitutional routes to union recognition. Unions must expect few favours from management in most enterprises, but when overt hostility of the State marries up with this 'permanent managerial opposition' the unions need to dig in, choose their battlegrounds and work towards at least a 'value neutral' approach by the State through a Labour/Liberal administration.

In the interim, amalgamations and concentration of union members is one route open to unions and the British 'problem' of multi-unionism seems to be *slowly* disappearing with the latest batch of mergers (although there are still too many small unions). The NUAAW merger with the T&G so that dispersed agricultural workers combine with the power of one of Britain's largest unions can only help. The merger of TASS and ASTMS in 1987 gave a membership (then) of some 600,000.

Recruitment drives and an intensification of existing membership groups continues unabated. The new image of the GMB with its replacement of 'Unity is Strength' by 'Working Together' is illustrative of the 'softer' trend.

Resurrection of the fringe benefits of a union and an emphasis on a Friendly Society approach may also pull in hitherto non-believers, particularly in the white-collar sectors. See Box LR2.9 on the Friendly Society.

Box LR2.9

Trade unions as Friendly Societies – arresting decline

In conjunction with the Labour Research Department, the trade union NALGO examined a range of benefits for fifteen of the largest TUC affiliated unions with a membership of almost 6,900,000 at that time. In addition non-affiliated organizations such as the Police Federation and the Royal College of Nursing were also surveyed.[1]

There is little point reiterating the detail of this piece of research as it goes on for some forty-three pages. We can summarize themes, though, which do indicate the welfarist vision of trade unions.

Strike Pay
All the affiliated unions had provision for paying strike monies. The majority of unions left the amount as a discretionary act of the Executive.

Benefits
A range of welfare benefits covered unemployment, sick pay, accident pay, incapacity, death/funeral expenses, convalescence, tools allowance and superannuation.

Convalescent homes
A two-week free stay is a widely available benefit but is little used by the membership.

Housing
'Special' schemes with a number of building societies do operate and one union had its 'own' building society. Preferential rates for mortgage interest rates were available for another union. Some liaison with Housing Associations also occurs for a small number of members.

Discount
Cheap tyres to free insurance advice characterize the discount schemes. The Survey questioned the uniqueness of these company discount schemes as they were on offer to many (non-union) organizations.

Holidays/travel
Some unions allowed some 5 per cent off holidays while four unions had their own holiday accommodation which they offered to members at a cheaper rate.

Legal services
All unions surveyed provided some facilities for employee-related matters concerning law. Advice and guidance was also arranged for non-employee-related legal matters by several unions.

Education
Labour relations/representative training occurred. A correspondence institute with technical/professional education was used by several unions. Weekend schools and scholarships were also provided.

Publications
All unions produced at least one journal while booklets on topics from equal opportunities to sexual harassment were produced by some.

Perhaps this area of benefits akin to those of a Friendly Society is one way of increasing membership – so long as the other trade union aims are not forgotten, for we would end up with a social cum welfare club only.

Source:
1   NALGO, 'Benefits of union membership – a discussion document'

The long-term future means not only dipping into the poorly organized sectors but maintaining a presence there, particularly in the private services such as insurance, finance, banking and distribution, until such time as recognition can be stimulated by a more friendly State.

Women workers and white-collar workers as a whole need to be addressed by the unions, for these groups are the growth areas of the labour market. Please see Box LR2.10.

BOX LR2.10

The great white hope – the white-collar trade unionist?

If trade union decline is to be arrested and the trend reversed, unions must court the growth area in employment, the white-collar worker.

Bain and Price give us a useful insight into the main schools of thought concerning this white-collar animal, for without an understanding of the animal, he or she cannot be courted properly.[1]

Three perspectives are given:

■ the brain–brawn view;
■ a functional approach;
■ an eclectic approach.

Brain–brawn

A dichotomy grew up between educated white-collar workers such as clerks and manual workers involved in heavy work. Lederer, a German sociologist, is cited as defining the white-collar worker on the basis of intellect, mental agility and non-manual work. Lederer's views may be more applicable to an earlier period of industrialization for many clerks and others involved in routine paperwork cannot really be seen as doing 'intellectual' work while some blue-collar technicians have more intellectually demanding work.

Functionalism

The job content is used to determine the white-collar employee and the work of Croner is applied. Administrative design, analysis, planning, commercial and supervisory/managerial tasks are noted. Croner notes that these duties were delegated from the owner and hence there is a status difference between white- and blue-collar workers. Such 'ownership' could not apply to public sector bureaucrats but the concept of the 'office holder' of the 'bureau' may be worth pursuing for it applies to large organizations in both the private and public sectors.

An eclectic approach

Girod, using Swiss data, suggests a difference in work milieu which is more 'bourgeois' in a white-collar environment. The second category involves the 'objects' of the worker's task. The blue-collar worker is concerned with material objects while the white-collar worker is concerned with people.

To Bain and Price, these analysts do not provide a definitive answer and they suggest that 'proximity to authority' may be a useful way of distinguishing white from blue. Yet we cannot get away from the difference in conditions: the white-collar worker can wear a good suit to work while the blue-collar cannot because of the greater propensity for hazards, etc. It tends to be the difference between the office and the factory. Yet, at the end of the day, both are workers – mere wage or salary slaves – owning little or no means of production. In spite of this, perhaps the real issue is that the white-collar workers and blue-collar workers see themselves as different animals. Furthermore, the white-collar animal may have more 'bourgeois' tastes and individual aspirations which a collectivist trade union may have difficulty tapping.

Source:
1 Adapted from Bain and Price, 'Who is a white collar employee?'

The TUC has a critical role to play in these turbulent years. On recruitment it must promote trade unionism to young people (training schemes and at school). Women and ethnic groups have been neglected – this must cease. Women, in particular, must be a key group in any recruitment campaign given the changes in the labour force. The internationalization of the labour market (post-1992) is really confirming what happens anyway, particularly with large multinationals such as Hoover at Dijon and at Cambuslang. This dimension is not lost by the TUC. The plan of campaign or the issues of the TUC campaign are highlighted:

- to improve the finances of unions;
- to expand/promote member services;
- to promote joint training with employers/other bodies;
- to develop a common bargaining agenda;
- to build up the union contribution to environmental problems;
- to develop trade union recognition taking account of the European dimension;
- to advance union recruitment and retention;[13]
- to input into the EU Social Action Programme.

The union movement needs a lead and the TUC must not shrink from its responsibilities. Will these policies be enough? Well, they may keep the ship afloat but it is still leaking. A closer domestic working partnership with its traditional ally, the Labour Party, should be its immediate priority and the next General Election needs greater labour mobilization than in the recent past.

We conclude this unit by looking at union effectiveness (see Box LR2.11).

Box LR2.11

The effectiveness of trade unions

Taylor[1] takes an historical perspective on UK trade unions and attempts to answer the question: have the unions been effective? The primary aim of trade unionism according to Taylor is wage determination. It is defensive and offensive. Yet Taylor is pessimistic on this 'free for all' in the private sector and on the rigidity of the state sector. The system is inequitable.

The system is in need of reform with more public debates and greater solidarity sought amongst and between the trade unions themselves. Negotiations are extremely short-sighted and do not go further than meeting the immediate goals of their members. This instrumentalism means that wider socio-economic issues are sidestepped. Higher pay resulted for some who were prepared to back up their goals with industrial action but this was at the expense not only of the weaker workgroups but of increased popularity for the Right and Thatcherism. (Taylor was writing in the late 1970s.)

Some blame the voluntarist tradition for failing to bolster the economy, but 'restrictive practices' cannot be solely to blame for Britain's malaise. Quite the reverse: the 1980s and 1990s have seen a neo-*laissez-faire* approach with a loosening of trade union 'restrictions', fewer members and less power, but the economic malaise has deepened.

Taylor points out a nice irony: unions and workers have responded to the enhanced individualism and market forces by becoming more materialistic – they have adopted the philosophies of their 'natural enemies'.

Taylor's hopes for the future lie in some harmonious relationship between unions, government and employers. Such corporatism has failed to get off the ground in the 1980s and 1990s. Their weaknesses in the face of managerial strengths combined with hostile administrations have increasingly outflanked trade unions. Marginalization and decline have occurred, not incorporation and growth. Having said this, the step to incorporation may also have led to an absorption of unions and a dilution of their freedoms. So they may be weaker – but they are still free albeit restrained and constrained by law.

If Taylor were to write this postscript he would probably say that the demise is of their own making. In part this would be correct but the interplay between the State and employers should not be forgotten and an 'alliance' between the two, as has occurred in the UK in the 1980s and 1990s, will combat even the strongest trade union force.

Source:
1   Adapted from Taylor, *The Fifth Estate*

Trade Unions – Effectiveness

Effectiveness tends to be goal oriented. When we examined the union goals of the 1960s and compared them with those of the 1990s we did notice some shortfall. The times are hard at the moment for the union movement but part of its whole rationale is to defend as well as to attack. It is currently defending on many fronts.

Some years ago, Blackburn[14] gave us a test of union purity perhaps rather than effectiveness, but we can examine the list in this context as well. He coined the ugly term 'unionateness', a qualitative term to supplement the quantitative aspect of density which we have examined at length. This 'unionateness' gives us a gauge to measure the commitment both of the unions and of the movement as a whole to some form of trade union ideology. It may still have some relevance – even more perhaps when numbers of members are declining. It covers the following.

- It must declare itself to be a trade union.
- It should be registered as such.
- It should be affiliated to the TUC.
- It should be affiliated to the Labour Party.
- It must be independent of employers for purposes of collective bargaining.
- It needs to regard collective bargaining and the protection of its members' interests as major functions.
- It needs to be prepared to be 'militant' and take industrial action.

The ideology of 'unionateness' should be enough to sustain the union movement in these difficult times. However, it does need to be allied to quantitative approaches on membership recruitment and retention.

The positive and negative roles of the State, the bias of much of the media and the often ambivalent/'pragmatic' role of management have been noted in this unit; we now turn to these other actors in Unit Three.

Notes

1 Marx and Engels, 'Bourgeois and proletarians', *Manifesto of the Communist Party*.

2 Adams, *Comparative Industrial Relations*.

3 Webb and Webb, *History of Trade Unionism*.

4 TUC, 'Evidence to the Royal Commission on Trade Unions and Employer Associations'.

5 Flanders, *Trade Unions*.

6 H. Pelling gives us an insightful approach to the early days of trade union development in *A History of British Trade Unionism*.

7 Adams, *Comparative Industrial Relations*.

8 Lloyd, 'Can the unions survive?'.

9 See Anderson, *Effective Personnel Management*.

10 Bain and Price, 'Union growth: dimensions, determinants and destiny'.

11 Lloyd, 'Can the unions survive?'.

12 Women and ethnic minorities have not been properly targeted by the trade union movement in the UK for it is still dominated by a male blue-collar vision of unionism.

13 Perhaps a more cautious route would be to build up the domestic base before developing the European scene.

14 Blackburn, *Union Character and Social Class.*

Unit Three

The State, Management and the Media

Learning Objectives

After completing this unit you should be able to:

- give an overview of the roles of the State in labour relations;
- relate these State roles to the dominant State philosophy;
- examine managerial roles in labour relations;
- understand the different managerial styles and approaches to the subject;
- relate managerial styles to the approaches of employer associations;
- construct a code of good practice for management;
- determine the roles and philosophy of the media in labour relations;
- apply the generic skills.

Contents

Unit Three

❝ By choosing the blunt and anti-social weapon of these 24 hour strikes the unions show themselves to be what they are – bullies motivated by political considerations alone.❞

London Evening Standard[1]

Overview

The previous unit illustrated the role of the State in union development. This unit builds on this role and considers a spectrum of actions of the State in labour relations. The prevalent philosophy held by the State is seen as crucial in guiding its actions in labour relations. An in-depth example of State intervention through its pay policies is used.

However, the main actor in the primary relationship apart from the union is the subject of this unit. The role of management, its objectives and philosophy and its actions, are covered. Research on the role is allied to the development of a guiding code of practice.

The unit concludes by examining briefly the impact of the media on labour relations. Clearly 'public opinion' is a feature in any democratic regime and the media are in a position to influence and reflect that opinion which may impact on any of the actors – particularly in times of dispute.

Figure 3.1 shows the unit in diagrammatic form.

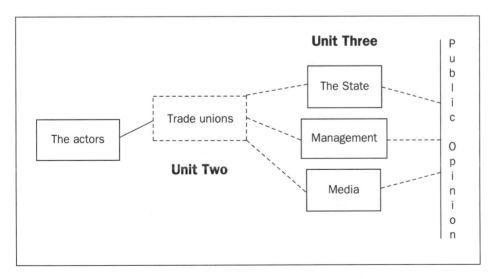

Figure 3.1 The main 'actors' in the system.

The State – Roles

As we have seen, the State as the third party has impacted quite considerably on union development. It has many other roles though. Anthony[2] suggests the following classification:

- employer
- paymaster/overseer
- buyer
- protector
- rule-maker
- peace-maker/incomes regulator
- manpower manager

The classification is quite sound but we can couple some of the headings together for our analysis to give

- employer/paymaster/overseer
- buyer–protector
- rule-maker and peace-maker
- economic manager – manpower and incomes

Employer/paymaster/overseer

The State is a huge employer of people, directly as in the armed forces and civil service and indirectly in nationalized industries and public utilities.

The State not only picks up the wage/salary tab for millions of workers but it is involved in capital provision and investment, policy directives, appointing the top management in certain sectors, price controls and of late wage controls or ceilings.

The example of the civil service is illustrative. During the First World War, a series of councils was established in the UK as a result of the work of the Whitley Committee. Full negotiation of terms and conditions of employment and pay now occurred with a safety net of arbitration if agreement could not be reached by the parties.

The State as an employer has a careful path to tread. It needs able and motivated state servants but it cannot set the pace on salaries compared with the private sector. Traditionally there has been some crude trade-off between lower pay in the sector with greater job security and index-linked pensions compared with private enterprise.

Strike action, where it is allowed, can be quite debilitating to the country as a whole. Teachers on strike, railway workers on strike or firemen taking industrial action can be cited.

Problems of comparability and fair treatment of state employees go to the heart of labour relations in this sector. Until its abolition, the Civil

Service Pay Research Unit (following the Priestley Commission of 1955) usefully assembled facts to give a fairer comparison with the private sector for civil service pay negotiators. *Ad hoc* provisions have prevailed in this area with several enquiries for teachers and nurses culminating in a Commission in 1979. 'Indexation' has also been used for the police and fire services. The absence of real comparability still troubles the sector.

The State also holds the purse strings in the health, education and local government sectors. The concept of service to the wider community must be balanced by the harshness of the marketplace. The remaining nationalized industries also suffer from this dilemma. The State may attempt to be even-handed in its treatment of staff in these areas but the pressures of the marketplace and the drive for efficiency are omnipresent. Again it is too easy for the State to dabble negatively in the labour relations of the sector.

Buyer–Protector

All things being equal, State projects should go to the lowest bidder. However, a 'protector' dilemma occurs when that low bidder is exploiting labour, contrary to the 'protective' vision of the State.[3] It can work the other way round as well for the State can deal with bona fide organizations which recognize unions, hence stimulating union recognition amongst supplier firms.

The protector role is perhaps more significant. Legislation can protect the rights of individuals (and groups) in health and safety, equal pay, discrimination, unfair dismissal, redundancy and maternity rights.

These individual rights tend to be enshrined in statute. The collective rights are more problematic and more open to manipulation by political parties. The example of Wages Councils providing a minimum wage for the poorest paid in the community and their abolition is indicative of this political manipulation. Another example involves trade union recognition. Under a Labour administration a constitutional means existed for unions to achieve recognition by employees through the apparatus of the agencies of the State. Again, this was curtailed by an incoming Tory administration. Collective rights are not as clear-cut as individual rights and can be curtailed under the guise of enshrining individual rights, as in the case of the closed shop.

Please tackle Activity LR3.1, and thereafter consult Box LR3.1.

ACTIVITY LR3.1

THE CLOSED SHOP

Activity code
- ✓ Self-development
- ✓ Teamwork
- ✓ Communications
- ☐ Numeracy/IT
- ✓ Decisions

The closed shop is an agreement between an employer and a trade union whereby all employees of a particular category *must* be union members.

Task
In the context of Professor Metcalf's quote below on the closed shop, debate the merits or otherwise of a closed shop from the perspectives of management and trade unions.

> But, in future, management will only encourage union membership or acquiesce in the face of a *de facto* closed shop where unions abandon adversarial industrial relations in favour of more co-operative modes, and where traditonal collectivism is tempered by concern for individuals.[1]

Source:
1 Metcalf, 'Can the closed shop ban open new doors for unions?'

Rule-maker and Peace-maker

As we have seen, labour relations have been seen by many, and in part by us, as rule making. The State is in a good position to make and establish clear rules – not only for its 'own' sector but for the labour force as a whole. For example, the 1971 Industrial Relations Act attempted to curb union power, defuse strikes, give some structure and formality to labour relations and put the whole system under the auspices of labour law. Value neutrality seems to be an aspiration of sociologists rather than a policy of differing administrators in the field of rule making within labour relations.

Peace making ought to be a fundamental aspect of the role of the State in labour relations. The State should provide a safety net – not only for its 'own' employees but for all at the place of work.

'Jaw jaw' must make more economic sense to a government than industrial 'war war'. Yet we have recent examples of teachers and ambulance workers being prevented from taking their cases to independent arbitration by their employers and by the State. Compulsory binding arbitration of the Japanese ilk may be a positive route by which the State could improve the settlement of disputes.

Left to themselves, the primary parties may not be prepared or be able to reach an agreement. Even where management has had the forethought and capability to develop methods and institutions for avoiding minimizing conflict, and even where there is a strong trade union movement and a well-developed system of industrial relations, many conflicts can be so severe as to require outside support to accommodate both parties, if not to resolve the issue.

It is felt that the 'solutions' to industrial conflict must rely on the actions of the primary parties to the conflict. Yet the State has a key role in conciliation, mediation, arbitration and holding inquiries into the dispute or conflict. This view takes a voluntarist stance with the State as a safety net.

To a great extent the issue may not just be between the interventionists and the non-interventionists of the State in labour relations. As we have seen, the State is not value neutral and labour law can easily degenerate into a political football – either through statute or by the interpretation of that law by the judiciary. Laws apart, we need some independent body to act as the 'referee' part of the State but yet outside of direct political interference. We are fortunate in the UK to have such a relatively independent body, the Advisory, Conciliation and Arbitration Service (ACAS), which manages on the whole to retain an objective line detached from the government of the day. This 'neutrality' could be questioned under its previous guise when it had the right to promote collective bargaining through trade union recognition, but as this no longer occurs the neutrality is not tarnished.

ACAS will be used to highlight these safety nets – see Activity LR3.2 on an evaluation of the role of a third party safety net.

One of the key roles of any independent third party is to give *advice and guidance*. The impartiality of this assistance can mean that the problem is contained or resolved before it becomes a major issue. There is also a more pro-active role as well, for joint problem solving can be stimulated by this advice.

The advice and guidance can cover such areas as collective bargaining. This can cover new procedures and negotiating machinery for example. Individual employment issues can also be resolved, for instance through common disciplinary procedures. Pay and conditions still cause many difficulties and advice/guidance can be sought in these areas. Improved consultation and involvement practices can also come under this advisory banner. In addition, change and its management has become an area under this advisory role which in turn seems to be linked to issues of the quality of working life.

BOX LR3.1

The closed shop

Talk to someone in a public bar about labour relations and two of the most common topics will be closed shops or strikes.

A closed shop is an agreement between an employer and a trade union whereby all employees of a particular category must be union members. So all non-trade-unionists are excluded from employment. Is this union tyranny attempting to form some form of labour 'cartel' infringing the rights of the individual, or is it a necessary prerequisite of union strength and effectiveness?

The answer to this question may relate in part to the so-called 'hard' or 'soft' theories. To the 'hard' theory the closed shop is part of the apparatus that gives a solidarity to the masses which is critical in times of strife. The 'soft' theory notes that management often encouraged the closed shop as a mechanism of order and stability as it gives a more disciplined approach to labour.

We shall not trace the legislative curbs on the closed shop in the UK in the 1980s and 1990s which were based on enhancing individual freedom and curtailing union strength. Suffice to say a hostile administration has all but sounded the formal death knell of closed shops in the UK, although they still exist on an informal basis. Instead we shall focus on the concept of the closed shop and attempt to answer our initial question.

The individual liberty view is that coercing a person to join a voluntary body is not a very liberal thing at all. Of course the side effect of this pro liberty argument is a torpedo on the ship of strong trade unionism.

The argument is perhaps broader. The closed shop certainly enhances the collective strength of trade unions for as we have seen the individual is weak vis-à-vis the power of the employer. Hence the collective strength may be an important pluralistic freedom where the freedom of the strong individual can become the exploitation of the weaker mass. So real freedom of collective association itself may be weakened by anti-closed-shop legislation.

Again, why should non-trade-unionists/non-subscription-payers/non-strikers have the same benefits as their unionized brethren in a firm? There is something less than liberal in this position.

From a manager's perspective, the closed shop prevents non-strikers turning up for work and crossing picket lines, etc., as well as the resultant difficulties after the event. However, this needs to be balanced: there can be no question that the closed shop makes industrial action almost 100 per cent effective. It can also restrict the labour pool where recruitment of workers emanates from only one area. Against this, the pool of workers often kept on file by the union gives a known skill level which may not be so apparent in the open market.

> The union 'hierarchy' may get a more disciplined workforce prepared to follow the official line. This depends on the membership, the steward, the issue, etc., and so it may not be such a clear-cut issue. It can limit multi-unionism and 'poaching' between unions.
>
> So liberty or not, the demise of the closed shop as a tactic of government/management through legislation is certainly a key factor in the weakening of trade unions and in the weakening of strike solidarity in times of strife.

Conciliation means that a third party attempts to act as a facilitator to get the parties to reach their own agreement. Modification of views can be helped by an examination of the various options open to the parties.

The meetings are held in confidence and are informal. No commitments need be given, only a readiness to discuss the issue, and either party can bring the process to an end at any time. The conciliator can see the parties separately, less often together.

The agreements are down to the parties themselves although the conciliator can play a constructive role in forwarding suggestions from each side.

The conciliator can become involved in individual conciliation such as unfair dismissal claims, race discrimination issues, etc., or collective conciliation where both parties, union and employer, are involved.

One step up from conciliation in the interventionist strategy is **mediation**. Again the parties still retain control over the end result but now they consider the recommendations of the middle man. These recommendations are not binding on the parties.

Mediation is thus more formal than conciliation but it does provide a structure for both parties to discuss the issues. Terms of reference are noted before the mediation commences to ensure a lack of ambiguity and to clarify the issue.

Arbitration, through either a single chair or a three-person board, occurs with a view to settling the issue. The parties can present their case, comment and answer questions. It is more formalized than the other two mechanisms. Although not legally binding, it is customary for both parties to honour the arbitrator's decision. A 'compromise' award is feasible depending on what is seen as fair and equitable in the circumstances.

There has been a move away in some quarters from this 'conventional' arbitration towards more 'pendulum' arbitration whereby the difference is not split but one party 'wins' while the other 'loses' according to the swing of the arbitrator. Of course in disputes of right or principle, the traditional method of arbitration may come down on one side anyway as the difference (unlike disputes over terms and conditions) may be far more difficult to split down the middle. This new(ish) pendulum arbitration is often linked to 'new style agreements' with no strike deals and this type of arbitration as the final stage of the agreement (see Unit Four, Box LR4.4). Please tackle Activity LR3.2.

ACTIVITY LR3.2

A SURVEY ON THIRD PARTY INTERVENTION

Activity code
☑ Self-development
☑ Teamwork
☑ Communications
☑ Numeracy/IT
☑ Decisions

Assume that you work with an independent body involved with third party intervention. Some academics have conducted a survey on your work in the last year by seeking the views of users (both management and trade union). The results are shown below. They have been linked with the statistical records of your cases and clear-up rates.

Task
From this survey extrapolate themes and trends that
1 are acceptable,
2 need action,
and draw up an action plan to meet these needs.

Advisory services
(combines visits and survey work.)

1 Of all the organizations seeking advice, 35 per cent said that the advice was 'neutral'.
2 Advice presented well (90 per cent of users).
3 On the quality of the advice, 69 per cent agreed that it was either 'very good' or 'good'.
4 Was the advice meaningful or significant in changing things? Fifty per cent answered yes and 20 per cent said yes, marginally better.
5 Key issues were seen as individual employment (45 per cent); collective bargaining (25 per cent); pay (12 per cent); communications, etc. (10 per cent); change management (8 per cent).

Conciliation

1 Used in most sectors, particularly engineering, transport, newspapers and publishing, and food and drink.
2 Collective case settlement rate 69 per cent.

3 **Areas by causation**   %

Terms/conditions   50

Changes in work practices   10

Trade union matters   3

Trade union recognition   10

Redundancy   20

Dismissal/discipline   6

Other   1

4 Over 50 per cent were joint applications by union and management with another 38 per cent emanating from the trade union side only and 10 per cent from the employer side only.
5 On individual conciliation, unfair dismissal dominated (70 per cent).
6 Of the 40,000 estimated individual cases, 39 per cent were completed successfully and 28 per cent went no further.

Mediation/Arbitration

1 Job grading/evaluation dominated the 200 requests for mediation.
2 Discipline and dismissal amounted to fifty cases.
3 Some sixty cases for mediation involved pay/conditions.
4 The union side 'won' sixty, fifty were 'drawn' and management 'won the rest' of the mediation cases.
5 Some fifteen requests were made for arbitration in the period. The difference was seen to be split in nine cases while the union 'won' two and management the remainder.

Economic manager – manpower and incomes

Manpower planning or human resources planning is a critical aspect of manpower management at the level of the firm,[4] and it becomes even more important at the level of the State, where the utilization of labour should be a fundamental preserve of any government's economic policy.

The examples of training epitomize manpower 'interventions'[5] and economic management can be seen in income controls by various administrations. We shall develop the example of an incomes policy. First we give an historical overview of these policies and then an activity will be based upon this summary. See Box LR3.2 and Activity LR3.3.

BOX LR3.2

State intervention – incomes policies

One interventionist role of the State can be used as an example of the State, from time to time, taking an activity interest in labour relations. This box is linked to Activity LR3.3 and so themes only will be extrapolated from this UK example.

> We are unlikely to get serious debate on the objectives of an incomes policy whilst we continue to regard each period as a temporary measure, a mere hiatus on the way to some valhalla called free collective bargaining.[1]

An incomes policy aims to limit pay increases for a given round of negotiation. It can be linked to price controls/restraints as well.

The aims include alterations to the level and distribution of incomes with a view to 'moderating the rate of price inflation, controlling the distribution of incomes and increasing the efficiency of labour resources'.[2]

Incomes policies can be seen by the State as a mechanism for coping with the following:

- balance of payment deficits;
- stagnation;
- low exports;
- poor productivity;
- weak currency;
- inflation.

It tends to be some form of crisis management rather than some macro-planning of the economy. The UK experience can be summarized in the following terms.

- **1945–51** Labour government sought wage restraint. From 1948 to 1950 we had *de facto* a wage freeze with the exception of the lower paid, undermanned industries and skill differential problems. Qualified TUC support until September 1950.
- **1951** Tory Government suggested some link between wage increases and productivity. Rejected by unions.
- **1956** 'Price Plateau Policy.' Employers asked by Macmillan's Government to restrain price increases so that lower wage demands would follow(?).
- **1957** Council on 'Prices, Productivity and Income' aimed at reviewing these three factors to encourage wage bargaining and price fixing. Trade unions particularly hostile to the early reports.
- **1961** Imposition of a so-called 'pay pause', rigidly in the public sector and requested in the private sector.
- **1962** 'Incomes Policy – The Next Step' gave us a 'guiding light' of $2\frac{1}{2}$ per cent norm. Some macro-management for 'consultation and forecasting' established in the National Economic Development Council (NEDC – later NEDO). The National Incomes Commission was established to overview guidelines in incomes and to give views on wage claims. Trade unions refused to co-operate.

- **1964** Tripartite *Statement* on Productivity, Prices and Incomes aiming to keep income increases in line with productivity and stable prices.
- **1965–9** Series of *norms* – 3–3$\frac{1}{2}$ per cent and then zero. 'Exceptional treatment' again with a new body, the National Board for Prices and Incomes, to investigate these claims for exemption. 'Voluntary' restraint followed with union co-operation. In effect, backed by a series of Prices and Incomes Acts. 'Policy' collapsing by late 1969, hence the range of 2$\frac{1}{2}$–4$\frac{1}{2}$ per cent with 'exceptions' allowed.
- **1970** The new policy made little impact as pay claims 'exploded' through until the Spring. The new Conservative Government tried to encourage output and growth and to restrain pay in the public sector through 'efficiency' measures. 'De-escalation' policy formed with reducing targets (to 7 per cent). Public sector hit badly.
- **1972+** New strategy – 'standstill' on wages, prices, rents and dividends. Stage 2 involved deferred collective agreements. Stage 3, pay limits established as in Stage 2. New 'monitoring' body – the Pay Board and the Prices Commission. Conflict increased, e.g. civil service and motor industry.
- **1973** State of Emergency over fuel crisis.
- **1974** New Labour administration. 'Special cases' allowed, e.g. nurses and teachers, within a voluntary incomes policy. 'Social Contract' accepted by TUC. Pay Board and statutory controls of pay both abolished. Another new Labour administration.
- **1975+** On paper 'Social Contract' still there but price rises of almost 20 per cent and wage increases of 30 per cent. Ten per cent limit for next pay round. £6 per week flat increase/no increase for those on £8,500 per annum. Dividends also limited to 10 per cent per annum. Controls on rent.
- **1976–7** New phase, 5 per cent limit with a floor of £2.50 and a ceiling of £4.00 per week. Non-wage benefits to be included.
- **1977–8** Pay limit of 10 per cent of national earnings (no figure given for negotiations). Government sanctions against deviant companies are threatened.
- **1978–9** A 5 per cent 'guideline' with the now established twelve-month rule between negotiations. Some pay anomalies sorted out, e.g. university teachers. The low paid could receive more than 5 per cent if their weekly earnings did not exceed £44.50. Reduction in hours possible. So-called 'Winter of Discontent'.
- **1979+** New Conservative administration. On paper no stated policy. In effect, constraints on funding in the public sector. At the time of writing a new stated limit on public sector pay of 1.5 per cent is in operation.

Sources:
1   Cowan, 'A pay policy for all time'
2   Discussions with Kessler, 'Incomes Policies', MBA Seminar

---

ACTIVITY LR3.3

INCOMES POLICIES

Activity code
✓ Self-development
✓ Teamwork
✓ Communications
✓ Numeracy/IT
✓ Decisions

Task

Study Box LR3.2 on State intervention – incomes policies.

By group, or on your own, derive themes from this historical overview which may act as 'lessons' for any State contemplating introducing a full incomes policy for all employees in the country.

The State – Philosophy and Labour Relations

This scan of the possible role of the State in labour relations emphasizes that the State is potentially a very powerful actor in the overall drama. Some of the roles do not marry up: the employer/protector, the manpower manager/the paymaster, the peace-maker/the incomes regulator. The State may have difficulty reconciling some of these ambiguities. The difficulty is compounded by the predominant philosophy or approach to labour relations of the government of the day. A clear ideological perspective becomes enmeshed in these roles and certain roles become dominant at the expense of others. Some are deliberately ignored. We shall examine the philosophies first and then we can apply them to the roles.

Some interesting insights into the politics of labour relations are provided by Box LR3.3.

BOX LR3.3

The politics of labour relations

As we have seen in Unit One, the power/political consideration is never far from labour relations. Crouch emphasizes this political dimension by looking at the role of government in industrial relations.[1]

The objective of government is essentially economic according to Crouch and this translates itself into four related, if not wholly compatible, aims:

- full employment;
- price stability;
- a favourable balance of payments;
- protection of the exchange rate.

The current UK Tory administration has failed in three of these four points perhaps in part because of an over-emphasis on price stability at the expense of the other dimensions. Either way these aims are sound for most governments.

These economic aims are polluted by political ideology. The balance between the objectives and the approaches to meet the objectives is conditioned by the socio-political perception of the political parties in power at a given time.

The Right seek a free market scenario. A return to the *laissez-faire* dictum of a bygone age means

- minimal State interference in labour relations;
- a pool of unemployed to weaken the trade union power base and their negotiation tactics;
- legislative curbs on the trade union movement to prevent or constrain strikes and disputes;
- a curtailment of 'political unionism' with trade unions, where they exist, being involved with industrial issues;
- a re-affirmation of managerial prerogative and the 'right to manage'.

Variations on this theme occur. The 'wetter' conservatives still accept the free market policies but unions can also be **incorporated** via tripartite (State, unions and management) measures. The more extreme Rightists would see this corporatism as a betrayal of the free market.

The leftwing view looks to greater socio-economic planning by the State. The hard Left is very committed to worker participation, if not control, of workplace regulations and of the means of capital and distribution. The 'softer' mainstream Left has more of a pluralistic vision:

- economic stability and growth can be assisted by State intervention in the economy and in labour relations;
- unions have a legitimate right to be recognized at the workplace;
- collective bargaining is a critical part of this union involvement;
- the Labour Party has some commitment to represent organized labour;
- the Labour Party has a more ambivalent attitude towards legislative controls over unions;
- management need to manage but management by consent and through agreement is favoured.

Crouch turns to policy alternatives for the State in labour relations. These seem to have two dimensions: the position of trade unions and the wider industrial relations system. Two types of system are propounded: a 'liberal' approach and a 'corporatist' approach whereby the unions become more involved with the activities of the State. Perhaps the dynamic of the other actor, management, is lacking in this scenario.

The 'liberal system' can be characterized by strong unions and free unfettered collective bargaining or by a neo-*laissez-faire* approach. The 'corporatist' option is likewise divided with bargaining corporatism occurring and unions trading their members' demands for more say in State economic policy. The weaker unions appear under corporatism where the unions are more absorbed into the State apparatus.

Interestingly, Crouch writing in 1979 suggested that monetarism and high unemployment would lead to corporatism. With hindsight, as we have seen (Unit Two) corporatism has not really occurred under these conditions in the UK of the 1980s and early 1990s but instead we have had more trade union marginalization and more macho management coupled with rampant *laissez-faire* tactics of government.

So the neo-*laissez-faire* approach has been more typical of the 1979 UK situation with high unemployment and weak disorganized labour subordinate to the employer through the market system. Tight monetary control and the regulation of public spending have stimulated unemployment and contained demand.

Crouch rightly foresees a problem: if and when recovery occurs the trade unions will attempt to make up lost ground for this period of (Tory) inspired deprivation. The next Labour Government may be in the unfortunate position of picking up the task.

Source:
1 Adapted from Crouch, *The Politics of Industrial Relations*

There are many philosophies of government with their own political cum ideological stance. Three (perhaps four) seem to stand out:

- Collectivism – compulsory
- Collectivism – voluntary
- Individualism

Collectivism – compulsory

This is a tripartite vision: the State, the trade unions and management all come together under some corporatist approach. Differing interests are diluted for the sake of social cohesion and uniformity. The unions, in particular, lose their independence, if not their identity. The 'common good' (defined by the State) dominates. Totalitarian regimes from Stalinist Russia to Nazi Germany fall into this category. Some crises make for corporatism as during the world wars. In the 1960s the 'common weal' was often advocated by employers and Conservative Ministers in the UK. In the 1970s the Labour administration 'encouraged' union participation in economic matters – but even then this policy fell short of 'pure corporatism'. This compulsory collectivism has not been the mainstay approach of the State in the UK.

Collectivism – voluntary

The UK norm for most of the twentieth century until the late 1970s has been that of a voluntarist tradition. The role of the State is more remote in this philosophy. The main parties voluntarily enter into an arrangement. When, and if, this arrangement 'falls down' through disputes or whatever the State acts as a 'safety net'. It can afford more of a neutral stance but it can come down on one side or the other and this tended to occur when governments started to invoke a plethora of labour relations legislation which had a distinct political colour to it.

Box LR3.4 gives an illustration of voluntary collectivism in the context of the UK. There is a clear change to individualism and we develop this in the next section.

BOX LR3.4

UK system – traditional features

As Britain was the first country to industrialize, it had the first industrial relations system. Consequently there have been several key themes in the UK system. These are perhaps changing since the late 1970s but we need an overview of history to determine whether the changes are permanent.

- **Collective bargaining** Priority has been given to this form of joint negotiation compared with say state regulation or regulation by one party.
- **Voluntary** The parties freely enter into agreemeents through voluntary means rather than being compelled by the State. When the relationship 'broke down' traditionally the State got involved, e.g. arbitration.
- **Minimum of government interference** The State has not really got involved in, say, minimum wages, etc.
- **Absence of law** Courts have largely been 'out' of industrial relations from 1906 to the 1970s.

This system was much admired by many observers. It gave economic freedom and *relative* industrial peace. It was flexible and the responsibility lay squarely on the parties to the system.

Increasingly though in the 1950s and particularly the 1960s the system began to come under challenge. Governments pushed by economic difficulties from inflation to strikes have intervened in, for example, pay policy to legislation. The 'threat' also came from below with the increasing role of the steward *vis-à-vis* the full-time official and the shift to plant bargaining.

By the late 1970s and 1980s the traditional features seem to be blurred, if not altered out of all recognition.

Individualism

This involves placing the individual (not the group) to the fore – at best a revamped form of nineteenth-century liberalism, at worst a recipe for selfishness and of beggar your neighbour. The freedom of the individual acting with the minimum of restraint or constraint from others epitomizes this view. It is allied to a view of the marketplace dominating all human interaction. The morality and practice merge. This reminds us of the early European imperialists fusing their religious zeal with a practical lust for gold.

Individual rights must dominate and 'combinations' in the marketplace, such as unions, must be curbed if not eradicated as they distort the natural supply and demand of the market. This looks like a recipe for *laissez-faire* policies with the government pulling out of its responsibilities for labour relations. In the event, certain interventions, such as legal constraints, do occur but withdrawal of safety nets has also occurred in the UK since 1979.

We can therefore summarize how the philosophies actually impinge on the rules before moving on to management, the next set of actors. This summary also shows that even within the philosophies there is a clear political interpretation (which is not always consistent with the overall philosophy) depending upon the political party in charge of government. See table 3.1.

Table 3.1 The State – Philosophies and roles in labour relations in the UK

Role	Philosophy		
	Collectivism (compulsory)	Collectivism (voluntary)	Individualism
1 Employer/paymaster/ overseer	The State is omnipresent.	The State is a 'responsible' employer (on paper).	The market dominates – hence privatization, etc. 'Roll back the State'.
2 Buyer/protector	On paper it is the planner.	Protective legislation for all is important. The State can influence power as well, if it wishes.	Individual protection emphasized – but even then unfair dismissal terms worsened of late in the UK.
3 Rule-maker/peace-maker	If 'disturbances' occur, the State can preside.	Sets the parameters and acts as a safety net. Sets the ground rules.	Little scope here for intervention.
4 Economic manager – manpower and incomes	It is *the* key employer in Leftist regimes and is strong on economic management in both Left and Right variants.	Depends on political complexion. Some Leftist attempts to manage the economy and parties (Left/Right) have attempted to intervene on prices.	Little scope for intervention in manpower utilization. Some unemployment policies as regards training. Interferes with 'own' employees' pay – not with others.

Management

Management can mean various things:

- mobilizing scarce resources to meet the end goals of an organization;
- those who physically carry out the process above;
- the functions or the activities from control to motivation;
- more recently the roles or interactions between people from liaison to decision making.

The popular definition derived from Mary Parker Follett and noted by Stoner and Wankel[6] is to see management as achieving results through other people. Whether this definition is adequate to describe all management is debatable, but for labour relations it will suffice for the moment to get us started on the detailed analysis. There could be a great debate as to whether the managers of labour are carrying out the 'normal' managerial functions or roles but we will leave out this discussion. We can note the specialist input of the labour relations advisor and the main work of the area falling to the line manager. (Refer to Box LR3.5.)

BOX LR3.5

The management of labour relations

Purcell writing in the early 1980s argues that labour relations are more than mere 'problems' at the workplace point of production.[1]

He identifies four 'managerial' issues which should be fruitful areas of research:

- corporate decision making and industrial relations;
- levels of bargaining;
- control mechanisms;
- managerial ideology and styles.

This is still a useful agenda for our time as well and these issues are developed elsewhere in this unit. The thoughts of Purcell should be enlarged upon. Further, we develop these themes in the main text.

Corporate structures are seen to be changing with multi-divisional units led by a strategic core at head office. Budgetary control and the profitability ratios of these 'strategic business units' have swung to these cores at head office, hence labour relations should follow the locus of decision making.

So labour relations embraces corporate strategy and the financial economics of the firm at the centre and not just at the fringe. This shift may be more strategic than operational, of course, and the divisions/units are still very much concerned with operational issues, both managerial and labour relations. The macro-strategy, of course, dictates the play and Purcell is correct to point this out.

The relationship and trade-off between corporate bargaining and trade arrangements and the localized or plant industrial relations systems follow on from this moving locus of power. Interestingly there is a current debate about centralized versus decentralized bargaining but the issue is greyer than that as the real locus of corporate power will still lie at the centre in spite of delegated decision making to the units. Perhaps this emphasizes the point that the subject matter of labour relations is increasingly being relegated to terms and conditions of work rather than the nature of work itself.

Management as we see it in this unit has a control fetish in labour relations. Purcell rightly sees job evaluation as a powerful tool[2] as the differential issues (if not payment) may be more easily resolved. The structuring of work and reward, particularly performance pay, have become key issues of the 1980s and early 1990s.

The managerial approaches to labour relations, the ideology (if it exists) and the way that things are done (the style) have become writ large in this period since Purcell was writing.

At the same time, the management of labour cannot be seen in isolation; the other actors, in this case declining trade unions and a *laissez-faire* government, acting in a turbulent external environment must impact on what management can and must do in labour relations. We shall now develop Purcell's themes.

Sources:
1   Adapted from Purcell, 'The management of industrial relations in the modern corporation'
2   See Livy, *Job Evaluation*

Decision making is covered in Unit Five as are levels of bargaining. We shall develop the overall management role in employee relations, touch upon ideology and style and examine this control theme. Before we can do this, we must note that management has tended to be less overt and open about its philosophies, aims and actions in labour relations compared with trade unions. We shall need to derive some of these themes through its behavioural patterns. Fortunately, we can also use employer associations, a collection of firms coming together for trade and labour relations purposes, as examples of managerial action for we know a fair amount about these associations.

Management's role in labour relations

The basic role of management in any organization is to husband the resources in an efficient and effective manner. Ultimately this is for the benefit of task accomplishment and the goals of the organization. The management of labour relations thus falls into this category.

It is made more complex by the existence of a dynamic labour relations system and by the potential opposition of trade unions with links to the likelihood of an interfering State. Rather than reiterate the whole system – which, of course, is relevant – we shall select some key factors which impact on the role of management in labour relations. They include the following points.

- Management can often be reactive in labour relations, following unions rather than giving a lead. The *strength and degree of unionization* is important. A powerful union bloc may stimulate a more cautious role on exercising managerial prerogative.

- The *power dynamics* and the history of *past relationships* and disputes patterns, etc., between management and the unions must be relevant. A troubled history may make for a low trust factor and a 'defensive' stance by either party.

- The external environment, particularly the *product market* and the role of the *State*, may impact on the role of management with drives for efficiency and monitoring of prices and incomes policies, etc.

- The *degree of formality of labour relations* will be important. Some organizations conduct their collective relationships in a very bureaucratic fashion and I have been party to 'gentlemanly' debates about Clause 2 and subpara 3, section 3. In another firm, I suspended a disputes discussion owing to continued foul language from the union side.

- The approach to *decision making* and *bargaining* will be relevant. A problem-solving approach (see Unit Five) will lend itself to a 'distributive' frame of reference while a traditional approach to bargaining will reflect a more power-oriented approach.

- The existence of a *supportive employer association* for advice/guidance/dispute resolution, etc., is relevant.

- The *level of skill and expertise* of the managers of labour and their degree of training are important (we shall come back to this later in this section).

- The *structure of the organization* and its tolerance of ambiguity as well as the scope for managers in the hierarchy to make decisions and agreements are very important.

- The prevailing *philosophy of management* (see the next section) and its style is a factor.

- The concept of *control* and the extent to which this is a fetish of management must be taken into account.

- The *behaviour* of management must be considered.

The philosophy and style of management and this control theme will now be developed but first we give some rather disturbing views of top managers on labour relations. The research is a little dated but anecdotal experience in industry, consultancy, training and teaching managers means that it still strikes a chord (refer to Box LR3.6 on the role of top management in labour relations).

BOX LR3.6

The role of top management in labour relations

Winkler's research into the attitudes and behaviour of directors in labour relations shows great misunderstanding of, if not a cynical contempt for, employees and their institutions.[1]

The research can be summarized as follows.

- Apart from some daily contact with secretaries, etc., most senior managers had no *real contact* with employees; this was compounded by the social segregation outside work akin to a class-stratified society.
- There was *little concern for the workers' lot*. Their interests, views and goals counted for next to nothing.
- Employees were seen primarily in *cost terms* and 'shopfloor therapeutics' (attitudes/motivation/participation) counted for nothing.
- *Order* not conflict was the expected norm as we have seen amongst people holding a unitarist perspective (see Unit One).
- *Labour relations information* emanated from the normal management hierarchy, crises, consultation and bargaining; key managers with worker empathy and the mass media were important sources.

So this social distance was linked to a state of ignorance whereby those further down the managerial hierarchy could deal with any 'local difficulties' which might arise in labour relations and leave the top management to direct the affairs of the organization.

If these perspectives still prevail, particularly the abdication by top management and the attempt to build 'buffers' via labour relations specialists and other forms of managerial systems, the result is that they do little to enhance the vision of the effective management of labour relations.

Source:
1 Adapted from Winkler, 'The ghost at the bargaining table: directors and industrial relations'

Management of labour relations – philosophy and style

We have covered the unitary–pluralist themes in Unit One. If management is adopting more of a unitarist view it means:

- an emphasis on its 'right to manage';
- trade union derecognition if possible and grudging acceptance as probable;
- an inability to grasp the dynamics of conflict and settle it accordingly through some negotiations.

The style or approach to labour is very much tied up with the underpinning frame of reference or philosophy. (See Box LR3.7 on a question of style.)

BOX LR3.7

A question of style

The interesting work of Purcell and Sisson[1] building on the earlier work of Fox[2] noted the following types of style in management – employee relationships.

Traditional	An authoritarian approach to staff. Clearly anti-union and opposed to recognizing unions. Perhaps latter-day unitarists.
Classical conflict	Unions are here but perhaps management could live without them. Constant challenge from unions and conflict predominates between managers and unions.
Sophisticated moderns	A more subtle managerial approach. The unions are here so we need to accept them and involve them. Effective communications and consent are important to 'break down the barriers'. This aims at getting the workers 'on management's side' and is an indirect form of control.
Continuous challenge	This is a conflict zone. Workgroup controls clash with managerial prerogatives in this battle for control.
Sophisticated paternalists	Trade unions are not normally seen as 'necessary'. The good employer looks after the interests of the workers through 'progressive personnel policies'. Management pursues its objectives in an unfettered manner. This looks like a human resource management variation.[3]

Sources:
1   Purcell and Sisson, 'Strategies and practice in the management of industrial relations'
2   Fox, 'Industrial sociology and industrial relations'
3   Anderson, *Effective Personnel Management*

A control fetish?

Most of these styles with their underlying frames of reference are about the control of labour.

All business organizations are evaluated by economic criteria and this financial vision is also percolating down to 'not for profit' enterprises as well where 'surplus' replaces the motive of profit. Managers must control the factors of production to achieve this surplus. Trade unions exist to limit this control over labour and indeed to advance their rights as representatives of working people as well. Groups and individual workers also use day to day informal controls[7] to 'make out' at the place of work.

Control really means attempting to get events to conform to plans. Control as an authority concept is more debatable but we can look at control from a goal-related perspective which is perhaps less debatable.

To complete this unit on control from a management angle, a broad perspective is required. Both labour and management have rights and prerogatives. The approach of Goodrich[8] is very useful with his floating 'frontier' between the two parties. Ultimately, we are not dealing with a slave/serf economy and we need motivated employees. Management can only gain this acceptance in the long term by giving up some of its control. The vision of sharing control to maintain that control in the long term has been a feature of the British ruling elite's emphasis on maintaining its power for centuries. Through bargaining and joint decision making some control is being shared out and the objectives of the business/enterprise or organization have greater chance of success without control being equated to some hang-up about authority.

We shall come back to this control relationship in our last unit. Now we turn our attention to real examples of the management of labour in practice through an analysis of the latest trend towards human resource management. Please see Box LR3.8. Thereafter we turn to employer associations as illustrations of management practice in labour relations.

BOX LR3.8

Human resource management – a managerial challenge to traditional labour relations?

Since the early 1980s, if not before, human resource management (HRM) has eroded the position of personnel management as the specialist activity concerned with the employment of people at the workplace.

The philosophy of HRM is different from that of personnel management as it is more managerialist and less concerned with people for their own sake; people become a resource like a piece of furniture or whatever that can be used (utilized) by the organization.[1] To Torrington and Hall 'it is . . . totally identified with management interests, being a general management activity, and is relatively distant from the workforce as a whole'.[2]

Above all else it holds a unitarist perspective seeking an integrated culture – from a managerialist perspective. There is little scope here for pluralism or divergent interests.

Power, conflict, separate interests are subordinated to the possibility or probability of 'a covert form of employee manipulation dressed up as mutuality (harmony)'.[3]

Armstrong[4] elsewhere argues that personnel management is not that different from HRM. There may be something here, for both are manipulative. Yet the philosophies differ: personnel management may not be pluralistic *per se* but it can accommodate divergent views, while HRM seems to be set on the unitarist rock.

So HRM is seen as a more exploitative, if subtle, attempt by management to move the 'frontier of control' in its direction. As such, it is a threat to trade unions and to the pluralistic frame of reference which may guide labour relations.

Sources:
1   See Anderson, *Effective Personnel Management*, in this series (Unit One)
2   Torrington and Hall, *Personnel Management: a new approach*
3   Fowler, 'When Chief Executives discover HRM'
4   Armstrong, 'HRM: a case of the emperor's new clothes?'

Employer associations – managing labour in practice

To a great extent, historically the role of employer organizations or associations means dealing with labour relations outside the scope of the firm. Indeed, labour relations tended to have a focus outside of the firm[9] during the nineteenth century. We find a general move away of the focus of power from the employer association to the plant or company during the twentieth century for the following reasons:

■ social change;

■ an increased size within the plant;

■ bureaucratization;

■ a 'managerial revolution' taking over some of the owner's responsibilities;

■ complex pay systems;

- more powerful unions at plant level;
- more areas being co-determined.

However, given the secrecy surrounding the management of labour relations, a study of these associations is quite revealing about the behaviour of management in labour relations. Please refer to Box LR3.9 and complete Activity LR3.4.

BOX LR3.9

Employer associations

Trade unions by definition are mass organizations and in many ways their power lies in their numbers, their ability to mobilize and the ability to act in a concerted fashion. In a sense they need to be proselytizing institutions. The same cannot be said for employer associations.

These organizations of employers cannot be seen as employers' trade unions. They are a collection of firms, already quite strong in their own right, coming together for mutual support and aid both for labour relations and commercial matters.

Unlike trade unions their history is cloudy and there is an air of secrecy about them. The associations, unlike unions, have a low profile and the public perception of their actions is minimal. Indeed, many new students to the subject do not know that they even exist! They can afford to be lobbyists rather than activists and they do not have to attempt to put their somewhat clandestine activities in a favourable light.

Their history and origins seem to be obscure. In the UK, we know that they were around in the late eighteenth century and were certainly established in localized pockets by the early nineteenth century. They may have been more tacit agreements by local employers than formal associations as such.

By the mid-nineteenth century stronger 'model' unions presented a clear threat to employers. Some associations attempted to crush this threat; others attempted to give sustenance to their fellow firms. Towards the end of the century the following techniques are evident.

- **Black listing** A list of deviants/strikers would be circulated by the association to stop them being employed (and employable elsewhere).
- **Blackleg labour** Financial support was possible through the association but 'scab' or 'blackleg' non-unionized labour could be employed to curb strikes within one member's factory.
- **Non-union membership to lockouts** Some attempts to curb union membership existed with clauses that employment was conditional on not being a union member. If things became 'intolerable' sympathetic lockouts could be used but considerable loss would be involved here and so it was not a favoured long-term tactic.

The growth of bargaining structures and industry type of bargaining during and after World War II stimulated the growth of these associations and they moved towards a bargaining role rather than some counter-revolutionary mode.

Currently, their roles include commercial matters such as advice and guidance in imports/exports to labour relations. Their labour relations functions include:

■ collective bargaining – particularly the basic terms and conditions of employment which can be 'added' to at the local level;

■ disputes handling as part of the disputes procedure outside the firm;

■ guidance on interpretation of agreements and legal advice in labour issues;

■ health and safety at work;

■ training;

■ research;

■ lobbying government and advisory members on legislation, etc.

To a great extent employer associations has been identified with national/ industry bargaining. With the relative demise of this type of bargaining (see Unit Five), their negotiating function may be weakened but they still retain other important roles in labour relations and commercial matters, so they will not disappear from the scene.

ACTIVITY LR3.4

EMPLOYER ASSOCIATION (+/−)

Activity code
✓ Self-development
✓ Teamwork
✓ Communications
☐ Numeracy/IT
✓ Decisions

After reading Box LR3.9 on employer associations, outline the main arguments for and against a company joining an employer association.

Towards good practice in labour relations

Philosophy
First of all any concept of good practice for the benefit of all parties concerned needs some guiding philosophy. It is suggested that a **Pluralist** frame of reference is more suitable for managers than other perspectives, for the following reasons:

- it allows the recognition and existence of other legitimate parties;
- it can lead to greater cohesion even though different interests are accepted;
- it allows conflict to be handled in a more constructive format;
- it recognizes that ongoing bargaining means that decision making is joint in many areas and this can lead to greater acceptance of the decision process similar to a Japanese approach.

The **sophisticated modern** style[10] follows on from this understanding. It may be manipulative – but all the approaches have this dimension. This approach does allow conflict to be reconciled with harmony; it allows the presence of unions and may reduce the power of strategic groups. It also facilitates control but the style is based more on consensus and joint acceptance than some autocratic variation of slavery or 'industrial' feudalism.

ACTIVITY LR3.5

A CODE OF GOOD PRACTICE

Activity code
- ✓ Self-development
- ✓ Teamwork
- ✓ Communications
- ☐ Numeracy/IT
- ✓ Decisions

Task
Given your knowledge of the aims and actions of management and unions, draft a code of guiding principles for both parties which will not only meet their diverse aims but allow them to live together.

You should consider the basic objectives of both parties and work through some mechanisms to achieve these aims. The assumed perspective is pluralistic.

A code of conduct

Very few attempts have been made to codify these principles into working codes of conduct. Certainly some firms have taken some of the philosophy of the 'sophisticated moderns' and encapsulated it in their policies and procedures. Others have trained managers and trade unionists to seek to adapt their behavioural patterns to meet these principles. First we look at the code of practice, then we develop policies and we conclude by examining useful training inputs in this area. We shall do this by completing activities. Please refer to Activity LR3.5, 'A code of good practice' and then tackle Activity LR3.6 on policies at the London Brewing Company.

ACTIVITY LR3.6

THE LONDON BREWING COMPANY

Activity code
- ✓ Self-development
- ✓ Teamwork
- ✓ Communications
- ☐ Numeracy/IT
- ✓ Decisions

The London Brewing Company has some 7,500 employees and sales of almost £800 million per annum. As the name suggests, it was founded in London, and the head office remains there. Times have moved on, though, and given its national and increasing international market, it should perhaps be renamed 'The UK Brewing Company'.

The company moved out of London into geographical 'divisions' after the Second World War. With acquisition and the removal of some of the fiercest local competition through a policy of attrition, the six geographical divisions became regional companies responsible for their own costs and profitability. Increasingly each of the regional companies has been given fuller autonomy. Apart from the corporate plan, capital/investment projects and the overall marketing plan, each company is virtually independent.

The focal point of each regional company is a brewery, so there are six breweries altogether making over forty-five different beers and lagers. On the retail side there are 4,221 tenanted public houses, thirty-two shops specializing in selling wines, beers and spirits, and eight 'inherited' inns-cum-restaurants, all in East Anglia. The pubs and inns are controlled by the regional companies while the shop side is controlled by a specialist company based in

Stevenage, Hertfordshire. Each of the companies has a regional board of directors, whose chairperson is on the main board in London.

The monthly meeting of the labour relations committee of the brewery, chaired by the Director of Personnel and staffed by each of the regions' Personnel Managers with the Company Production Director an *ex officio* member, had been considering the labour relations policies of the whole firm.

An agreement on what constituted labour relations had been made. This was seen as 'all matters concerning the relationship between managers and trade unions which are subject to the joint regulation between the company and trade unions'.

After some time and discussion, the overall objectives of the company's employee relations policy had been thrashed out:

- the achievement and maintenance of efficient work levels and productivity;
- the promotion of harmonious working relationships and the avoidance of conflict;
- the control and monitoring of labour costs, e.g. wage drift;
- the operation of this policy to avoid conflicts;
- the channelling of conflicts when they arise and the promotion of satisfactory relationships for all the parties concerned.

However, problems existed which needed to be resolved. Where did the line managers' responsibility end and that of the staff specialist start? Who should chair labour relations meetings at unit (department) or regional company or overall company (HQ) level? Were there different types of meetings needing different chairs, e.g. consultation compared with negotiation?

At company (HQ) level who should negotiate for the company and over what issues? Was the advice from the centre binding on other non-HQ managers? Where did policy emanate – locally or at the centre? Should there be more labour research at the centre? Where did the responsibility for training in labour relations really end (and start)?

What subjects could be discussed at local company level and at unit level? How much latitude should be allowed to non-HQ managers in the interpretation and application of agreements?

Which level should now negotiate the following: basic rates, hours of work, sick pay, redundancy, dismissal, overtime, shifts, amendments to agreements, start/finish times, working methods, operational issues not in the main agreement, payment 'plussages', local shift patterns and trade union recognition?

Who should have authority to make the decisions over:

- union recognition,
- major strike decisions (concede or otherwise),
- increases on basic rates,
- major innovations regarding consultation, pay or on any issue of labour relations?

Task

Using the threefold division of the Company (London HQ, the regional companies and the unit (department of the regional company)) your task is to draft a policy which will take into account good practice, the stated objectives of the firm and a mechanism to resolve these responsibilities – subject to decision/authority issues by the threefold division of the organization of the whole brewing company.

Solution

■ Line/staff responsibilities:

■ Role of labour relations specialists:

■ Functional allocation of labour relations at company (HQ) level:

■ Regional company level:

■ Unit (regional company departmental level)

■ Communications – labour relations

■ Training – labour relations

■ Subject matter – by level (×3) of negotiation

HQ

Regional company

Unit

■ Specific subject matter appropriate to level

HQ, company level

Regional, company level

Unit/departmental level

Training managers in labour relations – as an adjunct to codes, policies and procedures

To conclude this section, the basic responsibility for labour relations in the organization must rest with management. A skilled approach to the subject can minimize conflicts from strikes to absence and can increase the morale of the labour force by consistent non-arbitrary decisions in the often sensitive area of labour relations.

Working in 1984, Jennings and Undy[11] found that some 66 per cent of their sample (2,000) were expected to deal with trade union representatives. Their survey showed that specialist help was often available but 48 per cent of the sample noted that the specialist in labour relations was never present at these union–management sessions. They reported great confusion over line managers' perspectives on company policy and procedures.

It is fitting to finish this section on management as a key player in the system by examining some learning needs in the area of labour relations as training and development are both seen as critical components in effective labour relations (see Activity LR3.7).

ACTIVITY LR3.7

TRAINING MANAGERS IN LABOUR RELATIONS

Activity code
☑ Self-development
☐ Teamwork
☑ Communications
☑ Numeracy/IT
☑ Decisions

A comprehensive needs analysis has been completed by AApma (table 3.2). Senior managers (thirty), line managers under these top managers (250), first level supervisors/foremen (forty) and specialists (ten) had all been analysed. Their needs had been isolated and the percentage requiring some form of training in labour relations had been noted by job level against a specific knowledge or skill need. Attitudinal training was not specifically requested as it was felt by the Board to be somewhat 'unsavoury'.

Task
Your role is to collate these findings and write a report based on these statistics for management to consider. Priority areas should be noted.

Table 3.2

	Senior management (30)	Other line management (250)	First level management (40)	Staff specialists (10)
Identified knowledge areas				
National labour relations	45	60	12	3
Labour law	50	90	80	25
Company labour relations system	18	81	61	8
Company policy (labour relations)	10	83	98	31
Company procedures and agreements	25	89	79	25
Disputes/grievances	60	82	32	50
Discipline/dismissal, redundancy	35	93	81	38
Pay/job evaluation	20	70	10	31
Collective bargaining	49	60	10	2
Consultation/participation	63	51	12	32
Other, e.g. job design	10	8	3	25
Identified skill areas				
Change management	80	95	31	60
Negotiation	10	65	35	62
Research in labour issues	19	21	1	80
Consultation	63	50	3	30
Disputes handling	59	95	40	56
Discipline/dismissal, redundancy	10	98	84	40
Problem solving (labour relations)	41	83	66	15
Communication	58	63	10	35

Needs are expressed as a percentage of the above totals.

The Media and Labour Relations

This is the last 'actor' that we shall consider before moving on to the processes of conflict and power in the next unit.

The sinking of the Maine in 1898 may not have caused the American war with Cuba but real damage was done to public opinion by the 'Yellow Press' which whipped up the clamour for war amongst the masses. The relationship between media and public opinion and the impact of that public opinion on decision-makers is debatable. The media can forge and also reflect public opinion. But even then main actors may not take much notice of that opinion. Yet the public relations battlefield is wide open and all parties involved in disputes, for example, may attempt to get neutrals on their side to sway the opposition.

We need first to examine some perspectives on the media. (Please refer to Box LR3.10.)

BOX LR3.10

Media perspectives

A machine: stimulus–response

This is a stimulus–response type of argument. Like alcohol or drugs, we not only become 'hooked' on the stimulus, but it gives a chain reaction. Perhaps in small quantities the drug is not harmful but by definition the mass media must be quite powerful stimuli. Of course we are not empty vessels and the stimulus–response view of behaviourism must be tempered by some form of critical judgement of the receiver.

Opinion leaders and followers

It could be argued that the group leaders/opinion leaders are in more active touch with the media, or certain types of media, than the mass of the population. This is an active–passive dimension and presupposes both the power of the leader to influence and a herd (mentality) of the wider population.

Free choice: recipients' satisfaction and world views

The mechanical stimulus–response approach is contrasted with a view that free choice and personal satisfaction dominate our lives including the use of different types of media. Unfortunately many people may not have this independent free thought or the opportunity to put it into effect. At the same time, there is some choice as to which newspaper we read, to reinforce our own world view perhaps rather than to derive satisfaction.

Drip-drip approach

This is a cumulative type of approach, perhaps used by advertisers with their music, colour and movement. It takes account of the psychological needs and wants of the audience and a wider social perspective of income, demographics, etc. So the media is only one factor in our creation of a social situation.

The media are wide ranging: television, radio, magazines, newspapers, advertising, books, video, cinema, music, computers, cable/sky, Ceefax and Prestel, etc. How do all these impact on labour relations? It depends on the view taken of society to some extent. One vision is to see the media as being representative of the ownership of the means of production and distribution. Their imagery reinforces this control and authority system, peddling drivel, gameshows on television, horse racing and scantily clad women in some newspapers. This would consolidate the domination principle and help create some false consciousness. The acid test here may not be just the ownership of the media but their actual content.

A more liberal perspective is to see a free media, from newspapers to advertising, as part of industrial choice and freedom. The buyer is important here and can vote with his or her purse. So consumers' needs and wants dominate and the media are there to meet these demands almost from a marketing perspective. There is no Machiavellian plot to consolidate the ideology of the elite (perhaps to enrich the elite though) but the system is market led – a place where consumers (buyers) and media meet and compete with one another. If they do not meet consumer needs/wants the media will no longer have the right to exist. The ownership is not important in this view for it is customer needs which dominate as well as freedom – of the individual and of the media. The content of the media is not devoid of input, of course, but it must strike a chord with its audience in this marketplace. This consumption of events, or the view that the media know what the consumer wants, is advocated by the owners of the media.

A more realistic view of much of the media is that specialists give a 'product/service' which they feel meets consumer needs. This is a product oriented rather than a marketing vision and emphasizes the satisfaction of consumer needs through given inputs – standardized products. In turn these products are 'owned' by an elite.

In labour relations these 'standardized products' are particularly acute in the news reporting of this subject. Further, if we start making a content analysis of actual reporting on labour relations issues and an analysis of the tone and image as well as the commentary itself, we find that much of the reporting does not pass a test of objectivity.

Hence, many views exist concerning the role of the media in labour relations:

- the media are a servant of the ruling elite or establishment;
- the media must be kept in private hands (monopoly?) to avoid an extension of State 'dictatorship';
- the media are there to be used by the actors in the system as a form of extended public relations;
- the media are there to provide an objective commentary on current affairs;
- the media are there to educate and enlighten;
- the media exist to entertain;
- the media exist to lobby;
- the media are there as a reflection of freedom of speech in a democratic state.

Whatever they are, the media tend to fail to live up to Jack Barbash's[12] vision of seeing things through the eyes of the participants – at least in the area of labour relations. Newsworthiness, however defined, is the key aspect linked to the political and ideological editorial stance of the proprietor cum editorial board.

We seem to end up with half truths, distortions, deliberate falsification in some circumstances, an anti-union slant by most and a pro-managerialist vision in other commentaries. The unions are not handling their public image very well or managers do it better. Perhaps this managerialist bias inherent in the media over labour relations cannot be overcome as the media barons put their common employer interest first and objective news reporting second. A more Machiavellian view would be to see them deliberately manipulating news to distort the facts for public consumption.

Only a few UK quality newspapers such as the *Observer*, the *Guardian* and the *Independent* give a semblance of objectivity and depth in their coverage of labour relations matters. The *Financial Times*, in spite of managerial bias, does aspire to and meet an objective approach to fact finding in the area. Most of the media do not. Indeed, Seaton[13] notes that the role of unions 'is being eroded and distorted by the effects of increasingly hostile reporting'.

The classical example of media hostility to unions is demonstrated by the so-called (media term?) 'winter of discontent', a period which helped to tumble an already shaky Labour administration. Causation was almost ignored at the expense of the results or impact on the economy, individuals, and society, etc.

Another example of biased reporting which was upheld by the Commission on the Press in 1975 showed that 715 column inches out of some 800 column inches were geared to the impact and the processes of a strike in British Waters Board. Only a paltry fifteen column inches were given to the reasons behind the strike.

The Glasgow Media Group[14] studied the main television channels. Some of their research findings on the BBC (perceived by some to be the bastion of fair play) were as follows:

- union membership was seen to be a minority of the working population (at that time it was not);
- inflation seemed to be only wage related in its causation;
- strike action was against the 'common good';
- unions were seen as strike prone and a managerialist view was taken of the results of industrial action.

In fairness to television and radio they may not be able to present the full picture given timescales, etc., but they can report events fairly. The popular press in the UK is virtually in the pocket of the Conservative Party. At the time of writing the *Mirror* may be going the same way. Conservative trade unionists do exist, of course, but the party line, of late anyway, cannot be described as pro trade union. This is reflected in most of the popular press.

The reporting media (rather than the entertainment and advertising media) seem to adopt a conscious posture of speaking for 'the national interest'. The 'poor consumer' is struck by industrial action on the rail network while the causes of the issues are often given a cursory mention – if any mention at all.

'Newsworthy' items in labour relations revolve around conflict – strikes, disputes and disruption. Labour relations become a 'problem', being perceived in terms of the consequences of a given industrial dispute rather than from some wider perspective which may also involve causation and gestation. The reporting media seem to take up an 'independent' consumerist stance against the twin tyrannies of organized capital and organized labour. But the real 'problems' seem to be that trade unions are perceived as hellbent on pursuing their own narrow sectional interest (against consumers, against the public or against the national interest). There is little sympathy and not much empathy towards trade unions in this coverage.

At the same time, trade unionists and managers can use the media as well. When impasse occurs in collective bargaining or when 'leaks' have to occur, we have witnessed both sides using the media as an extension of their bargaining role. This happens in some bitter conflicts also – the picture of mounted police attacking miners is legend. So the main actors attempt to manipulate the media as well.

However, the real manipulation is writ large in the media. Does this constitute a conspiracy? The Marxists would say yes, while the Liberals would add that it 'influences' rather than 'conspires'. As an historian by training I tend not to go down the conspiratorial view of historical development, but much of the media reporting on trade unions and on conflict has all the hallmarks of such a conspiracy – dressed up in 'the consumers need to know' or whatever. There is certainly bias in the media on labour relations in general, and conflict specifically also gets a very bad press. We shall now turn to conflict – hopefully from a more objective stance.

Notes

1 *London Evening Standard*, quoted by the *Guardian*, 16 April 1993.

2 Anthony, *The Conduct of Industrial Relations*.

3 A fair wages resolution (as in 1946) would be one way out of this dilemma.

4 See Bramham, *Practical Manpower Planning*, and the subsequent book, *Human Resource Planning*.

5 See, for example, NEDO/MSC, 'Competence and competition, training and education in the Federal Republic of Germany, the United States and Japan'.

6 Stoner and Wankel in *Management* note this as 'the art of getting things done through people'.

7 The work of Roy is quite enlightening on this subject of informal controls. See, for example, 'Quota restriction and goldbricking in a machine shop'.

8 Goodrich, *The Frontier of Control*.

9 Clegg, *The Changing System of Industrial Relations in Great Britain*, makes this point and cites evidence of the 1891 Royal Commission.

10 This 'sophisticated modern' approach has been noted by Purcell and Sisson, 'Strategies and practice in the management of industrial relations'.

11 Jennings and Undy, 'Auditing managers' I.R. training needs'. See also Jennings et al., 'Managers and industrial relations: the identification of training needs'.

12 Barbash, *The Elements of Industrial Relations*.

13 Seaton, 'Trade unions and the media'.

14 Glasgow University Media Group, *Bad News, More Bad News* and *More Bad News Vol. 2*.

Unit Four

Conflict

Learning Objectives

After completing this unit you should be able to:

- appreciate the importance of conflict in labour relations;
- determine the environmental causes of conflict;
- extrapolate features leading to a greater propensity of conflict from research;
- examine the merits of using a model to predict conflict;
- analyse collective conflict;
- overview managerial views of conflict and its 'avoidance';
- apply the generic skills.

Contents

Overview

Conflict

Approaches

► The harmony approach

► The conflict approach

► The convergence approach

Conflict Causation – Specific Schools of Thought

► Political

► Economic

► Social

► Technical/technological

Conflict – A Predictive Model?

Conflict – A Range of Options

Collective Conflict – Disputes/Grievances

Collective Conflict – Strikes

Managerial Strategies – Conflict 'Avoidance'

Unit Four

❝ Conflict of interest is inevitable between employer and employee because there is an authority relationship in which the aims of the two parties will at least sometimes conflict.❞

R. Dahrendorf[1]

Overview

Conflict involves a struggle over values, status, power and scarce resources. As the basis of the employment relationship is seen to be one of divergent interests, such conflict is seen to be inevitable at the workplace. The extent, form and type of conflict will vary and working accommodations exist in order for the basic relationship to continue, but this does not detract from the inevitability theme, as one party will attempt to gain the desired values and to neutralize if not injure its rivals in the process.

This unit develops the importance of the concept of conflict to labour relations. It looks at the effects of conflict, both negative and positive.

Causation not resolution is the subject of this unit. Hopefully resolution (not eradication) would take causation into consideration and we shall examine the resolution of conflict in Unit Five. Some models of conflict put forward by researchers are examined as a mechanism of understanding this divergence. As individual conflict is considered elsewhere in this series,[2] the focus here is on collective conflict. Management may cause or stimulate this conflict but it will certainly be asked to resolve the divergence in most cases. Hence the study of conflict causation and gestation is critical to the effective management of labour relations. We examine strikes and, unlike many other books, we analyse the more routine (and numerous) disputes which management may face in labour relations.

Figure 4.1 overleaf shows the unit in diagrammatic form.

Conflict

The divergence of the basic employment relationship is seen to make some degree of conflict inevitable at the workplace. Coser's[3] definition of conflict is used:

> *a struggle over values or claims to status, power and scarce resources in which the aims of the conflicting parties are not only to gain the desired values but also to neutralise, injure or eliminate their rivals.*

115

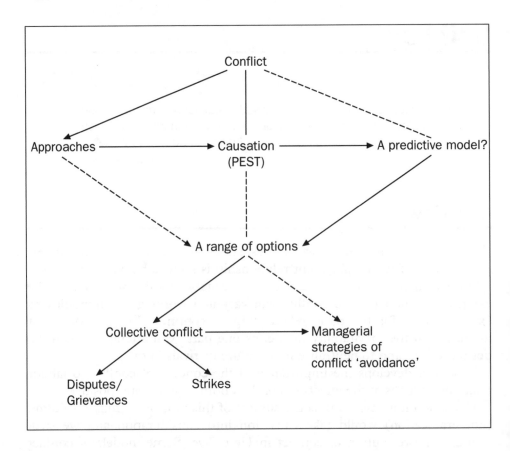

Figure 4.1 Overview of the unit.

The term 'rivals' gives a sense of healthy competition but sometimes the conflict manifestation involves more malevolent undertones allied to coercion. 'Elimination' may be a little too strong for many industrial conflicts for normally both of the primary parties will eventually have to settle down together again. At the time of a protracted dispute we may pray for the elimination of the opposition.

To Coser values are important. This is accepted. The perspective in this book is that of divergent values and a *power struggle* over the share-out of relatively scarce resources. At some times in history industrial conflict spills over to a political dimension and the share-out of resources becomes inadequate because the issue often becomes the actual ownership and not the distribution of the resource.[4]

Box LR4.1 gives a 'chronological' approach to grievances. Thereafter we go deeper into causation and gestation.

> **BOX LR4.1**
>
> ## A chronological approach to disputes/grievances
>
> Life is not smooth and neither are disputes. Disputes will not run to form as the power dynamics and coercion (overt/covert), the sanctions (real/threatened), can change the chronology very quickly indeed. There may be 'phases', though, which we can identify if, and it is a big if, all these sanctions/coercion etc. are ignored. Again the phases are very logical – emotion often runs riot in real disputes.
>
> | | |
> |---|---|
> | Environment | This is both the wider context of the dispute and the immediate scene which may act as the trigger. |
> | Trigger/change | Many disputes are triggered by one party changing something such as an agreement or custom or failing to change, for example, a payment plussage, etc., or making a demand on the other party which is deemed 'unacceptable'. |
> | Response | The trigger acts like a stimulus and the other party in good Pavlovian style responds. |
> | Positions | Polarization often occurs in arguments at this stage. |
> | Sanctions/threats | Sanctions may be employed to help the other party change its mind. |
> | Trade/compromise or power struggle | Negotiation may occur or a war of attrition will apply and the most powerful at that time will dominate over this issue. Rationality may also prevail in argument.(?) |
> | 'Peacetime' | 'Treaties' may be made until the next time a battle beckons. |

Approaches

Our view of society will dominate our perspective of conflict as the work organization is a subsociety and a reflection of the wider dynamics of an industrial society. Essentially there seem to be three visions:

- a harmony approach;
- a conflict approach;
- a convergence approach.

The harmony approach

This is important to labour relations as so much thinking (unwittingly?) is based on this approach. The work of Parsons and Shils[5] epitomizes this viewpoint. Harmony, solidarity and cohesion are the trigger words with an emphasis on **core values** and **shared norms**. However, by over-emphasizing order, they may well be over-reacting against disorder.

Inherent in this view is some form of **exchange relationship** based on trust and mutual aid between labour and management. Conflict is explained away as a mere aberration, the responsibility of deviants and the result of 'poor leadership', inadequate communications and a reactive management not able to eliminate industrial troubles.

The conflict approach

This view also has some form of 'exchange' logic but the differing interests can only be served and satisfied by encroaching on the interests of others which will not be mutually beneficial.

Differing interests and force, not consensus, inspire behaviour. The social structure is a dynamic changing concept and equilibrium, if it exists, is a transitory stage as relationships at the end of the day are based on dissension. Group interest will predominate, leading to power relationships with advantage or disadvantage for both parties.

These relations set the stage for conflict which, in turn, generates forces of order leading to the formation and maintenance of rules. These behavioural norms and regulations pattern behaviour and attempt to reduce or minimize the consequences of conflict. So factors influencing consensus and accommodation can operate within the conflict approach. The end product of this conflict is an on-going power struggle between those with and those without advantage. The Marxists would see this as a bitter struggle to the end, while the Radicals would see it as a continuous phenomenon.

The convergence approach

This is more of a pluralist vision. Conflict is seen to be inevitable but harmony co-exists with it as well. Disparate interests exist but they can be reconciled. There seems to be more room here for compromise and working accommodations than in the more radical view of conflict.

At the same time it paints a more representative vision of industrial reality than the unitarist cum functionalist views of the 'order' theorists. Power is important to this perspective as well as to the Marxists.

Conflict Causation – Specific Schools of Thought

We shall quickly scan some of the applied research and documented literature in the area of industrial conflict to give us some perspectives on causation, using political, economic, social and technological dimensions.

Political

One of the leading analyses of conflict came from Marx.[6] He saw the basic contradictions of the capitalist system which would lead to the inevitable and violent synthesis of social revolution. The Marxist vision of society rests at the macro level of the country whilst the organization is merely seen as a microcosm of the wider society with its divergent interests. There is little attempt to fuse the relevance of the Marxist analysis of wider societal conflict to the immediate needs of organizational analysis. Likewise, there was no reflection of Marx's views in the first managerial theories which were developed concerning the management of large-scale business enterprises. Arguably, the frame of reference of these managerial philosophers was that of a managerial manifesto anyway, and conflict was merely an aberration which could be overcome by adhering to 'proper managerial principles', so these viewpoints of the managerial theorists would hardly be worth discussing from a Marxist perspective.

A political vision concerns the exercise of power. The non-exercise of power or 'powerlessness' may also be in this category. The alienated worker of Marxist thought has moved increasingly to this view of 'powerlessness' in the literature of conflict. Work under this view strips life of its meaning and hence a reaction from apathy to open conflict ensues. The equation is that boredom plus frustration equals aggression. Conflict is therefore a form of catharsis, a relief from powerlessness and monotony in a boring world.

This lack of power and resultant monotony comes from the minute subdivision of tasks in ever more complex organizations. Baldamus[7] sees it as a result of workers not being able to work in a 'natural' personal rhythm.

Roy's[8] study also emphasizes the 'making out' by the workers in this game of work to beat this 'powerlessness'. A form of informal conflict at work is ongoing as managerial norms of productivity and efficiency are absorbed but yet rejected by the workers in their games of work.

To Friedmann[9] 'tension' is the critical factor and he notes the lack of specialist knowledge required by (some) workforces. This 'tension' is explained by the lack of opportunity to complete the job, the so-called 'zeignarnick effect'. Blaumer[10] identifies four categories of work alienation: powerlessness, isolation, self-estrangement and meaninglessness.

There may be another power struggle going on – not just that of owner–worker but between managers as a group and workers. With the changed patterns of workplace ownership and the rise of a managerial class taking over many of the traditional functions of the owner of the enterprise,[11] conflict might be seen between managers as a power bloc, not necessarily representing their own interests nor that of the owners, and the workers. Dahrendorf[12] coined the phrase 'service class' to describe the middling ranks in which many managers can be placed. A conservative vested interest in the status quo particularly when confronted with an alternative decision-maker, the trade union with its collectivist views, could characterize this internal organizational power struggle.

Economic

Industry sector – instability
Turner[13] writing on the motor industry argues for a positive relation between the economic instability of the trade and proneness to conflict. Cameron's study of the docks[14] also indicated that fluctuations in workload caused by the economics of the trade furthered strife.

Improved terms and conditions
Smelser[15] feels that strikes, not conflict as such, tend to be economic in motivation, essentially to improve terms and conditions. Samuelson[16] takes a different view and argues that strikes do not better the conditions of the labour force in the longer term. Of course, the economic motivation may be there, even if not 'realized'.

Relationship to unemployment/full employment
The economics of the marketplace are never far from the buying and selling of labour. Shortfalls in demand can stimulate labour unrest owing to layoffs, short-time and redundancies. Alternatively, full employment policies could make for a higher incidence of strike activity, as organized labour bargains from a position of relative strength. The economic insecurity – security dimension is certainly an important factor in conflict causation.

Social

This can be seen in social pressures outside of the place of work and in the work organization itself. Roberts,[17] for example, widens the contextual background and argues that history impacts on strike frequency, intensity and the form of industrial action. To Kerr and Siegal[18] the background milieu is also a dominant factor. Their classification of industries by proneness to strike is in particular related to the type of industry and its immediate environment: mining is high, textiles medium and agriculture low. In certain relatively 'closed' communities such as the docks and mines, the trade union becomes a 'working class party' for the area.

The social aspect within the firm is epitomized by the psychological approach. The early work of Viteles,[19] for example, sees conflict as a manifestation of inferiority linked to a loss of the individual's identity and to role conflicts. Argyris[20] refines the status difficulties between the organizational and individual needs, arguing that a collision occurs between the two demands. Adulthood requires independent thinking activity but bureaucracy with its specialization and task direction necessitates a passive subordinate position by its 'officials'.

Even if an 'ideal type' of bureaucracy is considered, the tension between task and people demands at the level of the individual permeates this line of thought. To Stagner and Rosen[21] relationships at work are vast, and hidden below the surface are many inherent conflicts which would not necessarily be revealed in outward decisions and disputes. Perception is critical to Stagner and Rosen and their 'dialogue of the deaf' may have relevance to conflict situations.

Technical/technological

The sociological milieu, to this school, is linked with the technological status of the plant or industry. The early pioneering work into Durham coal mining remains a classic while Woodward and Sayles have developed this 'production process school'[22] into a leading approach to organizational analysis. In particular, Sayles looks at the workgroup size and its strategic position emanating from the production system, with Woodward looking at the type of production process: batch, mass or process. So, the interaction of technology and environment is seen to affect job design, the organizational structure and the resultant levels of conflict.

Now examine Activity LR4.1 which applies some of these themes. Thereafter, reference to Box LR4.2 illustrates the 'balance sheet' of conflict at work. We shall then move on to a specific predictive model of conflict at the workplace as well as a less predictive approach.

ACTIVITY LR4.1

CONFLICT

Activity code
- ☑ Self-development
- ☐ Teamwork
- ☑ Communications
- ☐ Numeracy/IT
- ☑ Decisions

A senior manager's conference on the theme of labour relations at the debate was becoming more heated as the weekend went on.

The firm had a 'troubled' history – there was complete agreement on that. Constant stoppages of work, disrupted production flows, bickering, dispute after dispute over seemingly trivial matters culminated in a complete stoppage for a fortnight which cost the company millions of pounds in lost revenue. The penultimate debate of the Sunday was just finishing.

One approach was that the administration was faltering. The finance people argued that clearer organizational objectives, detailed specialization of work, more systems of monitoring performance and greater authority to management was the answer. 'The system as it was, is not logical', said Smythe-Jones, the Director of Finance. 'We need more rational objectives, so everyone knows what they are doing and these outbursts of conflict will go away. The workers are too emotional and we pander to their emotions. Greater rationality and this conflict will disappear.'

The production argument was not unsupportive but it went for a harder style of management. 'You're right,' said Fred Jones, the Production Director, 'at the end of the day it's all about our authority – we must exercise it more. We can't get rid of conflict, though, but better work structuring, tighter authority levels and more specific allocation of tasks will mean more control. If things stay as they are, the procedures will help to resolve the conflict but we need the correct division of labour and more structure about our authority.'

The Marketeer had her turn. 'Look, the customer is the business as we all know and that customer comes from outside of here – your views are all too blinkered. We need to look to the external environment. Look at the history of this firm – it's always been like this. The attitudes are in-bred from home. The workers take their views from their community. We need to change their views – or change the location of the place. Perhaps our goal should be to recruit more younger people from a different catchment area. Change the environment and this stupid conflict will go.'

'It's more than the environment, though, Anna,' said the Personnel specialist. 'We treat these people like slaves and yet we expect – no, demand – their obedience. It's like something out of a Dickens novel. We must build up their jobs – not break them down. We must stimulate their interest and increase job satisfaction. There is too much talk of the task, the structure and the environment and not enough about the people.'

The Chief Executive Officer summarized. 'We must move on to the next area. It has been a fruitful debate – but along functional lines. It would be useful if you could summarize your views and give an indication how you feel that they can resolve these damaging conflicts.'

Task

Your task is to summarize the four perspectives and relate them to a school of thought. Note the advantages/disadvantages of each and their possible application to the understanding, if not the resolution, of the conflict which is occurring in this firm.

BOX LR4.2

Conflict – a balance sheet?

The negatives of high levels of collective conflict at work are well known and most managerial and journalistic sources focus on this area.

- Conflict disrupts the production/operation.
- Conflict may mean lost orders as the customer goes elsewhere.
- Conflict means time and energy spent in resolving the issues when perhaps they could have been more gainfully employed elsewhere.
- Conflict can mean a souring of longer-term relations between managers and managed.
- Conflict can impact on quality/quantity of the product/service.
- Productivity/efficiency levels may be reduced in the longer term as well as during the immediate conflict.
- Conflict can be stressful.
- Conflict can always escalate and the whole organization can be disrupted and may collapse.
- The culture of work becomes even more hostile awaiting the next conflict point.

Conflict has some positive aspects as well:

- it makes the ground rules clear and explicit;
- the issue gains a wider audience;
- steam is let off, so it may act as a long-term stabilizer in a system;
- we may hear and may come to understand the position of the other party;
- we may be prepared to modify our own position through the resolution of that conflict;
- conflict helps to identify the real power holders/groups (if not known before);
- conflict can mean a quick device for achieving a solution;
- it is a vehicle of change;
- total suppression of overt collective conflict will mean more covert and individual conflicts which will be more difficult to manage.

Conflict – A Predictive Model?

Megginson and Gullett[23] put forward a predictive model of union–management conflict. The model is a system – alter one aspect and there is a knock-on effect to the other factors of the whole. The model is divided into 'givens', which they assume will exist in every situation of conflict, and 'variables', which can alter situation by situation.

The 'givens' are as follows:

- differing goals/value systems;
- competition for scarce labour resources;
- the status of representatives;
- the political nature of the unions.

- *Goals/value systems* Management aims to maximize efficiency, profits, etc., while unions aim to advance/protect the interests of their members. So different goals are assumed. This is probably correct but common goals such as a 'successful factory' may also be shared as well. Differing value systems between the collectivist workers and the individualistic managers are seen to exist. Again this may be more applicable to non-service non-white-collar workers, and the 'cult of the individual' has been actively promoted to all social classes during the 1980s and 1990s in the UK.

- *Competition for labour* The power of organized labour is seen to be reflective of the state of the labour market. For example, if the labour market is 'tight' the workers' power increases, and vice versa if the marketplace is 'slack' with a pool of unemployed.

- *Representatives* By definition the opposing representatives take their respective 'sides'. Of course, there is some cross-over in reality and 'objective' labour relations managers do exist as well as reasonable union officials who are prepared to see the other side's position.

- *Unions – political nature* To these writers unions are very much political bodies trying to influence members in a course of action, a united front, and coping with internal wrangles and in-fighting between officials.

The variables are seen as follows:

- the legitimacy of each party;
- past relationships;
- the approach to labour relations;
- personalities involved;
- external influences: customers, government and public opinion.

The variables in detail include the following.

- *The legitimacy of each party* The perceived acceptance of the other party's existence and right of existence is important. In management circles this may relate to the unitary–pluralist perspectives that we have covered.[24] It can also mean a grudging acceptance by both parties of each other's reason for being.

- *Past relationship* The history between the parties will haunt relationships unless it is a 'green field site' and even then past lives will impact on present realities. If there is a history of hate it may still resurrect itself over the most trivial of issues.

- *The approach* Essentially they divide relationships into two orientations: power based or problem solving.
- *Personality* The leaders, their views and prejudices should also be taken into account.
- *External influences: Customers, government and public opinion* This is self-explanatory.

Please tackle Activity LR4.2 on conflict and inevitability.

Given the view being presented here of labour relations which involves both conflict and rule making, it may be worthwhile merging the predictive systems view in Unit One with the overall systems suggested in Unit One with this predictive model of conflict. There are shortcomings particularly in the environmental analysis in this 'pure' conflict model and it fails to give adequate coverage to the role of power in the whole framework. Let us attempt to merge the views and see what we come up with which may explain rather than predict rules and conflict within the labour relations system.

See figure 4.2.

ACTIVITY LR4.2

'CONFLICT AND INEVITABILITY'

Activity code

☑ Self-development
☑ Teamwork
☑ Communications
☐ Numeracy/IT
☑ Decisions

Task
Review the model of Megginson and Gullett which we have just described. Isolate their 'givens' and their 'variables' using these factors; analyse by yourself or in a group which of the factors, if any, make for an inevitability theme about conflict, and give the rationale behind your/the group response.

Factor	Conflict inevitability	Comment
Differing goals and value systems, etc.		

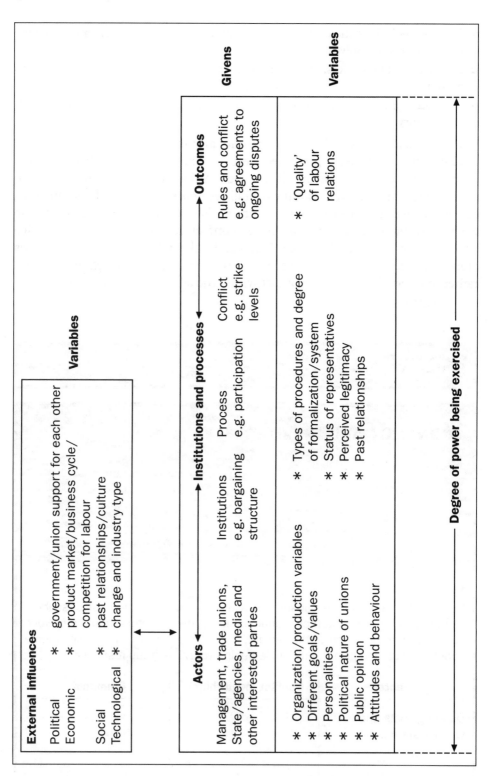

Figure 4.2 Labour relations – a detailed framework for analysing rules and conflict.

Conflict – A Range of Options

A whole range of potential types and methods of conflict exist. The individual can become involved in 'withdrawal from work', ranging from total absence to working at a given (reduced) pace/output, etc. The union can involve itself in collective disputes, individual grievances in procedure or 'working to rule', overtime bans, 'blacking goods' of other strikers, token stoppages, wildcat strikes (if legal) and longer strikes or total withdrawal of labour.

Management can get involved in locking labour out, cutting overtime or bonuses in a punitive form, 'blacklisting' trouble-makers, ensuring that no union members are employed, dismissing shop stewards on spurious grounds, offering promotion to troublesome union lay officials or giving 'early retirement' to known 'deviants'. A strike of capital is possible – refusing to invest in a plant or country until such times as 'guarantees' on peace or whatever are given. Ultimately, management has the final sanction of closing the place down. We shall focus on the common issues of disputes and strikes.

Collective Conflict – Disputes/Grievances

Individual grievances can merge with 'principle' and a collective dispute can occur. Although we shall centre on the issue of disputes, the principles of 'grievance bargaining' are not too far removed from handling disputes, so it will be fair to examine disputes and grievances as a whole.

A dispute can be 'constitutional' in the sense that it remains in procedure and the procedural mechanism is used to attempt to resolve the issue. It can also involve industrial action (by either party) and no real procedural recourse. It can combine both a constitutional format and the overt use of sanctions, threats or coercion. There is an argument that even if the dispute remains in procedure there is always the ghost of sanctions or threats hovering around in this power play.

The International Labour Organization (ILO)[25] has defined a dispute/grievance as an issue which

> *affect(s) the condition or employment of one or several workers in the undertaking when that measure or situation appears contrary to the provisions of an applicable collective agreement or of an individual contract of employment, to work rules, to laws or regulations or to the custom or usage of the occupation or country.*

The research in this area is often American, and although there may not be total transferability everywhere else the core management–union relationship and principles are transferable to other countries. Equally some transferable British research is worth citing. We examine first the British work and then the in-depth American research.

Hyman,[26] for example, has carefully reported disputes in procedure in the engineering industry in Coventry. The specific details of each case make interesting reading on the concerns of individual disputes. In a more limited fashion Marsh's[27] study of the York Engineering Conference also provides useful data. The work of Eldridge,[28] particularly in the steel industry, gives a wider perspective of disputes rather than proceduralized-only references.

The American research into disputes is more plentiful than its British equivalent. This may be because of the more legalistic approach to labour relations and hence greater availability of written data. The research is typified by a constant striving for 'solutions', and by a listing of the causes of grievances with the 'givens' and 'variables' to help understanding, and perhaps with a view to the removal if not the 'eradication' of these causes of dispute.

The work of Kuhn,[29] in the rubber and electrical industries, concentrates on workgroup bargaining over grievances – what he terms 'fractional bargaining'. For Kuhn, like Sayles,[30] the power of the workgroup is writ large. The group must feel itself to be seriously aggrieved before it mobilizes its latent power. Strategic groups planning sustained tactics and controlling essential resources with strong feelings of autonomy characterize this type of bargaining. Technology is an important mould of workgroup attitudes, and four characteristics are conducive to this type of 'frictional bargaining' or grievance/disputes situations. The jobs tend to be individually paced, so changes in methods of work and standards are ongoing; as the work is specialized, considerable interaction occurs between the task groups; the work tends to be divided into equal-sized departments and there is a sequential division of labour in the processing of the product.

Peach and Livernash[31] concentrate on the steel industry. Their study consists of departments with high and low rates of written grievances in separate plants. Their aim is to analyse the causes behind the differing rates, within and between plants. High grievance rates are classified under the following themes: environmental influences, union influences and managerial influences. The environmental aspect ranged from an incentive scheme with non-standardized tasks and earnings inequities, frequent product and process change, to close attention to the task. Second, a history of union–management conflict was identified, particularly in large urbanized plants. The formal union influence was weak, allowing the more 'radical' to take a lead. The third influence, management, involved little informal problem solving; inactivity on the first rungs of the management hierarchy; and active labour relations specialists away from the scene of the dispute. Poor consultation, weak discipline and an inequitous incentive scheme aggravated the grievances.

Lawshe and Guion[32] use attitude surveys to show a non-causation theme. Their concern is with the views behind the *process* of disputes bargaining. Some four hundred management- and labour-oriented individuals were surveyed to assess their similarities and differences towards grievance procedures. Later Ash[33] and Sulkin and Pranis[34] did look to correlations between high and low grievances. 'Differences' were ascribed to the personalities of the individuals who submitted the disputes/grievances. These 'psychological' studies do not link up with the procedural and wider organizational studies.

Ross[35] links the procedural disputes with the process of events of the actual dispute. He coins the term 'distressed' grievance procedures to describe a situation of an overload of issues, the over-bureaucratic use of the disputes machinery and an over-reliance on third party settlement.

We shall now apply some of this research in a series of scenarios derived from real organizations. See Activity LR4.3.

ACTIVITY LR4.3

DISPUTES AND DECISIONS AT THE *FREE PRESS*

Activity code
- ✓ Self-development
- ✓ Teamwork
- ✓ Communications
- ✓ Numeracy/IT
- ✓ Decisions

The following conflict scenarios have taken place within the printing and publishing centre of the *Free Press* newspapers. These scenarios go back over a period of ten years.

Task
You will be presented with the facts behind the dispute. In the first two cases you or your group should take a manager's perspective, in the next two a union's point of view and in the final case you should take the view of a neutral, perhaps a third party or an academic. You will be asked to make a decision at the end of these scenarios.

'Sick money'
Individuals working shifts had an earning protection guarantee whereby holiday pay was paid inclusive of shift monies. There had to be a twelve-month

service rule and the individuals must agree to change shift from their normal rota. The union wanted the scheme to include sick money, for only the basic rate (not shift payment) was included in 'sick money'.

Management decision

The dispute over the disputes procedure

The company view was that the disputes procedure was a company-wide document going back to 1971. The union acknowledged that this was the main disputes procedure for the firm as a whole but in the production section a special procedure was in force.

To reflect job changes, operational changes and the Measured Productivity Scheme within the section a special speedy procedure was in operation. The only difference was that at the end of the procedure, or during the procedure if stalemate prevailed, the union or management had the right to take the facts of the dispute to an independent third party. This was not for a decision as such but the facts would help in making an external decision.

The management view was that the main agreement must prevail. This was a local deal made in 1973 and, as the bonus scheme no longer operated, this agreement – a procedure which was specifically meant to deal with bonus-only problems – was no longer in operation. Further, neither party had invoked this 'local' procedure during the whole of the 1980s and the 1990s to date. The union disputed this fact saying that it felt that it was using this procedure at the moment.

Management decision

The distribution issue

The vehicles were getting old. Some were quite dangerous and the vans tended to break down under the punishing schedule of distributing the newspapers. The management had a rotating scheme for vehicle replacement, three per year, but this had fallen away under 'cost savings' and had not been used for some two years.

The union decided to 'black' six vans. The union insisted on new vans to replace these vans. The management responded that if a driver refused to drive any van, he or she would be 'off the clock' (i.e. not paid). The union responded by noting that if this occurred a full-scale strike would be called.

Trade union decision

Sales Reps – numbers

The company said that it did not co-determine staffing levels with the union. It did. The 'spare' sales rep for holiday/sickness cover was not going to be replaced, according to the Display Manager. This was a form of consultation, said the Display Manager, not a negotiation. The Father of the Chapel (FOC) put the issue into dispute. One week later, the reps agreed not to co-operate in covering each other's 'territory' in the event of sickness or holiday absences. Management said that the item was in dispute and so such action was 'intolerable'. The FOC responded by noting that the 'spare' rep did the coverwork, not the reps, and so they were merely doing their job.

Trade union decision

Hours

The union view was that the operative should be a night-shift worker. His starting time took him into the night-shift banding as he started at five minutes before 5 o'clock in the evening.

The company view was that the shift times were 6–2; 2–10 and 10–6, and hence 5 o'clock was not night-shift. He was a middle-shift worker. The union responded by saying that when he worked overtime, at company request which was quite often, he worked a ten-hour day and this was certainly night-shift.

Your third party decision

Collective Conflict – Strikes

We have purposively differentiated strikes from disputes. In essence a strike is a culmination of a dispute but disputes can take place without any industrial action if the dispute always remains in procedure.

As a form of discovery-learning, we shall look first to a range of strike statistics for the UK and overseas and thereafter examine the implications, the theories and the issues surrounding strikes. Activity LR4.4 gives a range of statistics on strike activity. Your role is to extrapolate trends from this range of data and construct a report on strike incidence, causation, historical trends and parallels.

ACTIVITY LR4.4

STATISTICS

Activity code
- ✓ Self-development
- ✓ Teamwork
- ✓ Communications
- ✓ Numeracy/IT
- ✓ Decisions

Task

1 Examine the statistics on strike activity in figures 4.3 and 4.4 and tables 4.1–4.4.
2 Extrapolate trends and construct a report on incidence, causation, historical trends and parallels between the countries and industries.

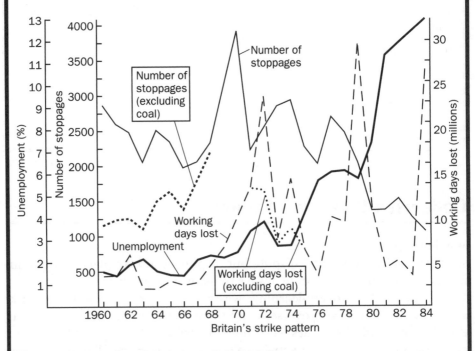

Figure 4.3 Stoppages of work due to industrial disputes.

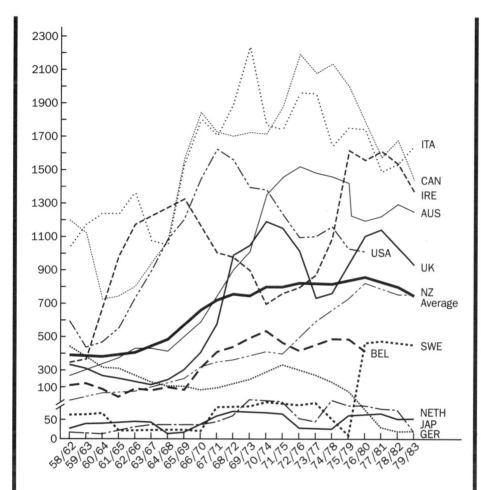

Figure 4.4 International comparison of working days lost (mining, manufacturing, construction and transport): five-year moving average (working days lost per thousand employees).

Table 4.1 Changes in working days lost per thousand employed, 1978–87

Reductions (%)				Increases (%)	
Sweden	−70	Ireland	−50	Denmark	+108
Netherlands	−67	Spain	−49	Norway	+93
France	−58	Canada	−46	Finland	+73
Australia	−58	Portugal	−43	New Zealand	+57
Italy	−56	Greece	−38	Germany	+25
USA	−50	UK	−26		
Japan	−50				

Table 4.2 British strike statistics: annual averages from 1900 to 1988

	Number of strikes	Workers involved (thousands)	Striker-days (thousands)
1900–10	529	240	4,576
1911–13	1,074	1,034	20,908
1914–18	844	632	5,292
1919–21	1,241	2,108	49,053
1922–5	629	503	11,968
1926	323	2,734	162,233
1927–32	379	344	4,740
1933–9	735	295	1,694
1940–4	1,491	499	1,816
1945–54	1,791	545	2,073
1955–64	2,521	1,116	3,889
1965–9	2,380	1,208	3,951
1970–4	2,885	1,564	14,077
1975–9	2,310	1,640	11,663
1980	1,330	842	11,964
1981	1,338	1,499	4,266
1982	1,528	2,103	5,313
1983	1,364	574	3,754
1984	1,221	1,464	27,135
1985	903	791	6,402
1986	1,074	720	1,920
1987	1,016	887	3,546
1988	781	790	3,702

Table 4.3 Pattern of strikes, 1980–90

	Number of strikes	Workers directly involved (thousands)	Working days lost (thousands)
1975–9			
Annual average	2,319	1,639	11,664
1980–90			
1980	1,330	830	11,964
1981	1,338	1,512	4,266
1982	1,528	2,101	5,313
1983	1,352	573	3,754
1984	1,206	1,436	27,135
1985	887	643	6,404
1986	1,053	538	1,920
1987	1,004	884	3,546
1988	770	759	3,702
1989	693	727	4,128
1990	620	285	1,903
Annual average	1,071	935	6,730

Table 4.4 Incidence rates from stoppages of work in progress in 1987 and 1988, United Kingdom

Industry group	Working days lost per 1,000 employees	
	1988	1987
All industries and services	164	162
Energy and water	505	453
Manufacturing	313	115
Services	117	182
Agriculture, forestry and fishing	–	–
Coal extraction	1,691	1,413

Table 4.4 continued

Industry group	Working days lost per 1,000 employees	
	1988	**1987**
Extraction and processing of coke, mineral oil and natural gas	1	–
Electricity, gas, other energy and water	53	30
Metal processing and manufacture	67	65
Mineral processing and manufacture	30	53
Chemicals and man-made fibres	69	28
Metal goods not elsewhere specified	119	85
Mechanical engineering	66	223
Electrical engineering and equipment	41	52
Instrument engineering	13	33
Motor vehicles	2,165	652
Other transport equipment	3,188	255
Food, drink and tobacco	86	70
Textiles	318	75
Footwear and clothing	50	104
Timber and wooden furniture	8	7
Paper, printing and publishing	7	36
Other manufacturing industries	20	18
Construction	16	21
Distribution, hotels and catering, repairs	1	1
Railways	88	17
Other inland transport	73	201
Sea transport	9,500	109
Other transport and communication	2,350	3,204
Supporting and miscellaneous transport services	71	56
Banking, finance, insurance, business services and leasing	–	–
Public administration, sanitary services and education	64	243
Medical and health services	27	5
Other services	16	32

Source: Derived from Department of Employment, 'Tables on strike incidence, British strike statistics and patterns of strike activity'

A strike is a temporary stoppage of work with the aim of coercing the other party to take or to refrain from some action. The ultimate sanction is 'to vote with one's feet' but the strike is significant in that it means a break with the psychological work–effort bargain. We cannot assume rationality because the loss of earnings incurred in the strike may not (probably will not) be made up by the new settlement (unless overtime is worked as in some organizations to make up for late orders/supplies, etc.). For the most part the immediate economics of striking, from the workers' perspective, does not seem to tally. Money is docked by the employer for days of action, strike pay may not be forthcoming and welfare benefit for the family from agencies of the State can be difficult to get. To recoup this loss would mean a very successful strike in terms of the final settlement. Of course, it is not just about rationality. Please complete Activity LR4.5.

ACTIVITY LR4.5

WITHDRAWING LABOUR AT THE SMALL ENGINEERING COMPANY

Activity code

✓ Self-development

☐ Teamwork

☐ Communications

☐ Numeracy/IT

✓ Decisions

The 'team' within the Small Engineering Company was essentially made up of semi-skilled men. At one time they would have been called fitters' assistants/mates but now flexible working patterns had made the men a pool or 'team' which could work in a lesser skilled capacity in any of the departments within the firm.

The 'team' of ten men worked under the direction of Jim Jordan, the foreman, and his deputy Fred Coot.

Billy Hickman worked in the 'team'. He was a good worker but the men regarded him as surly and he was a bit of a loner, preferring to eat his sandwiches at meal time away from the rest of the men. He had worked for the firm for eleven years, first as a mate and then as a semi-skilled man, and he had been in the team for four years – since its inception.

The promotion of Jim Jordan to a supervisor in another section was followed very quickly by the departure of his deputy Fred Coot who left the firm. Harvy Ronan took over as the foreman for 'the team'. This left a vacancy for the deputy's position. This was filled by a member of the team, Tim Framework.

Hickman was incensed by Framework's appointment and he contacted the shop steward to complain about this 'corruption'. The shop steward gave him very short change and told him to 'grow up'. Hickman was most unhappy – Framework had been a casual worker and been with the firm about 'five minutes' (one year). His resentment now turned to blind rage. His union would not help him and the management of the engineering firm had obviously connived at this whole farce.

He took it upon himself to write to the new foreman Ronan who was unaware of the whole 'problem'. The letter read as follows:

> I am incensed at management's action in appointing Framework above me. I have given many years' loyal service to the firm and work very hard. The union is not supporting me so I'll take the action myself. As a protest I will not attend work next week.

When he returned from his absence which was not paid, the Labour Relations Officer, Marsh, dismissed him for 'individually going on strike which could not be tolerated'. The shop steward did not defend Mr Hickman as relationships had completely broken down between the local union and Mr Hickman. The steward did tell Marsh that he would not contest the issue. Hickman left the company after the meeting with Marsh.

Task

1 Analyse the dynamics of this situation.

2 As a senior manager of the Small Engineering Company what view and action would you take after receiving notification of this event with the details stated to date?

Yet when we start looking at the ostensible reasons for strike activity, pay and payment figure large. It could be that strikers use pay as a focus of their real grievances rather than some more abstract argument which would be difficult to rally around.

To Knowles[36] strikes are caused by 'basic issues' such as wages, 'frictional issues' such as discipline and 'solidarity issues' such as union principles.

Strikes may be linked to a range of 'causes':

- job protectionism;
- class conflict;
- a need to share in decision making;
- a coercive tactic rather than an end within itself (with no justification other than tactical advantage);
- union recognition/derecognition;
- job loss/redundancy;
- excessive discipline by management;

- a decaying pay structure;
- a lack of equity;
- mishandling of change by management;
- a reaction against management, government, other unions (demarcation) and against the official line of the union (unofficial action, if legal).

From the research we can note the following themes on strikes.

- Industry/community strike proneness, shared grievances and worker solidarity within a community, such as mining, may make strike action more likely.
- Poor machinery for handling conflict – the absence of developed procedures for consultation and negotiation can stimulate strike activity.
- Establishments with a predominance of manual workers or more highly unionized establishments or larger-scale establishments are more likely to have strikes.
- Authority and control were important in another study, with 'commodity relationships' sparking off the issue.
- The change management tactics and the so-called break-up of the 'indulgency pattern' to new rules of work stimulated strike action elsewhere.

One of the most in-depth studies of strikes was carried out by the UK Department of Employment Research and Planning Division (see Box LR4.3).

BOX LR4.3

Beneath the theories – a statistical approach to strikes and their causation

---

UK trends
- A colossal study examined strike activity in the UK from 1893 to 1976.[1] Its depth is still of value and can be used as a benchmark.
- Upsurges in strike activity occurred before and after the First World War, in the late 1950s, early 1960s and in 1969–70.
- If strikes in coal mines are excluded (they are quite significant though) there has been a stable level of stoppages but a 'take-off' occurred in the 1960s.
- Large-scale official stoppages are a feature of the years of large numbers of strikes. For example, 1972 can be cited.
- Between 1966 and 1975 the UK average in mining, manufacturing, construction and transport was 775 working days lost per 1,000 employees. Canada, the USA, Italy, Finland, Australia and Ireland had higher rates. If all industries are examined, Italy, Canada, the USA, Ireland and Australia were higher.
- The pattern of strike activity was uneven: in the high strike period (1971–3) some 98 per cent of establishments were strike free.
- Some 0.25 per cent of all plants in manufacturing accounted for some one-quarter of recorded stoppages and almost two-thirds of all 'man days lost'.

- Coal mining, port and inland water transport and up to 5 per cent of plants in manufacturing were the 'culprits'.
- Strike incidence tended to rise with plant size only in certain categories – electrical, engineering, vehicles, textiles, timber/furniture and 'other manufacturing industries'.
- On occupational classification, a detailed study was carried out from 1966 to 1973 and it showed that the number of stoppages per manual employee was almost ten times that of non-manual workers.
- The reasons given for strike activity were as follows:

	Manual	Non-manual
Wages	52	58
Fringe benefits	2	6
Union matters	8	11
Redundancy	3	6

- 'Poor' strike records of a plant in a locality did not spread throughout the geographical area.
- A study of inter-industry differences in strikes using multiple regression techniques showed that economic factors were important in explaining strike activity. Labour intensity, large average establishment size, a high proportion of male employees and high average earnings were positively associated with higher levels of stoppage. Union density and unemployment (note the period though – 1966–73) were not supported in a consistent fashion.
- Basic economic issues, pay and job security, were the causes of strikes in this period of the study, not 'frictional' issues.

Source:
1 Adapted from The Department of Employment, 'The incidence of industrial stoppages in the UK' and 'Distribution and concentration of industrial stoppages in Great Britain'

Managerial Strategies – Conflict 'Avoidance'

In spite of the advantages of conflict which we have considered, most managers see collective conflict in the same terms as the 'Black Death': it should be avoided – almost at any cost. A whole range of strategies have grown up that do not necessarily avoid collective conflict *per se* but fine tuning of the mechanisms can mean possibly lower levels of such conflict. Some examples include the following.

- *Job evaluation* may make the payment system more equitable and less prone to disputes.
- *Participative leadership* approaches may take the harsh edge off some conflicts.
- *Job redesign* may make for a more intrinsically interesting job.
- *Direct communications* policies of involving people in decision making may remove some of the barriers between managers and managed.

Now refer to Activity LR4.6.

ACTIVITY LR4.6

AVOIDANCE STRATEGIES

Activity code
- ✓ Self-development
- ✓ Teamwork
- ✓ Communications
- ☐ Numeracy/IT
- ✓ Decisions

This activity consolidates the unit.

Task

You should summarize the three general themes concerning conflict causation in this unit, e.g. philosophy: harmony, conflict and convergence. The political, economic, social and technological dimensions can also be summarized, and then the predictive model, etc.

Thereafter you must examine the causation from the perspective of *avoidance* strategies. That is, what can management really do to prevent these conflicts 'spilling over' at the place of work? Do not be concerned with resolution at this stage – only gestation. Note the degree of 'control' by management over these causes.

Approach	Key themes	Conflict avoidance strategy	Control potential
Philosophy			
Harmony			
Conflict			
Convergence			
Political			
Economic			
Social			
Technological			
Predictive model			

We end this unit by noting that many conflicts cannot be eradicated and strategies for avoidance may be difficult to engineer. Some managers do try to go down this route though. Please refer to Box LR4.4 on no strike agreements.

BOX LR4.4

'No strike agreements'

The early employer associations often attempted to curb trade union activity and potential strike activity by asking (demanding) employees to sign a 'document' that they would not join a trade union. The prevention of strikes by employer action is still on the agenda in the 1990s. The 'no strike agreements' or 'new style agreements' attempt to offer the facility of a strike-free environment.

A strong Japanese influence is present in these 'new style agreements' as harmony and complementary relationships are emphasized at the expense of conflict. Japanese companies in the UK such as Toshiba Consumer Products, Sango Hitachi and Nissan have been at the forefront of these deals with the craft unions.

Typical details of the agreements include:

- single-union recognition/bargaining rights;
- union members will not withdraw their labour in the event of a dispute;
- 'single status' deals with a harmonization of terms and conditions for both staff and manual workers;
- consultation/participation mechanisms are strengthened;
- labour flexibility clauses are entered within the deals (see Unit Six);
- pendulum arbitration is used if a dispute occurs between the parties.

So the unions get single status deals, compulsory arbitration and fuller consultation against the handcuffs of not striking. The employers have job flexibility, single-union deals (no multi-unionism) and less industrial 'trouble'.

To some extent we have had no strike agreements in our existing procedural machinery with both parties agreeing 'to refrain from industrial action until the disputes procedure is exhausted'. Of course this agreement was and is flouted by both parties. However, the 'safety net' is there with the new style agreements of pendulum arbitration.

Whether unions can deliver such a conflict-free zone in the long term is debatable. Even if they can sustain it, the conflict will probably manifest itself somewhere else from absence to lower levels of productivity. We need to monitor such agreements before we can be more definitive in our views.

Strategies for the reduction of conflict are perhaps easier. We now turn to these institutionalized and interpersonal methods of conflict resolution through rule-making and behavioural methods in the next unit. Yet before we leave conflict, we must reiterate the positive aspects of conflict. Please see Box LR4.5 on constructive conflict.

BOX LR4.5

Constructive conflict

Management seems either to avoid conflict or to contain it in the context of labour relations. Coser, however, argues that conflict does not necessarily mean negative results, for positive effects can be apparent.[1] These include, for example:

- since power can often be appraised only in its actual exercise, accommodation may frequently be reached only after the contenders have measured their respective strength in conflicts;
- unity and cohesion of the group can become tighter through conflict;
- norms can be adjusted and formed through conflict.

So there may be some utility in conflict within the organization, but most managers would not accept Coser's vision and would see conflict as 'dysfunctional', tearing away the body and soul of the organization.

Interestingly Coser widened the conflict debate by seeing the real enemy not as conflict *per se* but as rigidity and intolerance. The institutionalization of conflict and the tolerant flexible approach which we are advocating here can mean that we come to terms with most conflicts in labour relations.

Source:
1   Coser, *The Functions of Social Conflict*

Notes

1 Dahrendorf, *Class and Class Conflict in Industrial Society*.
2 Anderson, *Effective Personnel Management*.
3 Coser, 'Social aspects of conflict'.
4 The Soviet examples in 1917 can be cited in this context. Conflict in industry can easily spill over and encompass the whole society for the national strike becomes a clear political weapon.
5 See, for example, Parsons, *The Social System*, and Shils, 'Center and periphery'.
6 See, for example, Marx and Engels, *Manifesto of the Communist Party*.
7 Baldamus, *Efficiency and Effort*.
8 Roy, 'Banana time – job satisfaction and informal interaction'.
9 Friedmann, *The Anatomy of Work*.
10 Blaumer, *Alienation and Freedom*.

11 Burnham's concept of a 'new meritocracy' of professonals gives credence to some form of managerial ideology – perhaps independent of the owners. See Burnham, *The Managerial Revolution*.

12 Dahrendorf, *Class and Class Conflict in Industrial Society*.

13 Turner, *Labour Relations in the Motor Industry*.

14 Cameron, 'Post-war strikes in the north east shipbuilding and ship repairing industry'.

15 Smelser, *The Sociology of Economic Life*.

16 Samuelson, *Economics*.

17 Roberts, *Industrial Relations: contemporary problems and perspectives*.

18 Kerr and Siegal, 'The inter-industry propensity to strike – an international comparison'.

19 Viteles, *Motivation and Morale in Industry*.

20 Argyris, *Personality and Organisation*.

21 Stagner and Rosen, *Psychology and Union Management Relations*.

22 Amongst the more frequently mentioned names in texts and reviews within the socio-technical school are J. Woodward, L. R. Sayles, T. Burns, G. M. Stalker, M. Crozier, P. Lawrence and J. Lorsch. In particular Woodward, *Industrial Organization – Theory and Practice*, and Sayles, *Behaviour of Industrial Work Groups,* impact on conflict studies.

23 Megginson and Gullett, 'A predictive model of union–management conflict'.

24 See Fox, 'Industrial sociology and industrial relations'.

25 ILO 'Examination of grievances and communications within the undertaking'.

26 Hyman, *Disputes Procedure in Action*.

27 Marsh, 'Engineering procedure and central conference at York in 1959'.

28 Eldridge, *Industrial Disputes*.

29 Kuhn, *Bargaining in Grievance Settlement*.

30 Sayles, *Behaviour of Industrial Work Groups*.

31 Peach and Livernash, *Grievance Initiation and Resolution: a study in basic steel*.

32 Lawshe and Guion, 'A comparison of management labor attitudes towards grievance procedures'.

33 Ash, 'The parties to the grievance'.

34 Sulkin and Pranis, 'Comparison of grievants and non-grievants in a heavy machinery company'.

35 Ross, *Distressed Grievance Procedures and their Rehabilitation*.

36 Knowles, *Strikes: a study in industrial conflict*.

Unit Five

Rules and Conflict Resolution

Learning Objectives

After completing this unit you should be able to:

- examine a range of methods and processes to institutionalize conflict;

- make a critique of the range and nature of collective bargaining;

- conduct bargaining through both rational and 'bounded rationality' approaches;

- note the shortcomings of collective bargaining;

- analyse the structure of bargaining arrangements using two different approaches;

- examine alternatives to collective bargaining;

- utilize disciplinary, dismissal, grievance and disputes procedures;

- apply the generic skills.

Contents

Shortcomings of Collective Bargaining

Bargaining Arrangements

Other Institutions/Processes

- ▶ Unilateral rule/decision making
- ▶ Statutory rule/decision making
- ▶ Tripartite rule/decision making
- ▶ Bilateral rule/decision making
- ▶ Informal rule making

Procedures

- ▶ Discipline and dismissal procedures
- ▶ Grievance and disputes procedures

Unit Five

> ❝ Constant efforts are required to mitigate conflict ... to create and preserve smooth running relationships, and to provide acceptable mechanisms of compromise, accommodation and adjudication to settle disagreements and to lead with organised group conflict which explodes or threatens to explode, into open warfare. ❞
>
> *A. Kornhauser et al., Industrial Conflict*[1]

Overview

This unit sets out to cover the range of methods used to accommodate workplace conflict. It covers both institutions and skills or processes.

Collective bargaining is seen as a critical component of this accommodation and much effort is put into looking at the concept and what it actually means. Types of bargaining differ and we note this variety.

The process of bargaining may not be logical so 'bounded rationality' underpins the rational model.

The general shortcomings of bargaining are then expressed. We examine alternatives to collective bargaining. The unit concludes by looking at some examples of procedure with which many managers become involved in their day-to-day work.

Figure 5.1 shows the unit in diagrammatic form.

Institutionalizing Conflict

Blake et al.[2] usefully summarize the alternative methods open to management for the resolution of intergroup disagreement. Three basic assumptions and attitudes are identified.

If disagreement is inevitable and permanent, the parties 'dig in', and if neither capitulates three major mechanisms of resolution remain open: a win–lose power struggle; resolution by a third party; or an agreement not to determine the outcome, what they term 'fate arbitration'. This assumes that, although conflict is seen as inevitable, agreement may not be possible. In effect, conflict is seen in this book as inevitable, of course, but this does not presuppose that disagreement is inevitable.

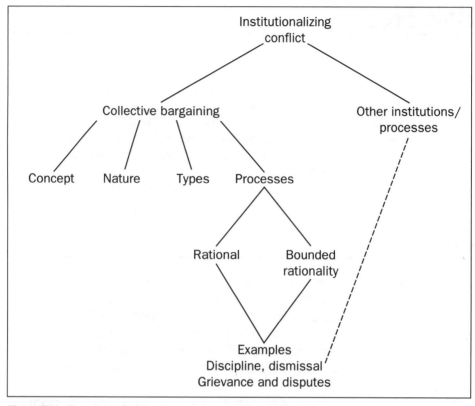

Figure 5.1 Overview of the unit.

Intergroup disagreement is then *not* seen as inevitable but agreement is not possible. In their words, 'these share in common, the maintenance of independence rather than any attempt to achieve interdependence'. The mechanics are withdrawal from the scene; a maintenance of indifference; or an attempt is made by the parties to isolate themselves. Isolation may mean eventual involvement and not on one's own terms as has occurred many times in international relations. For example, the sucking in of US assistance to Europe and to the world at large is a good example of traditional isolationism being curbed by military involvement.

Thirdly, cold indifference can be used but it will ossify positions with little or no scope for consensus. In their final category, they see a situation where agreement is possible in spite of conflict.

The methods of resolution include moving attention away from the real issues while maintaining 'surface harmony'. This occurs in many domestic relationships. The real issue does not go away but no breakdown occurs in the basic relationship. The authors, with a hint of missionary zeal, advocate a problem-solving approach with no rights and no wrongs. Yet their 'splitting the difference while retaining interdependence' with its compromise mentality is the hallmark of many settlements. In our terms this is collective bargaining.

Collective Bargaining

The concept

Group negotiation or collective bargaining is the hub of the whole industrial relations system. It is both the key institution and the processes which act as the interface between rules and conflict. Collective bargaining has been usefully summarized as:

> those arrangements under which wages (salaries) and conditions of employment are settled by a bargain in the form of an agreement made between employers or associations of employers and workers' organizations.[3]

Dubin[4] emphasizes the importance of collective bargaining for it is

> the great social invention that has institutionalised industrial conflict. In much the same way that the electoral process and majority rule have institutionalised political conflict in a democracy, collective bargaining has created a stable means of resolving conflict.

Perhaps Dubin's context suffers from a Whiggish perspective, a constitutional approach to history and political science, which enshrines if not glorifies parliamentary democracy.

But as a mechanism of social control in industry, collective bargaining has little equal.

The process of collective bargaining confirms the functional approach at the institutional level as well. Divergent interests are reconciled through this process. Inherent in this view is that different positions are taken by both sides, and movement occurs until the parties get closer before eventual agreement is reached. As movement from the original position will occur, the initial position will be unfairly high as a result. Demands from the opposing side should be ever decreasing as time and negotiations go on. Although maximization of one's interest is paramount, the context of the final agreement should not be lost. So following the main stages of the negotiating process as described by the work of Chamberlain and Kuhn[5] and Atkinson[6] in a British context, a logical model can be applied. (See the next section on the nature of bargaining.)

It is a land of claim and counter-claim, of target points and resistance points, of ploys, bluffs, threats and promises. Eventually, a range of 'acceptable preferences' should result and some form of settlement occurs, assuming no third party involvement and a willingness by both sides to move from their initial positions. If no bargaining occurs, sanctions, status quo or stalemate may result.

The nature of bargaining

An economic view

Labour is fundamentally weak *vis-à-vis* employers. In non-unionized sectors competition between labour becomes almost suicidal, according to this perspective, driving down the price of labour. To avoid this wholesale individual suicide, the strength of workers is enhanced by collective action and support to bargaining is based on the strength of the group, not the weakness of the individual.

Although this view was expressed by the Webbs[7] about a century ago it still has some merit. Of course individual bargaining can still coexist with collective bargaining and would be preferred presumably by more employers as the individual is weaker and the payment could be more 'flexible'. Or as Metternich, the nineteenth-century politician, would have said, a policy of 'divide and rule' can be applied.

A regulatory/rules view

To Flanders,[8] collective bargaining can be seen in the context of the power relationship and variables within the organization.

It becomes a method of joint regulation of the terms and conditions of work, if not of work itself. It is in essence a limiting force on the pure prerogative of managerial decision making.

A participative view

Chamberlain[9] accepts both an economic and a political aspect of collective bargaining and adds a democratic cum participative dimension. Collective bargaining becomes a form of industrial democracy in this system of industrial government with workers having some say in how their working lives are run.

A conflict view

We can take the views of Dubin[10] a little further. Collective bargaining is ultimately about reaching some agreement or working accommodation. It is a form of collaboration in essence. As such it takes the heat out of industrial conflict and puts conflict into 'constructive channels'. If left alone, conflict would spill over and destroy the organization if not the wider body politic. So collective bargaining is a conservative force preserving the status quo with some fine tuning here and there so that one group of workers gets a little more cake perhaps at the expense of the bread of another group of workers.

A status view

Collective bargaining can enhance job security and prestige of a workgroup. It can lessen (or deaden) the impact of arbitrary management with fickle uncaring views towards labour. It can thus reduce risk and protect the dignity of labour. Please refer to Activity LR5.1.

ACTIVITY LR5.1

APPROACHES TO BARGAINING

Activity code
- ✓ Self-development
- ☐ Teamwork
- ☐ Communications
- ☐ Numeracy/IT
- ✓ Decisions

Trade unions and management will probably have some fundamentally different vision and approach to bargaining reflecting their diverse philosophies and
styles. Even within management, as we have seen, a range of approaches is
quite likely. If some form of pluralistic vision is adopted by both trade unions
and management there may be more shared ground over the nature of bargaining.

Tasks
1 Assume that you are a trade union official. What guiding principles would
  you expect to have in your approach to bargaining?
2 Assume that you are an official of an employer association. What guiding
  principles would you expect to have in your approach to bargaining?

Types of bargaining

Ultimately collective bargaining means that some consensus is feasible in
spite of underlying conflict.

Oldfield's work at Mobil Oil gives us an interesting insight into different
types of bargaining.[11] He sees 'traditional' bargaining as a combination of
national and local bargaining. In times of full employment bargains are
struck locally to protect output while 'concessions, once gained, are
defended by the men like grim death. Any attempt to rationalise the
structure is usually regarded with the utmost suspicion and is usually met
by refusal to change.'

The basis of the 'traditional' methods is seen as 'money bargaining' with
pressure tactics from both sides, with ultimately demands and threats. The
'authority structures' of both sides perpetuate this method of bargaining,
particularly through conventions and deliberate ambiguity. (See Box
LR5.1 on bargaining.)

BOX LR5.1

Bargaining

In *The Strategy of Conflict,* Schelling looks to the concept of 'bargaining power'.[1] In bargaining, Schelling notes that 'each party is guided mainly by his expectations of what the other will accept'. The whole concept is based on one party making a 'sufficient concession' in order to strike a deal, for some deal is better than no deal.

The whole bargaining process is seen as invoking commitments (to a principle for example), threats (if you do that X will happen), promises (we will give you Y monies) and communication (advising the other party of your position – negotiating stance – and making signals at the right time to signify final positions).

If we accept Schelling's views, *expectations and counter-expectations in this exchange relationship are critical,* so imagined and real positions need to be communicated at various stages of the proceedings – assuming some desire to move and negotiate.

Source:
1 Adapted from Schelling, *The Strategy of Conflict*

To Oldfield an alternative approach is an integrated participative view. 'Joint discussion of a common problem in an attempt to find a solution that will meet the need of everyone concerned' is the essence of the alternative advocated by Oldfield. It is discussion, not argument, and it is based on a joint problem-solving method. This co-operative vision starts with identifying problems and finishes by going into the details of implementation. To summarize, 'the *how* has been worked out by participation and involvement and the *how much* can be negotiated with a great deal more understanding and confidence on both sides'.

Walton and McKersie

Another framework for understanding types of bargaining is provided by the American writers Walton and McKersie.[12] They see bargaining as a form of adjustment, an interaction between two social groupings, within labour relations. They identify four different types of negotiations:

- distributive;
- integrative;
- attitudinal structuring;
- intra-organizational bargaining.

Let us comment on each category in turn.

Distributive bargaining is power-based. The goals and aspirations of the parties are divergent. This is in line with Oldfield's 'traditional' classification. If one party gains, it is at the expense of the other as the pie is not infinite.

Integrative bargaining is more like Oldfield's problem-solving approach. Common ground is sought and common interests should prevail. This could occur, say, over health and safety matters or over productivity bargaining where a pie may not be involved or, if the pie is involved, it has the chance of becoming bigger. Oldfield's views may see the 'new look' of problem solving going on before the normal bargaining over 'how much' but the process should be less prone to conflict. Walton and McKersie probably would not put distributive and integrative bargaining into completely different 'boxes'.

Attitudinal structuring really involves the beliefs held by each party (management and unions) about each other. This would cross over Oldfield's twofold classification. The whole conflict–trust relationship will be affected by this attitudinal process – amongst other things. (See the framework in Unit One and the conflict models in Unit Four.)

Intra-organizational bargaining occurs *within* each camp and not between the main actors, management and trade union. For example, attempting to precondition your 'team', selling the package to others or negotiating your case with more senior people would fall into this category. Anecdotal evidence would note this to be one of the most difficult aspects of the whole process.

Collective Bargaining and Grievance/Disputes Bargaining

There is distinction between disputes of 'interest' and 'issues of right' as noted by Marsh.[13] Interest issues will tend to dominate 'normal' bargaining over terms and conditions while both interest and right (prerogatives of both parties) may be found in grievances and disputes. Kuhn[14] notes a form of bargaining in grievance settlement which may differ from that of the 'normal' contractual terms and conditions type of bargaining. When issues of right dominate, the scope for settlement and for actual negotiation may be circumscribed. This was the case in the study by Anderson.[15] So different types of bargaining may occur depending on the issue and the type of procedure and whether we are dealing with normal contractual negotiations or disputes/grievance bargaining.

That is, disputes over terms and conditions allow more latitude of settlement and disputes over rights are more prone to trench warfare with little bargaining and 'principles' to the fore.

Please tackle task 1 in Activity LR5.2.

ACTIVITY LR5.2

GRIEVANCE HANDLING AT MALMÖ – THE PROCEDURAL CASE

Activity code
- ✓ Self-development
- ✓ Teamwork
- ☐ Communications
- ☐ Numeracy/IT
- ✓ Decisions

Union A is a small union within Malmö Communications, a Swedish-based organization with its core business in telecommunications. Recently Malmö had taken over Peripheral Systems in the UK. Some 220 people work in the systems firm.

The firm is unionized and the relationship with the white-collar union was reasonable, while the relationships with the manual unions were more troubled.

Union A represented specialist technicians. Local management wished to install a new bonus scheme for these technicians based upon a combination of throughput and quality.

The old management at Peripheral Systems had been cleared out in the takeover and new individuals had been put in place. Savage cuts in labour and new human resource issues were now to the fore. The unions had been seriously weakened but union A, because of its strategic position with its key members/employees, was still a force to be reckoned with.

The personnel section (HR Advisors) contacted the local full-time official to receive his blessing over the new bonus scheme. The official had experience of this firm and he was quite glad to be consulted. He stated that 'he would be happy for the thing to go ahead on principle but the detail would have to be negotiated'.

The shop steward of the technicians was not advised of this phone-call. The previous shop steward had been promoted to a line management position and was now an HR Manager.

Given the historical climate of the place combined with the latest managerial initiatives the previous steward was not very popular amongst the technicians.

The previous steward, now the HR Manager, a line position, met with the new steward to discuss the quality initiatives of the firm. The meeting degenerated into a debate about bonus, not quality as such, with both individuals asserting their 'authority'. There was no agreement at the end of this informal session.

Next the HR Manager called the full-time official into the company for 'a chat'. The technicians, on hearing of this, felt that this was a breach of procedure and bad manners. The official met with management on an unofficial basis for he was conscious of the troubles within the firm.

The technicians refused to join this meeting. Later that day they sought a meeting with the HR Manager who was 'too busy'. The workers were incensed. However, a meeting was arranged for the next day. This meeting meant that the deputy steward would have to remain after his normal time. Payment was sought. It was refused. The meeting went ahead but with a technician deputizing for the deputy.

Management objected to the presence of the technician. The technician and the steward said that they had a right to have anyone at the meeting. Management insisted that this was out of procedure. The meeting was terminated after ten minutes without a discussion on the bonus/quality issue.

The technicians started to 'work to contract'. The full-time official was asked into the plant. He was 'busy' that week but would come 'early next week'.

The 'work to contract' began to impact on the firm. Letters were sent to the technicians asking them to work normally as the issue was still in procedure and being debated.

The steward asked that 'failure to agree' be recorded and that the letters should be withdrawn. Another session occurred, this time with the Managing Director, Tom Smith, and the steward with his deputy. Management talked about the action, the unions talked about procedure. The meeting with the full-time official now looked unlikely as Smith and the stewards could not even agree on the disagreement. 'Unless we agree the nature of this dispute, we can't resolve it' were Smith's last words at that meeting. The union seemed to be sticking to its breach of procedure stance.

Task
1 From the perspective of the full-time official analyse this situation.
2 How can it be resolved? (You may wish to tackle this part of the activity at a later stage once the unit has been completed.)

The Process of Bargaining

Most approaches to bargaining assume almost a rational approach to an issue where both sides have starting positions, ideal settlement points and realistic settlement points (see figure 5.2). This assumes a logical approach to an issue devoid of emotion, with stages of concessions, fallback positions and a sense of realism as to what can be achieved.

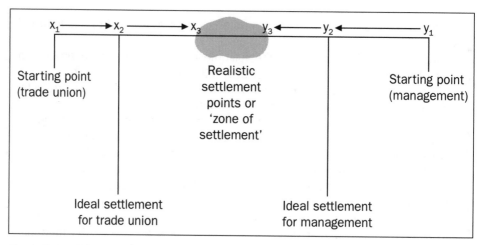

Figure 5.2 'Rational' bargaining approach: management, Y_1, Y_2 and Y_3; trade unions, X_1, X_2 and X_3.

Bounded rationality

The rational approach is made more complex in reality.

The **issue** at stake has been discussed and it is put forward that negotiation over a pay increase or some other matter of interest is easier than a deal over a more principled issue of 'right', such as who allocates the overtime shifts. The rational model may apply to the terms and conditions while the 'zone of settlement' may never be reached over a principle for neither party may move from its original position.

The absence or the presence of **procedure** can make a difference to the process as well. In one organization I worked with, the bargaining process was very gentlemanly with reference to subpara 3, 2(i) etc., of an agreement. In another, might was right – irrespective of procedure. Logic and rational debate counted for less in this organization.

The overall **climate** of the labour relations, their history and past successes/failures, can impact on the bargaining scene with one or both parties trying to make up for past debts. The climate is affected by the variables of the system of labour relations. For example, the product market in newspapers can give an urgency to negotiations as yesterday's newspaper is only useful for a fish and chip shop to use as wrapping paper.

This sense of urgency which I found also in the perishable products of the food industry can lead to a cheque book philosophy by management in response to trade union manipulation. The reverse side of the coin can be seen where a pool of unemployed exists, recession is striking home and job security fears are paramount. In this climate, management can be, and often is, far more cavalier.

The **approach** to bargaining by the parties is of importance. The traditional/participative and distributive/integrative divisions are major influences on the style and activity of the whole process. For example, a productivity cum efficiency bargain should mean a more harmonious approach compared with an annual wage round where claims are running high and profits are low.

The degree of **coercion** is relevant. Conflict, the threat of or actual sanctions, is never far from the bargaining table. Sometimes it may result if the negotiation ends in deadlock or alternatively it may be ongoing during the actual negotiation itself, although the other party may refuse to bargain under these circumstances. So muscle, not mind, from either party can distort the logical bargaining approach and push the 'zone of settlement' to the ideal position of the party using coercion.

The possibility of error, the costly impact of not getting a deal, coercion, the drain on resources and time can all lead to a degree of **risk**. Most managers interacting with others in the organization may not experience this degree of uncertainty. Perhaps buyers and marketeers do experience this as they interface with external agencies as a matter of course. Labour relations people also interact with external agencies, the 'hierarchy' of the trade union, and control over this group is almost impossible, so uncertainty and risk permeate the process.

To reduce this uncertainty a good knowledge of the **people** involved, their **styles** of bargaining and the **skills** of bargaining are essential. We shall develop this later.

Finally, the bargaining process can be quite **ritualistic**. We used to negotiate for months and months with claim, counter-claim, proposal, etc., going on infinitely it seemed. The expectation of the ritual may have inhibited settlement for the parties never quite knew, or were not prepared to accept, when an offer/proposal was 'final'. The senior management believed that 'jaw jaw' was far better than 'war war', so this inhibited a decisiveness as well, while the expectations of the labour force were exceedingly high and a lot of intra-organizational bargaining had to occur between the union officials and the trade union representatives, who in turn had difficulty 'selling' deals to their members.

The process of bargaining needs to take account of this and the 'rationality may be bounded' as a result. This is not an excuse to ignore a logical approach, but anecdotal experience shows that such logic will be tested depending upon the context in the bargaining.

A rational approach

There seems to be three stages to any rational or logical approach to bargaining:

- the preparation;
- the physical conduct;
- the end (which is often ignored).

We can use these headings as a guide although the previous restrictions on pure logic need to be noted.

Preparation

Preparation involved setting objectives and having a plan of campaign. The objectives must be clarified and they must be realistic. The intra-organizational structuring may be prevalent at this stage. Both parties independently need to identify the following:

- ideal finishing point
- realistic finishing point
- resistance points that cannot be 'traded'
- potential trading points (series of and what is wanted in return)
- this should give a 'zone of settlement'

The preparation by both needs to include some prediction of the other party's likely position. A written proposal drawn up or a grievance item obviously clarifies the matter beforehand. A feeling of what their likely line will be can help. We are now moving to the land of 'anticipated reaction': if they do X, we will do Y, and in turn they will do either Z or A, etc. We need to be careful in anticipating too long a chain, but putting ourselves in the shoes of the other person should help us to anticipate some of the likely postures and positions.

Good research and costing of the claim/proposal as well as examining the knock-on effect of given concessions are all critical elements of this stage.

Conduct

The aim tends to be to reach a settlement or at least to move the opposition along the route to settlement or to alter their expectations. As this is very much a skill-based approach, the conduct is best explained by examining an activity derived from reality together with boxes on research in the area with some recommendations on do's and don'ts.

Please tackle Activity LR5.3. This is best approached in three stages: the groundwork preparation, followed by reading the boxes on skills, and then physically putting the negotiation into practice, through role-play for example.

ACTIVITY LR5.3

NEGOTIATION – PREPARATION AND ROLE-PLAYING AT THE COLLEGE OF EDUCATION

Activity code
- ✓ Self-development
- ✓ Teamwork
- ✓ Communications
- ✓ Numeracy/IT
- ✓ Decisions

The College of Education has been granted decentralized bargaining rights over its main terms and conditions. The current lecturing agreement is as follows:

- 35-hour week;
- 36-week year;
- salary scale £15,000 to £28,000 p.a.;
- sick pay of one week after one year's service and so on up to a maximum of twelve years (i.e. twelve weeks);
- overtime is paid at a fixed rate of £22 per hour;
- the pension scheme is separate and non-negotiable;
- all petrol allowances/travel arrangements are decreed by management;
- research/consultancy of up to ten weeks is allowed provided a research paper is published by the College in-house publishers;
- formal holidays of six weeks plus statutory days is part of the agreement.

Tasks

1 Using a rational model of bargaining, prepare either a management or trade union case with appropriate steps.
2 This is suitable also for *role-play*. The ideal position of each party is given below and your group/individual task is to examine the different stages and to negotiate a settlement. Note that the lecturers can strike but a ballot will be required. The management would rather do without a strike as the term with thousands of students is about to start. Do not consult the brief of the other party.

Management

- The hours should remain as now.
- The weeks should be split up into two semesters to maximize the resources of the college. This would mean a 40-week year.
- All increases on the pay scales must be 'self-financed' by efficiency/productivity.
- No change in sick pay.
- Overtime should be abolished under 'professional contracts'.
- No change in pensions.
- No change in travel, etc. (RPI = 5 per cent, so management will determine the increase but not at this table).
- The college must have 25 per cent of *all* research consultancy fees.
- No change on holidays.

Trade unions

- The hours should be reduced to 30 (15 teaching, 15 administration, research, preparation, etc.).
- No change in the 36-week year.
- RPI of 5 per cent on the scales. Efficiency deals of about another 10 per cent should be sought (student numbers have gone up by 20 per cent).
- Sick pay is not a problem.
- Overtime should be paid at time and a half and the new rate should be £25 to allow for backdating plus a half (£37.50).
- The pension is low and paid on 3/80 of the salary while the norm is sixtieths so move to sixtieths.
- No problem over petrol, etc.
- The consultancy belongs to the membership and no deduction should be made.
- Holidays could be increased to eight weeks (plus statutory days).

BOX LR5.2

The skills of successful negotiation

The researchers defined a successful negotiator as one who was seen as effective by both sides with a track record of success and a low incidence of failures.[1]

The process of face to face negotiation was studied through behaviour analysis to differentiate the average bargainer from the successful negotiators.

Behaviours which are best avoided include the following:

- the use of *irritating expressions/words* such as 'this is a generous offer' or indeed saying gratuitously favourable things about themselves or their organizations;
- making a *counter-proposal* immediately after someone has made an initial proposal as this can be seen as a blocking tactic or as an effort to cloud the issue;
- *conflict spirals* with attack/defend posturing going on, which increases the tension in an already stressful situation.

More positive behaviours include seeking information from the other side, testing the understanding of a point with the other side, summarizing your case/argument and perhaps that of the other side (honestly), as well as demonstrating positive behaviour 'labelling'.

The role of planning was also examined aside from these pure process/interactive skills. The skilled negotiator was seen to spend a lot of time looking at the outcomes/options per negotiable issue *prior to the event*. The skilled bargainer looked for common ground or anticipated agreement and not just at areas of conflict. The potential longer-term impact of these considerations were also considered by the skilled bargainers more so than by the average negotiator.

Sequential planning of issues tended to be avoided by the skilled operator as each issue was seen as an independent entity with its own game plan. The researchers termed this 'issue planning'.

So a combination of the right process skills linked to structural planning skills was seen to be evident amongst the 'successful negotiators'.

Source:
1 Adapted from Rackham and Carlisle, 'The effective negotiator, the behaviour of successful negotiators'

BOX LR5.3

Negotiation – do's

Central theme
Try and concentrate on a main argument but use supportive and related themes as the main theme may fall. Keep some arguments in reserve, i.e. 'keep the powder dry'.

Proposals and rejection
Always precondition before making a proposal. Give the reasons for rejection before the actual rejection itself.

People and teamwork
Focus on the key decision-makers on the opposition team. Ensure that your team speaks with one voice. Adjourn, if necessary, to regroup.

Questioning
Ask questions and probe the level of commitment to the opposition's theme.

Counter arguments
There is a view that you should anticipate 'their' arguments and articulate them – 'I know what you are going to say on this'. Don't overdo this though, but it does deflect.

Summarize
To ensure understanding make summaries of points before moving on. Watch out for the false summary!

Listen
Be seen to listen and do listen.

Link
If necessary, the linking of issues can be used and the least important issue 'traded' at a later stage.

Issues
Try and 'think through' the consequences of making a settlement in a given area. If uncertain, there is a strong case for 'kicking for touch'.

Common ground
When nearing a settlement phase build upon the common denominators. The real issues of disagreement may not go away but a 'spin off' may occur.

Conflict/winning
Try and avoid personal attacks and ignore/deflect if possible (it is difficult). Ultimately try for a situation in which neither party feels that it has been beaten. Avoid humiliations and aim for a win:win situation.

BOX LR5.4

Negotiation – don'ts

Conflict
The situation is often tense and usually stressful. Don't allow a 'tit for tat' approach to develop or, as we call it, a conflict spiral.

Arguments
Be prepared but don't be afraid of 'thinking on your feet'.
Don't use irritating phrases about fairness.
Don't threaten people!
'Blunt' arguments rather than reject them out of hand.

Silence
Don't jump in to fill 'gaps'.

Rules and conventions
Don't allow the tone of the meeting to get out of hand.
Be bound by conventions and manners.
No personal attacks.
Avoid flippancy.

Proposals
Don't respond with a counter-proposal. Consider the proposal or reject via prepared arguments.

Adjournments
Adjournments that are too frequent and too long can show disarray and the other party may leave.

Offers
Never too early, and don't say 'this is our first offer'.

Motives
You may suspect motives but don't openly question them.

Decisions
Always give reasons first – then the decision.

Preparation
Don't forget to do your homework and remember the theory of 'anticipated reaction'.

The end

Some form of agreement or an acceptance of disagreement will end the process. The end can be approached by examining its triggers and the mechanics of selling an agreement or failure to agree after the event. We shall focus on getting a deal and assume that normal communication processes follow.

The end involves some relationship between the ideal position (which has been abandoned) and a trade-off between resistance points and potential trading points, to give on paper the zone of settlement. It can be difficult to reach this position.

The process to date has been ritualistic with positions being proposed by both. It now needs to turn to a more realistic conversation. A slow movement is possible using a hypothetical situation of 'If I were to do X, do you feel that an agreement is possible?'. 'Off the record' chats are useful as prescribed rules can be put to one side. The use of a deadline certainly focuses the mind but deadlines run out. An ultimatum as we know can move us into war, so these need to be used with great care, if at all. The consequences of 'breakdown' can be explained by both parties and threats are often alluded to at this stage. Too many threats can be counter-productive, so a comment about the potential consequences of breakdown is a better way forward.

If the line has been 'hard' to date it can be softened to show willing and, if necessary, some 'blockages' can be traded at this stage. A harder line at the end is likely to antagonize the opposition and may inhibit movement or settlement. An 'inducement' can sweeten the situation.

The fear of washing dirty linen in public, or third party intervention, may be enough to allow an eleventh-hour settlement to be reached. If no settlement/movement is possible and/or sanctions are being threatened or employed, the safety net of third party intervention can be quite reassuring (see later, Activity LR5.5 for example).

Making the offer/position public is another route for involving other interested parties. This is not to assume an agreement but to widen the communications and possibly to put pressure on the other side (if the solution is reasonable). The 'all or nothing' tactic is a high risk but it can work towards a settlement.

Briefly, once the deal is struck it has to be communicated. To avoid ambiguity this is best done in writing, whether it is an agreement over terms and conditions or the outcome of a grievance. Minutes, notes for the record or signed agreements prevail in this formal part of the episode. So many disputes that I have encountered come from breaches of agreements – perhaps unwittingly – by management. We shall turn to procedures including disputes procedures later. First, we conclude this key aspect of labour relations with a brief note on its shortcomings, and a longer discussion on bargaining structures. Both issues are very much in evidence at the time of writing.

Shortcomings of Collective Bargaining

To Flanders[16] there are three main limits of collective bargaining:

- there are few if any safeguards to the public interest;
- the growth of such bargaining has been inadequate;
- the institutions for conducting labour relations at the workplace are inadequate.

The national interest versus sectional interest was very much an issue of the 1960s. With the relative decline of trade union members and strength this has become less of a journalistic fad, but the freedom to bargain (and strike) may mean an imposition on other sectors of the community. I am not sure that this can be resolved for it is either a freedom or it is not. Appeals to common sense and reasonableness can be made and legislation to make agreements legally binding could further 'the national interest' – whatever that means. Yet it goes back to a freedom of association and that is as important as any national interest.

The growth of bargaining has actually declined since Flanders wrote his critique. The role of the State, as we have seen, is critical in this exercise. Strong union organization, a mutual recognition between the parties, 'responsible bargaining' and maintaining agreements can enhance the process but a hostile State and hostile employers need a lot of convincing at a time of derecognition rather than recognition of unions. The procedural items raised by Flanders follow in due course.

Bargaining Arrangements

How the bargaining is structured is very much an issue of the times. The issue of bargaining structures concerns the following:

- the potential degree of trade union recognition afforded;
- the locus or focus of power and decision making within and between the main actors;

- the degree of informality/formality of relationships;
- the scope and content of the prerogatives of both sides;
- the agents involved in the bargaining;
- the levels which apply;
- the form and content of the bargaining;
- limits/tolerance levels of acceptable behaviour, e.g. no lockouts;
- the degree of formality compared with custom and practice;
- the commitment of both parties to be bound by the results of the processes within the structure, e.g. arbitration.

Above all else the collective bargaining machinery allows codification and systemization in the fluid 'frontier of control'. As such it goes to the heart of institutionalizing conflict. (See Box LR5.5 on historical themes. Then tackle Activity LR5.4.)

BOX LR5.5

UK bargaining – historical themes

The historical perspective develops the concept of collective bargaining, its pressures and its merits/disadvantages, and it provides a context to the debate on the 'best' bargaining structure.

There is some evidence that collective bargaining occurred in the eighteenth century, particularly in shipbuilding for example, but much of the 'bargaining' was unilateral pressure based on a take it or leave it philosophy, particularly in the print industry.

By the nineteenth century it had become well established in the skilled trades of engineering, furniture-making, shipbuilding and printing. The pieceworkers in iron and steel, coal mining and cotton textiles also benefited from such bargaining.

However, for the majority of workers, even where trade unions existed, negotiation was often sporadic with many workers too weak to take advantage of negotiating opportunities for much of the century. Certainly the skilled workers and their 'New Model Unions' were an exception but even they were hampered by a lack of recognition at national level until well into the 1890s. The period between 1897, when the engineers agreed a national negotiating procedure, and the run-up to war in 1914 witnessed more and more national agreements. Yet the majority of workers had no such agreement and many were still unorganized while most of the organized groups conducted negotiations at local level.

Industry-wide agreements were stimulated by the war. Government control of sectors such as coal and railways and the Munitions of War Act prohibiting strikes as well as inflation, which meant wage readjustment, tended to lead to more national arrangements.

The Whitley Committee, established as a response to industrial unrest, sought to secure a 'permanent improvement' in work relations. The Committee stimulated major changes in the bargaining machinery with Joint Industrial Councils (JICs) in well-organized sectors where national bargaining could take place.

The system also percolated downwards to district and establishment level. Not only were pay and conditions on the table, but efficiency, research and education/training could be matters of concern. In the poorly organized sectors, Trade Boards, with statutory wage regulation, were established. Dispute settlement through a permanent Court of Arbitration would also be possible.

Between 1918 and 1921 some seventy-three JICs were established, yet some five years later only forty-seven were still operating.

Employers often favoured local negotiations and this can be illustrated by the coal employers after 1926. During this period we tend to see a decline in national bargaining but it still flourished in the State sector, and in industries such as cement, chemicals and flour-milling, owing to the scale of the sectors.

Wartime again revived central control and JICs seemed to flourish again. Government control was evident again through legislation to curb strikes and lockouts and to arbitrate in disputes. The low paid were also protected from outright exploitation through the 1943 Catering Act, the Wage Council Act 1945 and the Agricultural Wages Act of 1947.

The bulk of the workers were now covered by national bargaining arrangements.

Fuller employment after the austerity of the early 1950s led to more domestic or plant bargaining encouraged by unions and employers alike. This was in parallel with the national bargaining. The national pay levels often became minima for top up at local level in the private sector while still retaining their importance in the public sector.

The 1980s and 1990s have seen a drive backed by government away from national and central bargaining to plant bargaining and perhaps a philosophy which would prefer no collective bargaining at all, irrespective of the level.

The level of decision making in collective bargaining is the current issue of all these bargaining arrangements. Cadbury,[17] in his annual Hitachi lecture at the University of Sussex, argues that the shift to site bargaining and greater individualism is permanent.

> *Economic pressures and technology have altered the way in which enterprises of all kinds are organised and managed...*
>
> *These structural changes have had and will continue to have profound consequences for the pattern of industrial relations in this country...*

An important reason why these changes will not, in my view, be reversed is that they are reinforced by the third force, the determination of individuals to exercise more control over their own lives...

The shift in the focus of power is from institutions to the units within them and from collective organisations to individuals rather than from the shopfloor to management, which is the theme of new realism.

It is felt that there are clear intrinsic advantages of decentralized bargaining to management which outweigh the costs. We also need to examine contingency variables which may impact on the degree of decentralization, but first we look at the 'inner merits'. See Boxes LR5.6 and LR5.7 on these 'inner merits'.

BOX LR5.6

Decentralized bargaining – advantages

1 Shorter lines of communication. This may resolve disputes more quickly.
2 Diverse technologies and different product and labour markets can be accommodated by a local flexibility.
3 Local not national interests can predominate.
4 A vision of 'one company' and a unitarist philosophy may be easier to promote for management.
5 Managerial authority, particularly at less senior levels, is enhanced by dealing with the trade unions at local level.
6 Greater flexibility over terms and conditions is more likely.
7 Labour relations can be less structured and more informal.

BOX LR5.7

Decentralized bargaining – disadvantages

1 The right people with appropriate competence are necessary – both management and union. This may be more difficult than in a centralized system with 'national experts'.
2 In multi-site companies, parity claims can increase labour costs.
3 In multi-site companies, precedents can occur and leapfrogging from other plants will almost inevitably happen.
4 Strategic workgroups may be able to manipulate the plant structure in their favour whereas in centralized bargaining the group may be insignificant compared with the whole.
5 Uniformity of pay rates across a multi-site company may be difficult to hold and monitor.
6 Multi-unionism and trade union recognition could become problems if no central input occurs in labour relations.

Contingency factors are also relevant.

■ Management may seek control with a minimization of error. If so, this means that the locus of decision making will be central rather than local. The labour relations decision structure should mirror the managerial decision structure.

■ Uniformity of all major decisions in labour relations will be difficult to maintain under a decentralized regime.

■ The type of technology may be relevant. Mass production industries may lend themselves to more centralized decision making (unilateral or joint) while more advanced technology may find a decentralized decision format more acceptable, as in jobbing industries.[18]

■ The rate of change of the industry or the turbulence of the external environment may make for more decentralized marginal decision making which impacts on labour relations.

■ According to Greiner,[19] a decentralized structure will come as the organization goes through its life cycle and this will impact on the bargaining arrangements.

■ A participative managerial style may welcome greater local involvement.

■ Trade union power/authority bases must be recognized and reconciled with the level of decentralization.

We should now move onto other mechanisms for institutionalizing conflict and rule making. Before we do this, please complete Activity LR5.4.

Other Institutions/Processes

So collective bargaining is fundamental to the rule making–conflict interface which characterizes labour relations, but there are other institutions and processes which we need to mention.

Unilateral rule/decision making

Unilateral rule/decision making is the norm in non-unionized environments where management sets the agenda for decisions/rules. This is essentially unchallenged. Some form of discussion may occur but it is often consultation after the decision has been made.

Even in unionized environments, managerial rule/decision making will be unconstrained in the non-people aspects of work. For example, on business policy, finance and accounting, marketing and sales and the enterprise as a whole, management will have the monopoly over non-people decisions. In the labour-intensive areas of operations and production, the people decisions may have more of an input from the trade unions. But even this is often restricted to a 'poverty agenda' involving basic terms and conditions.

ACTIVITY LR5.4

THE LOCUS OF POWER

Activity code

☑ Self-development
☑ Teamwork
☑ Communications
☐ Numeracy/IT
☑ Decisions

Task

From a trade union's perspective outline the advantages and disadvantages of both centralized and decentralized bargaining. Give a conclusion on the 'inner strengths' of both levels of bargaining.

Centralized

\+   −

Decentralized

\+   −

Unilateral rules/decisions can be made by trade unions as well but these are of marginal relevance compared with the unilateralism of management. For example, in one plant that I was familiar with, the unions refused to work with non-union labour. A *de facto* closed shop existed but it did not officially cover contract labour on site. The decision not to work with the people and to down tools unless the contractor was unionized is an example of unilateralism coming from the union side.

Statutory rule/decision making

The law of the land will stimulate labour legislation from health and safety to protection from arbitrary dismissal and redundancy. As this will vary from country to country, and given the international audience of this series, we just note that it can constrain the prerogatives of both management (maximum hours/minimum pay) to unions (strike ballots/election of officials).

Tripartite rule/decision making

The government or its agencies may become involved with the primary parties in labour relations to form a threesome. For example, arbitration and to a lesser extent mediation can be seen in this light. Please tackle Activity LR5.5 on Arbitration.

ACTIVITY LR5.5

ARBITRATION

Activity code
☑ Self-development
☐ Teamwork
☐ Communications
☑ Numeracy/IT
☑ Decisions

You are the arbitrator. Make a ruling on the meaning of Clause 3 in the agreement below and determine the bonus to be paid per person per week for this year.

Clause 1
Payment (basis)

Staff Reduction Clause 1985 Agreement	£28.11 per person per week
Clause 3(a) 1986 Agreement on Technology	£25.50 per person per week

Clause 2
The remaining make-up of bonus is as follows:

(a) flexibility money
(b) pay for improved volume achievements, when and where confirmed, since commencement of any previous Agreement
(c) the continued use of flexible working
(d) the inclusion of the National Bonus of 1983

Total for (a), (b), (c) and (d)	£29.50

Clause 3

Also included in the bonus is a 10 per cent advance volume payment which will be taken into account when calculating any future advanced volume increase for the preceding year.

Any adjustment from the arrangements noted above, applicable either in 1994 or in any future agreed volume, will relate to Clause 2 (sections (a) + (d)).

The final bonus for this year will be .... Why?

Give the rationale.

Bilateral rule/decision making

This is the field of collective bargaining and other variants of employee participation (see Unit Six for participation *per se*). We have spent a considerable amount of time on collective bargaining, so we should focus on the procedures.

Before we do this we need to consider less formal arrangements of co-determination, namely custom and practice and the 'informal system'.

Informal rule making

Earlier we looked at the social action perspective. These theorists see rule making as an ongoing interaction where the written law, rule, agreement, procedure and policy are constantly undermined by a series of negotiations between the key players. The work of Zimmerman[20] is useful in this context.

Some managers regard custom and practice as forms of restrictions. To some extent they also restrict the prerogative of management but they exist because they were agreed tacitly or otherwise between managers and managed.

An example will be illustrative. Many years ago I worked in production in a paper plant. The men were scheduled to finish at 2 p.m., or 5 p.m., or 10 p.m., or 6 a.m. depending on the shift pattern. The work was quite dirty and the plant exceedingly hot. 'Wash and brush-up' time started informally. Instead of finishing at 10 minutes to 5 and walking up the hill to clock off for 5 the men stopped at 20 minutes to 5 and began to tidy up. Some stopped earlier. Almost three decades have passed since that experience and the day employees are probably finishing around 4 by now unless it has been pulled back. Customs and practice tend to drift via 'agreement'.

When management start to pull back an informal 'agreement' trouble often ensues. Gouldner's famous study[21] was noted earlier.

The informal rule making and breaking is ongoing in most organizations. You don't have to be an interactionist to accept these informal processes. From our perspective, the limits of formality, particularly procedures, need to be recognized.

Procedures

The procedures provide the constitutional mechanisms for preventing, channelling and resolving conflict. So they act as a form of power check on the parties. If one party exceeds its authority, the other has a constitutional means of redress. They can also act as judge and jury in the case of discipline/dismissal cases. They can give a platform away from overt conflict or sometimes where the parties can act through their rules, and they can act as a 'hierarchy of appeals' whereby other more senior (and more objective?) individuals not associated with an item can become involved. They can also be used as face savers for both parties.

Procedures can occur at various levels: local, plant, company and national. They can be informal, but increasingly they have become more formalized and in writing.

BOX LR5.8

Procedures

Recognition of trade unions
This often includes facilities for representatives and time off, etc. It may be incorporated into the preamble of the main negotiating agreement.

Negotiating procedure with information disclosure
Often encompassed as part of the main terms and conditions substantive agreement with annual updates on substantive terms and conditions being inserted into the main agreement.

Discipline and dismissal procedure
Self-explanatory with a hierarchy of appeals, timescales and types of 'punishment' which can be applied according to the offence/rule breaking.

Consultative
For example, we find agreements on procedures for handling technological change and the introduction of new equipment and work methods.

Bonus/incentives
I have seen a specific procedural agreement to handle problems with the introduction and maintenance of a bonus scheme.

Manning levels and job demarcation
Numbers and 'who does what' can be codified by these procedures. On manning I've come across a procedural agreement whereby the union office was contacted directly for every job vacancy. The union office then provided a list of potential candidates.

Redundancy/lay off/short-time working
Specific agreements on how to handle these situations are quite common.

Disputes and grievances
These need some attempt at reconciliation in most organizations. This constitutional approach gives a framework for resolution which does not necessarily imply actual coercion or threats of sanctions from either side. In reality, though, this dimension of overt sanctions/threats can still be present – unspoken perhaps in some cases and apparent in others.

A range of procedures can be found. Please refer to Box LR5.8 on procedures.

As a way forward we will focus on the two most common procedures that the average employee and manager will come into contact with – discipline/dismissal and grievance/dispute.

Discipline and dismissal procedures

To a great extent much of the employment relationship is about control. This can be demonstrated by the management approach to discipline and dismissal which is very much geared to its frontier in the control equation – in spite of labour legislation on dismissal.

So employees need legislative curbs on dismissal and trade unions take an active interest in the rule-making process. Certainly unions are represented in this procedure and often assist in drawing up the document in the first place but the prosecution, judge and jury all tend to lie with management in most cases with some external safety net provided by the State and its agencies.

The attitude towards discipline reflects the managerial style and approach to labour relations. A punitive cum authoritarian style linked to a legalistic approach to rules of conduct and standards of behaviour will do little for motivation and self-discipline.

Please tackle Activity LR5.6.

Constructive self-discipline encompassed within the attitudes and behaviour of mature adults must be the best way forward. Employees need to know the rules, the standards of conduct and the expected behavioural

ACTIVITY LR5.6

THE DISMISSAL

Activity code
- ✓ Self-development
- ✓ Teamwork
- ☐ Communications
- ☐ Numeracy/IT
- ✓ Decisions

Mandy looked over to her boss, John. He caught her eye and smiled knowingly. She hesitated too long, flushed a little, and smiled back. Rogers caught them. It confirmed what he had suspected all along – they were lovers.

Rogers was no prude but he was a gossip. He told everyone his suspicions but was ignored by most in the office as reading too much into a passing glance. Anyway, Mandy was engaged and 'old' John was married.

The seed was planted, though, and people began to see Mandy and John together – at lunchtime and in the evening. Rogers was right – they were lovers.

On its own this would never have bothered Jack Paynton, the Labour Officer, for he prided himself on having the objectivity of a sociologist. Rumour, gossip, maliciousness existed in every organization and he could not care less about Mandy and John. However, his personal views were soon tested.

Mandy was an able woman who worked like a Trojan. She was good and she knew it. The 'key tasks' of her job description were met every six months (the appraisal was every six months) and she had been recently promoted. To the world at large and to Rogers in particular 'she was sleeping her way to the top'. This was totally unfair of course but jealousy of her good looks and of John's good fortune meant that her colleagues had a tarnished vision of her. They complained first to their overall boss (John's boss) that Mandy was receiving special treatment. Her promotion was linked to her getting all the best jobs in the locality while others travelled miles. It was 'fixed' by John they said. They were now living together 'in sin' and they wanted to be together all the time according to the group gossip.

The rest of her peers refused to work with her and John.

A special meeting was called. The facts were outlined. Mandy was asked to transfer to another branch. She declined as she preferred to work for 'gentleman' John. The boss of the other branch had an awesome reputation.

Management looked around but could find no other suitable employment for her. The managers agreed that she would not have any earnings reduction in spite of the job being a slightly lower grade in the other branch. Mandy would not move. Her union representative was in a dilemma: he represented the group and Mandy. He could see both points of view and she was being a bit unreasonable.

Management thought so as well. An ultimatum was given to Mandy – move or be dismissed. She declined to move, so she was dismissed.

Task
Analyse this case.

patterns in an organization. The objectives of the disciplinary/dismissal procedure should be clearly stated and widely known. If the issue is rule breaking, capability, conduct or general behaviour the procedure must be applied fairly and objectively across the board.

On an anecdotal level, I remember being party to the discipline of two employees who had been guilty of theft. The shop steward put their case, and in the end he knew it was quite hopeless. At the end of the session, he noted that his membership could be watching out to make sure that everyone was treated in this way across the board. I gave him that assurance. Less than a month later two white-collar foremen/supervisors with long service were caught fiddling timesheets and signing on for one another in order to get extra shift monies. The pressure from wider management was to give them a final warning and some suspension (it was allowed in the procedure). It took me a lot of work to dismiss these men and a lot of heartache as well.

Rules must exist, of course, and people need to know them. Management must inform, remind and encourage (cajole) employees into accepting the standards of behaviour about the place. A minority, as in the wider society, will exhibit more deviant behaviour and the management of labour must meet this pressure head on.

Ultimately the discipline/dismissal procedure is about giving people parameters and making them conform to given standards of conduct. Punitive action is not the *raison d'être* of disciplinary procedures. Action must be taken in some cases, though, so it is important

- to have clear definitions of acceptable/unacceptable behaviour;
- to consider all the known facts as soon as possible;
- to give the employee the right to state his or her case with a representative present;
- to give and honour the rights of an appeal to an independent person (or a manager hitherto not involved in the proceedings);
- to use a system of warnings or 'stepped' disciplines for events which do not warrant instant dismissal.

Some 'offences' tend to be regarded as making the offender liable for instant dismissal (see Activity LR5.7 on discipline or dismissal). The rules need to be published and well known. Management should prevent the issue arising if possible and this requires uniform interpretation and ongoing consistency.

Too many rules may bring the whole system of rules and discipline into contempt, and they will be bypassed by many and cause difficulties in administration for management.

Procedures with first, second and final warnings with appeals, etc., are not enough; they need to be matched by clear rules, as few as is practicable, and by a uniform and fair-minded approach by all concerned, even against transgressors. Of course, even though a transgressor is being disciplined, he or she has the right to use the grievance procedure if he or she perceives that principles of equity are being breached.

ACTIVITY LR5.7

DISCIPLINE OR DISMISSAL

Activity code
- ✓ Self-development
- ✓ Teamwork
- ☐ Communications
- ☐ Numeracy/IT
- ✓ Decisions

Listed below you will find a series of misdemeanours. Clarify your stance on each item, give some rationale for your decision and decide to discipline or dismiss. Assume that you have gone through the procedural mechanisms.

- Injury or assault
- Theft
- Sleeping on duty
- Using drugs/alcohol
- Damaging property
- Smoking
- Making false statements
- Falsification of returns, clock cards, expenses, etc.
- Ignoring instructions
- Wilful neglect/wilful disclosure of organization's secrets

Grievance and disputes procedures

It has been put forward that some degree of conflict is inevitable in labour relations. Given this premise the onus may have to be on settlement rather than prevention. Even if the premise of inevitable conflict is not accepted, 'breakdowns' in the relationship will occur from time to time. On the other point about settlement, we increasingly find a human resource management vision permeating people relationships[22] and this school of thought may be more for conflict prevention or attempted eradication than settlement as such. Whatever viewpoint is taken, we still need some procedural mechanism for resolution from time to time.

The methods used can vary from *ad hoc* meetings to formalized sessions with rigid constitutions. Formality should prevail. I recall that I experienced a dispute on the disputes procedure where the unions accepted one localized procedure covering bonus with management advocating the centralized procedure which was different. Much energy was dissipated discussing the existence or otherwise of *a* procedure. So in this area it is best to err on the side of formality.

A grievance tends to be an individual complaint whereby some redress is sought. A dispute tends to be a collective issue with group ramifications. A grievance can easily become a dispute as it may have collective implications. The procedure tends to be similar in both circumstances and this can be transferred over to discipline as well. Both grievance and disputes procedures have a notion of a 'hierarchy of appeals'. If the issue cannot be resolved at the first level it goes onto the next in the hierarchy including more senior actors from both sides.

Marsh and McCarthy[23] give us two tests to apply to these procedures: 'effectiveness' and 'adequacy'. The 'effectiveness' test is some form of compromise action to an ordered behavioural pattern between the actors. The 'adequacy' test concerns a lack of overt conflict and a genuine attempt to achieve a peaceful settlement. So adjustment of differences and the minimizing of open conflict seem to be paramount. Other 'guiding principles' can be found in Box LR5.9 and an application of procedure can be seen in Activity LR5.8.

BOX LR5.9

Disputes procedure – guiding principles

If we can assume that peaceful coexistence and tension reduction (not conflict elimination) are the aims of the primary parties, we can look to certain guiding principles.[1]

Acceptable
There should be a genuine acceptance of the existence of the procedure by all concerned and a serious attempt should be made to reconcile differences.

Appropriate
It must be related to the needs of the actors in a given industry or organization. For example it must reflect the decision-making apparatus: there is no point in having a decentralized disputes procedure, for example, when the locus of decision making is at the centre.

Voluntarist
Agreement cannot really be foisted on the main parties. Of course third party intervention is important (see Unit Three) but the main parties must both accept the outcome in order for the agreement to be workable in practice.

So these agreements are 'treaties of peace and devices for the avoidance of war'.[2]

Sources:
1 RCTUEA, *Report 1965–1968*
2 Marsh, 'Disputes procedures in British industry'

ACTIVITY LR5.8

TOWARDS A MODEL PROCEDURE

Activity code
☑ Self-development
☑ Teamwork
☑ Communications
☐ Numeracy/IT
☑ Decisions

Task
From the discussions so far, establish a list of criteria which could be used as the basis of a model procedure covering disputes and/or discipline.

So, we have covered a range of methods and processes which facilitate the resolution of conflict. As far as effective labour relations are concerned much of management's time can be spent in this area. Yet management needs also to be pro-active in the area of labour relations. In the next unit we focus on a whole range of topics which are of current importance and which also allow management to be more pro-active. Having said this the mechanisms for the resolution of conflict go to the heart of labour relations and they must be understood and accepted by all the parties concerned. We consolidate this unit by looking at a range of scenarios derived from reality. Please tackle Activity LR5.9.

ACTIVITY LR5.9

SCENARIOS

Activity code
- ☑ Self-development
- ☑ Teamwork
- ☐ Communications
- ☐ Numeracy/IT
- ☑ Decisions

Task

Your role is to accommodate and resolve the issues below by a combination of procedures, agreements, disputes/grievance handling, negotiation and management decision making. This activity consolidates this unit.

1 To cover excessive holiday output, casual labour is employed. The full-time workers say that they will cover the work on overtime and refuse to work alongside the casuals.

2 The whole issue of higher earnings is involved in this scenario. Mr X seeks a transfer to a higher paid job. His manager's report is poor with bad time keeping and 'attitudinal problems'. He was warned but there is no formal disciplinary note on his file. You refuse to accept him. The union backs his claim as he has the experience of the task.

3 The Personnel Manager is walking through the warehouse section when he sees someone blatantly riding on a pallet truck. He does not stop the person but goes immediately to the supervisor and tells him to stop this action as it is unsafe – and the Personnel Manager is responsible for safety. The supervisor tells the man to stop. Within five minutes the remainder of the shift, singing loudly, all start riding around on their pallet trucks at great speed.

4 A number of notices have started to appear on the noticeboard citing alleged victimization and heavy-handed management. A supervisor catches one lady doing the posting onto these boards. The supervisor wants to discipline this individual. You advice is required.

5 Imi Morgan, a coloured worker, alleges that he is being ignored by his colleagues, that racist taunts have been made and that extreme rightwing literature has been placed in his locker.

6 The clerks in Unit B who are outside your jurisdiction are taking industrial action. The clerks in Unit A are not taking action but have similar grievances. Pressure is being brought to bear on the clerks in Unit A to join the action 'on their own behalf' – not as a sympathy gesture. As a Unit A manager what should you do?

Notes

1 Kornhauser et al., *Industrial Conflict.*
2 Blake et al., *Managing Intergroup Conflict in Industry.*
3 See Ministry of Labour, *Handbook of Industrial Relations.*
4 Dubin, 'Constructive aspects of conflict'.
5 Chamberlain and Kuhn, *Collective Bargaining.*
6 Atkinson, 'Bargaining: the rules of the game'.
7 Webb and Webb, *Industrial Democracy.*
8 Flanders, 'Collective bargaining: a theoretical approach'.
9 Chamberlain, *Collective Bargaining.*
10 Dubin, 'Constructive aspects of conflict'.
11 See Oldfield, *New Look Industrial Relations.*
12 Walton and McKersie, *A Behavioral Theory of Labor Negotiations.*
13 See Marsh, 'Disputes procedures in British industry'.
14 See Kuhn, *Bargaining in Grievance Settlement.*
15 Anderson, 'A study into the managerial control of labor disputes – the roles of negotiation, sanctions, overt threats and procedure in the process of disputes accommodation'.
16 Flanders, *Collective Bargaining: prescription for change.*
17 Cadbury, 'The 1980's: a watershed for British industrial relations'.
18 Woodward, *Industrial Organisation – Theory and Practice.*
19 Greiner, 'Evolution and revolution as organisations grow'. See the other non-people texts in this series: *Effective Accounting, Effective Finance, Effective General Management, Effective Entrepreneurship, Effective Enterprise, Effective Marketing, Effective International Marketing, Effective Marketing Communications* and *Effective Business Policy.*
20 See Zimmerman, 'The practicalities of rule use'.
21 Gouldner, *Wildcat Strike – A Study in Worker–Management Relationships.*
22 We spend a lot of time on this issue discussing the philosophy of human resources management and personnel management in the sister volume of this series. See Anderson, *Effective Personnel Management.*
23 Marsh and McCarthy, 'Disputes procedures in Britain'.

Unit Six

Some Current Issues

Learning Objectives

After completing this unit you should be able to:

- critically examine and analyse some key labour relations issues of the 1990s;

- apply the generic skills.

Contents

Unit Six

> " If democracy means anything it means the establishment of institutions in which an individual can influence his own destiny by having some share of control over his material and human environment. "

Tony Benn, Labour politician[1]

Overview

The relationships between owners/managers and labour have been usefully summarized as the 'frontier of control'.

This frontier is akin to an ageing meandering river which may separate two countries. The actual course of the river will change and so will the frontier between the states.

In terms of labour relations this analogy is preferred to visions of 'balances of power' as the latter ideas presuppose some steady state and the potential for equilibrium which is not really there as the real power base is weighted towards the employers, particularly so when in tacit or formal agreement with the State. With a significant pool of unemployed, recession if not depression, union weakness and employer offensives, the meandering river, of late, has been changed to meet the needs primarily of employers. This is reflected in the current approach by many employers in the series of issues selected for this unit. To paraphrase Flanders,[2] many employers seem no longer prepared 'to gain control by sharing it' for now they seem able to take it without consensus – with no vision of shares and stakes. Many employers seem to have gone down the route of individualism in an attempt to divert the river away from collectivism altogether.

However, an historical context is important: we should not view labour relations from the narrow perspective of the immediate present, for the past has a habit of catching up with us. Neither should we extrapolate current themes into an unknown future. The course of the 'frontier' can so easily change again, although the residual managerial base will still be more powerful than that of organized labour and definitely far more powerful than that of disorganized or unorganized labour.

Figure 6.1 shows the unit in diagrammatic form.

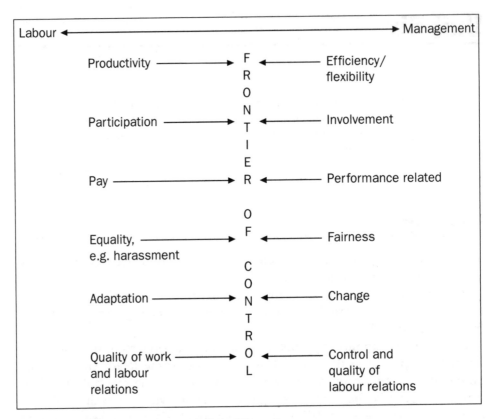

Figure 6.1 Diagrammatic representation of the unit.

Productivity/Efficiency and Flexibility

Productivity has to be of critical importance to any manager of labour. Towers[3] looks at it as the ratio per period of time between total outputs (or production) and the resources (or inputs) associated with those outputs. This can involve the better utilization of capital and other resources such as land, but here we will focus on labour productivity and in particular productivity cum efficiency bargaining and agreements.

The aim of productivity bargaining is essentially economic. It attempts to enhance efficiency by increasing the output over a period or reducing the hours worked over a period to produce a product. In the service sector, a concept of value can be used to give output derived from the total value of output (sales) minus the cost of raw materials. Labour productivity can be gleaned from the formula.

In the last unit, we examined different types of bargaining. In productivity bargaining the theme is reciprocity between the parties with the ultimate aim of efficiency and a share of the potential savings which accrue. So it is very much integrative bargaining. Indeed the relative decline of productivity bargaining may reflect a lack of consensus, with management no longer 'gaining control by sharing it'. It can now rely on more of a diktat; hence 'unilateral flexibility' is emphasized at the expense of negotiated productivity and efficiency. So in theory productivity bargaining is 'an agreement in which advantages of one kind or another such as higher wages, are given to workers in return for agreement on their part to accept changes in working practice or in methods or in organisation of work which will lead to more efficient working'.[4] What lessons can be learnt from experiments with productivity bargaining and what relevance, if any, do they have for the 1990s?

There are various types of productivity bargains but the core theme is the better utilization of resources. As the National Board for Prices and Incomes[5] noted '[it] concerns the relationship between the output of the organisation and its overall use of all resources' (i.e. including labour but not only labour). Wasteful practices can be bought out and duplication of effort can be reduced. Another variation is some form of stakeholding concept with lower labour costs emanating from an agreement with the savings being apportioned. Joint manpower initiatives from policy to planning the supply side of the manpower plan may be another variation.[6]

A range of agreements therefore exists:

- partial or comprehensive, covering a specific area or the whole plant;
- shopping lists to cut back on 'restrictive practices';
- efficiency agreements;
- joint union–management initiatives to plan for change.

Please see Box LR6.1.

BOX LR6.1

Payments by results and productivity/efficiency bargaining

Payments by results (PBR) is *not* productivity bargaining in all but name as considerable differences exist between the two concepts.

- Productivity bargaining like PBR aims to stimulate higher production by higher wages/salaries but, unlike PBR, it involves a change in working practices or conditions.
- PBR tends to emphasize quantity; productivity bargaining may emphasize quantity but quality is also involved.
- PBR may be introduced unilaterally by management; a productivity agreement is usually a result of protracted bargaining by both sides.
- PBR tends to concern a few areas while productivity bargaining tends to be many sided.

Various assumptions lie behind productivity/efficiency bargaining. In distributive power-based bargaining the cake is not infinite, and negotiation is concerned with the price of labour. It is zero plus bargaining. Productivity makes the cake bigger as both parties 'give' something to the cake. This concept has transferability to current labour relations as it supplements a power-based approach by both sides.

Economic growth can be behind the desire for productivity/efficiency bargains and this is relevant to the 1990s. The assumption is that it is desirable for people to enjoy more goods and services. So the economy must have the facility to improve the rate at which it transfers its resources (effort, raw materials, machinery, fuel and power, etc.) into more goods and services. So there is scope to improve productivity. Of course, such efficiency may be improved by other policies from mechanization to product standardization, but labour is more than a mere cost and its input can be isolated and improved.

For management, productivity/efficiency bargains aim to give a better utilization of resources. They involve not only cost cutting but the more efficient deployment of labour. Flexibility bargaining has taken over these themes (see later). The productivity initiatives in the 1960s and 1970s in the UK were very much geared to meeting skill shortages and tackling rising trends of overseas competition. There is a competitive angle here[7] for the internal labour resource can give critical competitive edge. This was recognized by the Prices and Incomes Board which looked to industrial regeneration and allowed self-financing productivity schemes to escape statutory wage controls. In the event this clause may have been abused by some employers and unions as bogus productivity deals may have flourished in order to bypass government controls on pay.

Trade unions and their members are interested in job security. Enhanced basic rates to reward skill and less emphasis on 'variable' elements such as overtime are inherent in these schemes. Again many employees have the competitiveness of 'their' companies at heart – at least to keep them in work. This is as relevant now as in the 1960s.

Managers wish to remove inefficient working practices and these are bought out through productivity bargaining. In the 1960s managers were 'claiming back' some of the perceived inroads into their prerogatives by the workgroups. Full employment and plant bargaining with strong shop stewards provided the context. This 'clawback through consensus' is less relevant in the 1990s, as 'equilibrium' (if there is one) has swung considerably in favour of management prerogatives while diktat may have replaced the need/desire to operate through agreement. Yet informal customs and practices may mean that some 'restrictions' still occur while often management and labour have jointly connived in maintaining so-called 'restrictive practices'. (See Box LR6.2.)

BOX LR6.2

Restrictions or restrictive practice

The 'restrictive practices' by organized labour can be seen in overmanning, withholding output, unnecessary overtime, job rights/demarcation issues and working to the letter rather than spirit of agreements.
 Why do they exist?

- An attempt to maintain job security.
- An attempt to control one's work environment.
- A base for strong bargaining.
- Tradition/group mores.
- Management using overtime as a tap and allowing these practices to go on.
- Workgroup controls over the effort–reward ratio.

Consequently managerial initiatives from human resource management strategies to 'cultural change' have tackled these 'restrictive practices'. Some negotiation over flexibility also targets this area.

It may be felt that some thirty years later we are still attempting to get rid of these 'restrictive practices' in some sectors. Yet some remain. Does this mean that the concept of productivity/efficiency agreements is flawed or are they unsuccessful? There is a clear problem in putting a price on a perceived abuse for it can easily reappear. The issue may also involve workgroup controls for these will continue irrespective of agreements although the worst 'abuses' may be eradicated.

However, there were clear gains from past productivity deals. Please tackle Activity LR6.1.

Further, the efficiency drive is still relevant and the *process* of this bargaining and the potential for gain-sharing is still relevant to the 1990s.

Fleeman and Thompson[8] give us an insight into this process. Perhaps the physical activity of doing it is more important in the long term than the material short-term gains for each party. For example, goals have to be established at the outset and senior managers have to get involved. This planning puts labour relations on more of a strategic level. Both parties look to mutually acceptable performance indicators and bargaining can be more 'rational' as a result. A problem-solving approach may become apparent but certainly trade unions are involved quite early in the process and management need to 'open the books'.

So this integrative bargaining over productivity and efficiency has much to commend it.

Labour flexibility is not new. Indeed it is inherent in these productivity agreements. Part-time working, a core labour force, a transient pool of labour supplementing this core, shift-working as well as moves against

ACTIVITY LR6.1

PRODUCTIVITY BARGAINING – GAINS AND LOSSES

Activity code
☑ Self-development
☑ Teamwork
☐ Communications
☑ Numeracy/IT
☑ Decisions

Task
Your task is to determine the potential gains and losses to the main parties (management and union) of implementing a productivity deal.

'restrictive labour practices' are all tantamount to flexible working. Of late, though, the degree of flexibility has altered: we have flexibility in numbers, hours, crafts and skills, pay and rewards, and moves towards harmonization.

The industrial relations system is ever developing and some recent UK changes which may be indicative of developed countries including the following:

- economic turbulence with worldwide slumps in the late 1970s/early 1980s and yet again in the late 1980s to date and costs, particularly labour costs, can be seen as one way of meeting this external turbulence;
- new technology and automation have continued unabated with a potential for deskilling of labour and for wholesale job cuts;
- product markets have become more fluid with rising international competition;
- sustained high levels of unemployment have created a permanent underclass and a pool of unemployed which in turn weakens an already weakly unionized sector;
- subcontracting and self-employment has risen as the 'shake-out' continues;
- part-timers, often females, and often seen as cheap labour, are available to fill any gaps caused by over-cost-cutting exercises;
- management seem to be taking a more aggressive approach in many firms;
- the trade union power base depleted by unemployment and hindered by statutory curbs seems unable to oppose plans for 'flexibility';
- privatization and compulsory tendering in hitherto secure areas of the public services have opened this sector to the vagaries of the market.

Curson[9] notes manpower surveys of UK employers in the 1980s and cites their 'labour strategies' as

- permanent reductions sought in unit labour costs against a background of market uncertainty and growing international competition;
- a reluctance to give commitment to increase permanent full-time staff;
- a need to look for 'novel patterns of working' against a background of a desire for shorter hours.

These strategies find expression in various attempts at gaining flexibility through

- numbers
- functions
- distancing
- pay/rewards

Numbers

The demand for workers fluctuates, particularly in some organizations. Numerical flexibility means a greater ability to increase or reduce the size of the workgroup. These measures include the use of part-timers, temporary workers, job sharers, subcontractors, homeworkers, fixed-term contracts, overtime/shift changes and flexible patterns of hours.

Functions

This removes 'artificial' barriers to allow the redeployment of employees to meet changing workloads. It means a relaxation of demarcation lines, retraining, and some multi-skilling whereby the worker is trained in a range of skills.

Distancing

This means reducing the core number of workers on a permanent contract and supplementing them by contracting out whole sections, such as canteens or cleaning, using the self-employed (saving employers' insurance rates) and franchising or giving some concessions.

Pay/rewards

We will develop this later in this unit under performance-related pay, but we find attempts to relate labour costs to output not through some productivity gain share as in the past but through individual pay and performance. Merit pay and performance appraisal schemes are slipping into many firms as part of this flexibility.

We find increasing examples of money being placed with people rather than with the job and others being paid selectively outside of the established pay structure.

This drive towards flexibility has resulted in the so-called 'flexible firm'. The core employees with their functional flexibility are supplemented with peripheral workers undertaking numerical flexibility. In turn, job sharing, part-timers and short-term contracts make up the next tier of 'outsiders'.

For management certain costs are incurred:

- training
- time
- monetary increases
- new procedures
- new methods
- new facilities

Yet the benefits far outweigh these costs:

- shorter planning cycles
- increased machine capacity
- reduced manning levels
- greater integration between departments
- increased output while fixed costs are contained

The costs seem to outweigh the benefits to trade unions and their members:

- wage cuts are experienced
- national bargaining is savaged
- protection for the lower paid is lost
- job security is threatened
- collective representation is made more difficult
- standards may be reduced as in public services, e.g. cleaning

The benefits can include

- a 'bigger' job
- possibly more equality (harmonization)
- the availability of better training
- more flexible hours
- employees who are more 'transferable' to other firms after re-skilling

For the core workers life may be acceptable but for the non-core peripheral workers this casualization process seems rather bad news. We need an adaptable labour force but we also need a highly trained productive labour force in work rather than a relatively well-off core and a poorer periphery.

So the integrative bargaining of productivity deals has much to commend it for all parties. In times of savage cost cutting, such productivity/efficiency deals allied to investment would be a welcome relief, a constructive method of dealing with labour costs rather than a destructive policy of laying waste organizations, if not communities, by short time, layoffs and redundancy. It may be a better option than enforced 'flexibility' which often has the hallmark of a resurrected nineteenth-century version of casualization of work – a deskilling process particularly for the non-core workers (see later, 'Quality and labour relations').

Participation and Involvement

Participation is essentially a stake in the decision-making apparatus of the organization while involvement is a managerial attempt to engage the support of the workers for organizational objectives. Both reflect the 'frontier of control' and the current move in the UK seems to be towards involvement rather than participation.

We shall develop Walker's[10] concept of the nature of participation, seeing it as four levels of 'democracy at work': ownership, government, terms/conditions and management. First a little more on the concept and the influences on the idea.

The concept

The term participation concerns having some share or involvement in the enterprise. As a minimum position there is some vision of democracy and, as a maximum stance, control with associated rights.

One key strand is that of decision making. Blumberg[11] notes this emphasis: 'What I am primarily concerned with is decision-making by the workers'. Walker[12] continues this theme but broadens it further to cover managerial functions (i.e. other than decision making) and also limits it as a concept to workers making inroads on managerial prerogatives rather than having a vision and agenda of their own.

The other key strand concerns the exercise of control. To Guest and Fatchett[13] the issue becomes 'those processes whereby subordinates are able to display an upward exertion of control'. This builds on more of a power dimension than straightforward quibbles about decision-making prerogatives but it may be linked to the degree/type of shared decision making which may finally result.

So participation is a process of involvement of workers in the exercise of decision making based on some form of joint control or power sharing.

The influences

The socio-political context of participation gives some historical 'feel' for the subject. The growth and relative influence of the trade union movement, the role and attitudes of management and the State, the changing social mix of the labour force with differing less deferential and wider expectations, must be linked to *realpolitik* at a given time to determine whether or not participation is on the agenda. For example, in the UK in the 1960s, strong unions often preferred collective bargaining as an option while more democratic styles of management prevailed which looked reasonably upon implementing some participative approaches. The State encouraged by a strong philosophy advocated 'forced participation'. These initiatives seemed to find an echo in the aspirations of many workers. In the 1990s, the union priorities seem to lie elsewhere, managerial styles may have hardened and a *laissez-faire* philosophy of the UK government seems to dampen any aspirations for greater participation, if it is prevalent, amongst the workforce. The European dimension and the Social Chapter and Charter are still with us though. Further it is felt that the issue of participation in some form or another is so fundamental to labour relations that it will remain on the agenda (see Box LR6.3).

BOX LR6.3

Towards a managerial rationale behind recent developments in participation

Marchington notes various reasons for the current interest in the subject.[1]

- To employers it is related to 'employee commitment' strategies.
- It is an attempt to undermine collectivity and collective bargaining and to move people away from their trade union loyalty base.
- It sweetens the pill of the employment contract and may be linked to conflict reduction strategies.
- There may be a link to 'change management' as involvement may reduce resistance/improve propensity to change.
- To employees, participation may meet social expectations of a greater say in their working lives (identified with the quality of working life).
- It may lessen the impact of managerial remoteness in large organizations and reduce worker alienation as a result.
- The Japanese 'economic miracle' with its participative practices may be copied as a tool of improved competitiveness of the enterprise.
- There is a growing weight of EC legislation and examples of participation which can promote the concept.

Sources:
1 Adapted from Marchington, 'Employee participation', and Marchington, *Managing Industrial Relations*

Classification schemes

Most commentators divide participation into 'direct' forms, where workers speak for themselves, the general aims and rules may not be codified and there is little external influence, and 'indirect' forms. Indirect forms are more formal and often involve external agencies and representatives who 'speak' for their constituents.

Another classification used by Poole[14] is to examine the source of the initiatives, management, workers, trade unions and the actions of governments.

Marchington[15] uses the twofold division of direct and indirect with the addition of 'financial participation'.

The scheme put forward here is a development of the classification by Walker.[16] Classification is into four areas:

- *ownership* – this includes co-operatives to more modest profit/share option schemes;
- *government* – representation on the Board at a policy-making level;
- *management* – a share in decision making;
- *terms and conditions of employment* – such as collective bargaining.

Let us enlarge upon this scheme.

The *ownership* category is hardly ever challenged at most workplaces and we have diluted forms of 'stakeholder' analysis currently very much in vogue in many firms. Shell operates a Save As You Earn Scheme with options to 'buy in' at the end of each savings period; profit-sharing schemes with X amount of shares allocated to staff and held in trust before release can be seen in Marks and Spencer; profit-related pay, a form of cash top-up based on the financial success of the organization, can be seen at Unilever; while most executives traditionally have had a stake in some executive share scheme with nominal sums being paid for the price of shares. Increasingly performance-related pay, as distinct from top-up, is becoming part of the financial package, but this is not ownership, even of a diluted kind.

Apart from the executive schemes, these share option schemes do not give real ownership. They may give greater identification with the organization, and may relate to productivity, but these points are also both debatable. So ownership is not really being challenged or shared under these initiatives.

The *government* and policy-making committees of an organization can be influenced by employee directors or representatives co-opted onto boards. Examples in mainland Europe are numerous.

The issue of worker directors is a contradiction in terms to many trade unionists. Collective bargaining is the 'proper' approach to impact on policy decisions of management; while many managers jealously guard their decision-making prerogatives at this level in the hierarchy. The opposition, particularly from managers, to the majority report of the Bullock Committee in 1977 may be indicative. Some experiments did occur in British Steel and the Post Office but the vast majority of British managers were reluctant, to say the least, to adopt such radical policies. Some unions noticed that 'their' representatives soon became engulfed with company affairs to the detriment of the 'pure' union outlook. Of course, involvement in policy making in the organization may restrict trade unions and their freedom of movement to challenge the policy further down the line.

The European 'model' of two-tier boards can overcome some of these difficulties. Participation in government is not participation in management.

The supervisory (or main) board has worker representatives sitting in on its policy-making role covering the direction of the business. The next tier concerns the day to day management of the enterprise. This board determines the mechanics of the operating policy and would not normally have employee representation.

Excluding collective bargaining agreements to which we shall return briefly, employee councils may be a useful mechanism of extending debate and consultation. Directors may sit on such a council and the subject range can be quite wide compared with the moans about canteen food often associated with Joint Consultative Committees. Company Advisory Boards on the Japanese model, which involve an element of both consultation and negotiation prior to fully blown collective bargaining, can give Westerners considerable scope in democratizing the decision-making process at work.

Collective bargaining, as we have seen, is a direct mechanism of 'government' of the enterprise and, depending on its subject and scope, can have an immediate participative influence.

Discussion and negotiation over *terms and conditions* of work through collective bargaining, as we have seen, provides an independent approach to participation and removes the union charge of being too close to management thinking in some of the other forms of participative government.

We now move to a more contentious area, that of participating in managerial 'functions'. Before we do this, we need to note that there are different degrees of participation in each of these classifications. The work of Tannenbaum and Schmidt[17] in another context may be relevant. Talking about leadership style, they note a spectrum of approaches from leader-centred to employee control. At one end of the continuum the manager decides and informs the group, going through phases of co-determination until the group itself makes the decision on its own. This continuum can apply to the four classifications of participation:

1 an advisory level whereby management tells workers what is happening, not necessarily before the event;

2 an advisory function before the decision is made;

3 full-scale co-determination by both parties;

4 unilateral determination by the workers/representatives.

Ownership is not really 'up for grabs'. Some limited (very limited) participation may occur at consultative level with shareholding but this is normally at management's discretion.

Government floats between unilateral determination with some constraint on managerial prerogative but this tends to be marginal unless some structural device checks the policy-making board.

Terms and conditions again in many firms are at the sole discretion of management. Unless strong collective bargaining exists managerial discretion will not be tempered by real worker participation.

The *managerial* area may be more fluid as informal worker controls and formal institutions may curb this prerogative. A range of managerial functions (not only decision making) allied to a range of participative schemes can be found.

However, many organizations operate at a much lower level of 'participation', and consultation (not negotiation) prior to managerial decisions often takes place through some consultative machinery or process. Please tackle Activity LR6.2.

From a trade union perspective, collective bargaining is probably the most appropriate form of participation. If we add consultation to this bargaining, most unions would be satisfied.

To a great extent the real debate about participation and involvement centres around management and decision making. The issue of control surfaces once again. A continuum of participation and decisions can be seen in figure 6.2. Assuming no State directives, this continuum would be impacted on by the whole system of labour relations but, in particular, the power dynamics, workers' strength, the type of representation, the potential scope for involvement and participation and, perhaps key, the predominant style and philosophy of management.

To conclude: formal participation seems to be quite limited in the UK. We seem to be far away from real control or democracy. The power-oriented participative approach has moved to a unitarist/commitment involvement approach by management. The real areas of concern, ownership and government, are really untouched by participative practices while managerial practices tend to reinforce this one-way approach of downward and unstructured (non-formalized) participation. It is only in terms and conditions and informal working practices that unions and employees seem to be really participating and this assumes a strong union base and a management prepared to negotiate with the unions over terms and conditions. Much participation seems to be a sham. For the more liberal or libertarian organizations, people managers may have a role in inputting some form of 'participation' based on communication systems.

Please tackle Activity LR6.3.

ACTIVITY LR6.2

CONSULTATION

Activity code
- ✓ Self-development
- ✓ Teamwork
- ✓ Communications
- ☐ Numeracy/IT
- ✓ Decisions

Your role is to draft the constitution for a Joint Consultative Committee.

You may wish to consider the following themes (with some examples) as a guideline.

1 *Purposes*
   e.g. efficiency
      better morale
      communication
      improvement
      participation etc.

2 *Scope*
   e.g. Type of issues which can be discussed.
      Does it include issues which are normally negotiated?

3 *Constituency*
   i.e. Who could attend?
      Union members only?
      All staff?
      All employees?

4 *Qualification* for voters and 'candidates'
   e.g. Length of service?
      Age?

5 *Composition*
   Who should be on the committee?
   Ex officio members?

6 *Meeting administration*
   e.g. Office holders
      Period of holding office
      Frequency of meetings, etc.

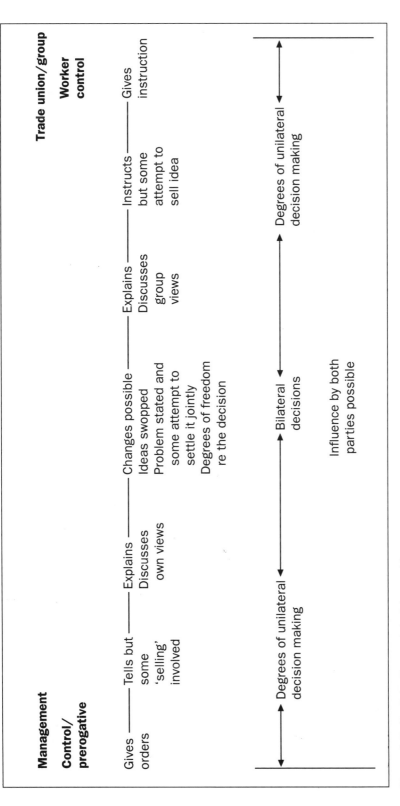

Figure 6.2 Participation and decision making.

ACTIVITY LR6.3

THE LABOUR RELATIONS SPECIALIST ROLE IN PARTICIPATION

Activity code
- ✓ Self-development
- ☐ Teamwork
- ✓ Communications
- ☐ Numeracy/IT
- ✓ Decisions

Task

Assume that you are a specialist manager in labour relations. You are required to draw up a list of principles that will help you introduce and maintain an employee participative cum involvement scheme in your workplace.

Performance-related Pay

The determination and allocation of pay are two of the most fundamental aspects of any system of labour relations. Wages and salaries usually constitute a major cost to any organization while labour looks for fair compensation for its energy, time, effort and skill/knowledge. To the organization, pay is more than a mere cost as it provides both a mechanism of control and an incentive. This reward management is very much an issue of the 1990s. To a great extent we cover pay determination and systems in the sister volume of this text,[18] and so we shall focus on a growth area, if not one of the most contentious aspects of reward management, performance-related pay (PRP). The objective here is not to give some encyclopaedic classification of different variations of PRP, but to examine its pros and cons within the context of a system of labour relations. We are not looking at how to motivate people either, for this is also covered elsewhere in the series.[19]

Managers look to reward systems essentially as a means of recruiting and retaining people and as a means of increasing workers' motivation and commitment.[20] We develop these objectives later. From the perspective of labour, the dictum of 'a fair day's pay for a fair day's work' (however defined) is also relevant.

PRP attempts to link financial rewards to

- individual performance
- group performance
- corporate performance

Concepts of fairness and equity seem to be abandoned in favour of this carrot-induced approach. Armstrong[21] is particularly good on the range of options open to us through different PRP schemes but we will concentrate on the philosophy and the impact of PRP. We touch upon some types of schemes later under 'inner merits'.

In the early days of industrialization without unions, the master determined the pay and its level without real input from the servant. The market dominated pay levels. With unions we find greater co-determination. Without unions we see a unilateral imposition by management taking account of pay levels, skill/expertise, supply/demand, going rates and the ability to pay. Excluding State regulation, we find the levels and types of pay in unionized environments taking account of these factors and the power dynamics of the system of labour relations. Yet PRP attempts to remove many of these factors and 'performance' (however defined) becomes the key component. Please tackle Activity LR6.4.

ACTIVITY LR6.4

PERFORMANCE-RELATED PAY AND NATURAL BEAUTY

Activity code
- ✓ Self-development
- ☐ Teamwork
- ☐ Communications
- ☐ Numeracy/IT
- ✓ Decisions

The Directors of Natural Beauty agreed that performance-related pay (PRP) had been successful in motivating their company as it had clearly motivated the Directors. They decided to review the whole benefits package for HQ managers and staff and in particular PRP.

They wanted to motivate all the employees, increase their commitment and encourage a results-oriented culture.

After scanning the literature in the area, a PRP plan was born. It would be based on the 'performance culture' which they had recently developed and would be linked to key objectives of each individual. An appraisal scheme would be implemented based on this reward orientation. The employees would be motivated by this additional money for the Directors looked to the money as a 'top-up' rather than the rationale for all pay increases. Once under way for some years it could well become the rationale for increased money but this was not the initial intention.

The merit pay would be based on the appraisal and so it would be an objective rating with key tasks for each person. They would check the business objectives and translate them all into individual key tasks.

Six months later the scheme had floundered. They spoke to the representative of the staff. 'There is a whole list of issues: the appraisal is seen to be based on "who you know"; the targets cannot be written up for some jobs like administration or work in the kitchen; the assessment of targets is arbitrary; some of us cannot reach these targets anyway and have given up; and, perhaps most importantly, it is not worth it – the staff prefer overtime and the management (whom I do not represent) prefer time off. Altogether we would rather give this PRP stuff a miss.'

Task
1 Analyse what is going on here.
2 Advise the Directors on their next step regarding PRP.

Ostensibly some may see the attraction in PRP with the hardest working/most able, etc., being rewarded the most. However, it is very divisive by definition and it may not only be a method of incentives for the most able, etc., but a device to turn the clock back to unilateral managerial pay determination. In many cases, unions can be ignored in pay determination through PRP, particularly when it forms *the* main constituent of the pay packet or cheque. Box LR6.4 quotes a trade union view within the educational sector.

Clearly unions would prefer free collective bargaining unfettered by such performance 'indicators'. The cost of living, 'comparability' with other 'like workers' doing similar tasks, productivity and efficiency (as we have seen earlier in this unit), the supply/demand of labour, time, and principles of 'betterment' based on low pay or 'improvement', etc., must be more preferable to most trade unionists.

Yet PRP in some form of another has been with us for some time – usually as a constituent part of the *make-up* of the pay system. Increasingly it is becoming *the* basis of the whole payment system. This has occurred for various reasons.

■ Weaker trade unions operating in a depressed economy with hostile labour laws have been given a 'take it or leave it' approach, as in the education sector.

BOX LR6.4

Aims of performance-related pay – a trade union perspective

A key one is the motivation of staff, in order to produce enhanced performance and thus benefit the functioning of an organisation overall. Additionally the introduction of PRP may be seen as an opportunity to change the culture of an organisation: increasing emphasis on hierarchical management relationships, focusing attention on individual rather than group performance, placing stress on measurable achievement rather than process, and last – but not least – undermining collective payment systems and bargaining.

It is also possible to view PRP as a cost effective way of spending a limited amount of money. Instead of making a – smaller – overall payment to everyone, a – larger – 'motivating' payment may be made to a few.

Source: NATFHE, *Performance Related Pay*

- A unitarist value system is prevalent amongst managerial advocates of PRP who sees such payment schemes as consolidating a new results orientation amongst the workforce.

- Increasing competition in the product market has meant even greater awareness of payment costs and PRP should be 'self-financing' to some extent.

- Decentralized bargaining structures and the break-up of national bargaining, as in the health sector, mean that greater flexibility can occur with less rigid wage rates/salary scales.

- Goals and standards have been emphasized through this type of payment structure and these 'targets' are often codified through some appraisal process.

- It can be used as a crude carrot/stick motivation whereby employees are paid additional monies in 'good times' and not paid such monies in 'bad times'. Perhaps the next motivational step would be to remove monies of poorer performers through wage/salary cuts!

- The Government actively encourages such PRP practices in the public sector (i.e. it withholds money if such schemes are not introduced).

Apart from the 'inner merits' of the schemes which we will consider quite soon, the actual results of PRP schemes look mixed. The performance indicators (quality, flexibility, profitability, targets, etc.) are often not clearly identified. Some types of employee, such as production workers on an assembly line dependent on the work flows of others, may have difficulty entering such schemes. Ongoing monitoring is necessary.[22] The 'blue-eyed boy' syndrome can apply. Teamwork may suffer in individual-based schemes. Most importantly of all, money may not be a motivation and PRP may not guarantee a more motivated or committed labour force. The research on the results of PRP schemes is not too encouraging (see Box LR6.5).

BOX LR6.5

Performance-related pay – the incidence and issues

- Almost 50 per cent of the survey had PRP for non-manual workers; in addition some 21 per cent used 'merit' money for non-manual workers.
- Non-management grades were less likely to be involved with PRP in the public sector.
- Private sector managers/professionals were twice as likely to be involved with PRP than their public sector equivalents.
- Only 10 per cent of public sector employees in clerical and administrative grades were involved with PRP. Some 56 per cent of equivalent jobs in the private sector were covered by PRP.

However, issues were noted. The impact of objectives was often difficult to gauge; the issue of motivation for the majority of people seems to be ignored; and little formal evaluation of the schemes seemed to be taking place.

Source: Adapted from *Personnel Management,* 'Report on PRP'

Is it just a question of fine tuning the possible schemes? To what extent do we have 'inner merits' of these schemes or are they internally flawed?

We have already looked at profit-sharing schemes from the perspective of participation. They may bind the individual in some loyalty theme to the organization and they may help identification with the firm. The rewards tend to be marginal though and remote from the average worker's day to day performance. They tend to degenerate into a 'holiday bonus' type of approach. So this is quite mixed in its impact on performance.

Bonus or achievement schemes by group, department, plant or company tend to fall into the same category. They may lead to tighter group/team cohesiveness but non-performers, workgroup output norms and control mechanisms as well as the removal of bonuses for poor performance can negate the positive impact of such schemes. However, they can provide a 'top-up' to the existing pay packets although control/monitoring of the schemes can be a full-time job.

The commission-only approach of some salesforce incentive schemes is not to be recommended as the basic physiological needs may not be met by such schemes. Again, as a top-up to core salary there may be some mileage in having a volume/sales commission for some direct marketing/sales employees. Indirect workers may be more difficult to place on a commission basis.

From the perspective of organized labour, trade unions have been involved in the negotiation of group bonus schemes for some time. Assuming agreement on targets, X times, X quality, etc., consultation and negotiation, and reasonable starting points for outputs and earnings with the bonus-only part of the overall package, this type of group PRP should be welcomed by trade unions. Profit sharing is more of a 'bonus' and tends to be perceived as such by trade unionists because the 'dividend' is beyond the realm of negotiation.

To trade unionists, individual PRP schemes may be more flawed. The paying or withholding of improvements, based on the level of performance, is apparent, particularly in large bureaucratic organizations and in the public sector. Provided that the goals are reasonable, known and negotiated, more trade unionists could probably live with this type of approach.

However, an individual salary/wage increase based on so-called competence or appraisal of performance may be harder to live with for many trade unionists. Some organizations give an increase for inflation and thereafter a 'merit' payment with a further reward for 'excellence' and a nil reward for being 'ineffective'. Sometimes this merit pay is the only pay made available with no inflation indicator. This type of approach is clearly in the realms of unilateral managerial prerogative and most trade unionists, particularly blue-collar workers, can see the potential fickleness of such schemes. Fickle or not, they are outside the realm of co-determination between the primary parties and individualize the contractual relationship, destroying concepts of collectivity.

From an organizational perspective, PRP may not be the answer either. We need to examine the aims behind any system of reward management by looking at the objectives of employers or what they want out of a payment scheme. The motivational aim of PRP seems to be quite insignificant compared with these other aims and there seems to be no guarantee of the motivational influence under PRP anyway. (Please see Box LR6.6.)

BOX LR6.6

Payment structures

Employers aims (no order of priority is suggested)
- To attract and retain people.
- To meet the needs for productivity/efficiency.
- To meet the 'going rate' of the marketplace.
- To meet the need for flexibility.
- To keep down costs.
- To avoid/reduce conflict.
- To reward skill, experience, professionalism.
- To be fair, equitable and consistent.
- To reward effort.
- To get value for money.
- To recognize talent and long service.
- To reward merit/achievement/results.

To conclude this section, PRP is certainly with us. It has been with us for some time but it is now seen as some panacea of the 1990s by some employers. The payment impact looks mixed and its potential success even more mixed. The unions can cope with the group scheme, all things being equal, but the individual schemes are certainly more open to abuse and manipulation.

The agenda may not be pay at all. It seems a backdoor assault on collectivity. The Association of University and College Lecturers,[23] an educational union, cites the Institute of Personnel Management survey which we mentioned earlier and adds an interesting twist to the whole argument about PRP with its possible hidden agenda:

> *The Institute of Personnel Management on the other hand, in a recent survey of over 800 companies found that 'PRP was fundamentally lacking in effectiveness and of limited use'. The survey goes on to state that 'PRP rewards the individual and acts as a demotivating force for the majority'. Given the philosophy in higher education of team work, and the collectiveness and co-operation which is the embodiment of the nature of our work, it is clear that PRP could destroy, not enhance, our service.*

Equality: Fairness and Sexual Harassment at Work

Discrimination in employment from age to sex, from negative approaches to people with disabilities to race, if not social class, means a tremendous waste of the potential contribution of people at work. The Institution of Personnel Management in its Code[24] notes that the issue of discrimination is not going away:

> *investigation shows that a considerable and unacceptable level of racial discrimination in employment still exists and that sex discrimination is dwindling only very slowly. [The] results are . . . increasingly apparent in disillusionment among ethnic minorities and women, in social unrest, and most importantly in the employment context,* ***IN THE MISUSE AND/OR WASTE OF HUMAN RESOURCES***.

A topical area that we are going to focus on is victimization and harassment.

Harassment is all about power or the lack of power. Paddison[25] tells us that 'anyone who is perceived as different, or is a minority, or who lacks organisational power is vulnerable to harassment'.

We are dealing with the integrity of the individual and the dignity of labour. Harassment is linked to a form of bullying and abuse and it may cut across the primary employment relationship identified here between managers and managed as co-workers may well be involved.

Harassment is concerned with power over a group or individual and this power may have to be met with a stronger power to reduce or eliminate harassment. The case of sexual harassment may be indicative of the issue.

Sexual harassment is a difficult area for the labour relations manager to come to terms with as intent on behalf of the perpetrator may not be present yet the effects and the impact may be felt by the recipient. We can have fun, jokes and flirtation but it may be received as an attack on the personal territory of the individual.

Clearly harassment involves perceptions of behaviour, but if that behaviour is not wanted, not reciprocated and the other party is advised of this situation, then harassment is involved.[26]

The individual recipient of these unwanted actions can suffer from anxiety, anger, stress, humiliation, fear and degradation. This may result in decreased morale and poorer work performance or higher labour turnover and absence rates within the organization.

The law can attempt to combat the issue. Given the assumed international audience we shall not consider this area but it is an important backdrop to the whole subject. Policies on equal opportunity are favoured organizational responses to the issue (see Activity LR6.5). Please refer to Activity LR6.5, Towards a policy on sexual harassment at the Water Works.

ACTIVITY LR6.5

TOWARDS A POLICY ON SEXUAL HARASSMENT AT THE WATER WORKS

Activity code

☑ Self-development
☑ Teamwork
☑ Communications
☐ Numeracy/IT
☑ Decisions

Task
Draft a policy on sexual harassment taking into account the main issues raised in this section. The organization is the Water Works, part of a local government institution.

Remedies do include the use of law but the labour relations manager and trade unions have a positive role in improving the situation within organizations where harassment is or could be a problem.

- Counselling needs to be established so that male/female employees have recourse to some informal process rather than formal grievance machinery.
- Individual employees need to be aware of their rights and their obligations to their co-workers.
- The right to say 'no' must be enshrined in the culture of the organization.
- The potential transgressor needs to be made aware of what he or she is doing to others by management. (He or she may not be aware.)
- Procedures exist and management and unions must have the moral courage to involve these rules.
- A climate of non-acceptance of this behavioural norm must be encouraged by all managers of labour.

At the end of the day, this unacceptable behaviour can be 'outlawed' and new norms can be encouraged, if not demanded, by both unions and management. 'Model policies' may not be the answer. Attitudinal change and behavioural acceptance of new norms backed up with policies, procedures and laws seem to be the way forward to protect women and men at work from such harassment.

Training can play a key role in changing norms and attitudes. Communication from management on acceptable codes of conduct backed up by monitoring procedures can facilitate change. Trade unions and their membership as a whole must not tolerate such practices and must be supportive of managerial actions against harassment. Laws and procedures are necessary but the softer organizational normative change may be more long lasting.

We started with harassment in general. There are lessons in coping with such harassment in Activity LR6.6. It needs a bold ongoing initiative between managers, managed and trade unions to counter such unacceptable practices. You should now tackle Activity LR6.6 on sexual harassment at KD Designs.

ACTIVITY LR6.6

KD DESIGNS – HARASSMENT?

Activity code
- ☑ Self-development
- ☑ Teamwork
- ☑ Communications
- ☐ Numeracy/IT
- ☑ Decisions

Harry Southgate is a manager with KD Designs. He is in charge of a section dealing with customer care and service. Harry's staff is predominantly female. There are three supervisors, two women and one man. The supervisors work on a shift basis as do the rest of the section.

'Garry the Groper' had a reputation for being a 'bit of a lad'. Although Garry Ahad (or 'Groper' as he was known) was married and had been in the supervisory position for some time he had a deserved reputation for always patting young women and brushing up against them. He was a flirt – he knew it and they knew it. He was always making comments on their dress, asking the more attractive ones out for 'a drink' and cracking lewd jokes. He was good looking and he knew it. His manner, though, was very affable, his repartee was enjoyed by many and to date even if he had upset people no-one complained about him. Harry was aware of Garry's reputation but he was seen as a loveable rogue and the women seemed to like his behaviour for he was not serious after all.

An opportunity for secondment to a Project Team meant more money and a change of environment for Garry. He grabbed it. He was replaced by Philip Stone. His nickname was 'Creepy Phil' as many in the Accounts Department where he worked felt more than a little uncomfortable with him. He seemed to stare people out, undressing women with his eyes and making some lewd comment as he did so. Most women kept away from him and he would keep his office door open – if they could – when they went to see him.

'Creepy Phil' was in his 40s and single. He was not particularly good looking, a bit quiet, a bit of a loner and very intense with narrow staring eyes. He knew about Garry and what Garry had got up to and decided to do exactly the same.

He would wink, touch and stroke people's hair. His innuendoes and lewd comments started to cause some concern to the other female supervisors. Female staff became increasingly uncomfortable and some felt threatened. The whole thing culminated in an argument with Jane Seymour. The argument was over work schedules and Jane's inability to meet a quality deadline. She claimed that he began to pick on her after she had refused his advances on three previous occasions. She was taking the case up with the union. Phil said that she was not doing her work properly and if she had a complaint about harassment she should have followed the existing procedures of the firm.

Task

Assume the role of the manager, Harry Southgate.

1 Analyse the dynamics of this situation.
2 What can be done about (a) Phil and (b) Garry?
3 Determine the role of counselling in these circumstances.
4 How would you go about tightening up procedures?
5 Draft a new procedure to deal with cases of sexual harassment.

Labour Relations: Change and Adaptation

As we have seen there is nothing as continual as change. The whole system of labour relations is set in the dynamic of internal and external variables which impact on the levels of conflict and rule making. The pace of change in the 1990s has increased and 'the management of change', with its inherent flexibility and ability to adapt to turbulent competitive and business environments, is one of the most significant people issues facing management today – and, by implication, facing workers.

The process of change impacts on the industrial relations system to a great extent and we shall examine change, lessons from organization development (OD) and the implications for labour relations. We shall focus, particularly in activities, on technological change which is often seen as the sharp end of this overall turbulence.

Pressures for change can be seen as some coalition between external and internal forces within the organization. Kessler and Bayliss[27] sum up some of these forces in the UK:

> *Self reliance, individualism, the curtailment of public expenditure, the play of market forces instead of the restraints and directives of public policy, the prerogatives of management instead of the power of trade unions, centralisation of power instead of pluralism.*

We shall not go through a lengthy note on current pressures behind change but several examples from the UK will suffice. Politically we have seen a government intent on promoting individualism and destroying collectivism through anti-union legislation. Economically we have suffered under a recession with mass unemployment, unsurpassed business failure and increasing competition from abroad, while at the same time the industrial base to fight back has been decimated. Socially, the self-help vision of Thatcherite Britain has taken a grip, particularly in the bungalow-minded visions of some of the working masses in the southeast of the country. Technologically the pace of change and new methods of work has been unsurpassed this century.

Internally, within the organization the 'organic' flexible form of structure and philosophy to adapt and adopt has taken hold. The OD approach is worth noting in this context.

To Bennis[28] OD is 'a response to change, a complex educational strategy intended to change the beliefs, attitudes, values and structures of organisations so they can better adopt and adapt to new technologies, markets and challenges'. This managed change can be divided into content, the physical changes sought by management and process, the mechanics of getting these changes introduced. So it has a managerialist frame of reference from the outset.

It does call upon an 'open socio-technical system' which ensures that the organization does not have an inward-looking feel to it. This reminds us of the open system approach that we noted in our labour relations model at the outset as the organization is in constant interplay with its environment and vice versa.

Unlike our system of labour relations, though, the perspective is one that draws mainly upon the human relations school of management, seeing people as important in their own right, recognizing their needs and developing their potential at work. It is also unitarist, seeking an harmonious whole united for a common (managerialist) purpose with a single group in authority and almost passive participants (workers) motivated by common goals. The system being proposed here is far wider than this perspective as it recognizes conflicts of interest and views trade unions not as some interlopers but as legitimate representatives of the working masses. Does this mean that there are no lessons from OD to labour relations in handling change? Clearly one route of management is to endorse this OD perspective. As we have seen earlier the human resources management vision draws upon similar guiding philosophies.

The work of Kotter and Schlesinger[29] indicating methods of overcoming resistance to change can be widened to illustrate *approaches to change*. These include

- coercion
- manipulation
- education
- support
- participation
- negotiation

These strategies can be illustrated by labour relations examples in many organizations: unilateral managerial moves to local bargaining, single-table negotiations, single pay spines, imposed pay deals and the derecognition of trade unions. 'Leaner' organization structures, individual rates of pay, performance-related pay as we have seen, single status agreements, flexibility of labour and a 'take it or leave it' approach with no consultation, let alone negotiation, have been seen to prevail in some organizations. Many managers have used a combination of the coercive/manipulative routes linked to softer communications and education/training to force change.

Of course, this may be far more reflective of an authoritarian management than of sound OD principles, for the study of OD would suggest the following:

- sound analysis and diagnosis;
- planned 'interventions';
- a longer term strategic view;
- top management involvement;
- an awareness of the power structure;
- behavioural change based more on member consensus than on planned coercion.

So one route of change is this planned coercion. Another route is planned consensus through OD or a planned approach to harmony/conflict through the existing labour relations system.

The OD approach attempts to change attitudes, values, norms, goals and ultimately relationships by changing the technical and structural variables influencing people's behaviour. So it is manipulative but perhaps not coercive. Team working, changing jobs or intergroup relationships, reducing group conflict and attempting to alter the organization's personality to some pre-ordained ideal state are all part and parcel of this approach. Above all else, it is integrative, emphasizing the fusion of needs between managers, employees and customers. It emphasizes co-operation, not conflict, between workers and management.

The labour relations approach being pursued here can take account of the co-operative aspect of the employment relationship but we need to come to terms with the fundamental conflicts within the relationship. These conflicts will not go away, so the way forward in change management is to adapt a planned approach to harmony/conflict through participation and negotiation. The latter route is to combine coercion and diplomacy. Now the *planned coercion* by management is a sign of the times but coercion will ultimately beget coercion and a cowed labour force in the short term; while the *planned consensus* of the pure OD route does not take account of the plurality of interests and the dynamic of conflict within labour relations, interacting with the view of consensus.

The work of Walton and McKersie[30] may be from another time period, but their sophisticated study of the relationship between managers and managed is worth citing as the way forward for a *negotiated route towards change*: as the authors rightly claim '[the four sets of actions] account for almost all the behaviour in negotiations'. As we have touched upon their work earlier, we will be brief. 'Distributive' bargaining involves maximizing one's share in the context of fixed payoffs. 'Integrative' bargaining involves a less conflict-dominated scenario and common concerns over 'an issue' dominate. The 'desired relationship patterns between the parties' can be gauged by the level of trust, respect and friendliness/hostility, if not legitimacy. This is conducted through 'attitudinal structuring'. Intra-organizational bargaining aims at gaining consensus and support within your own 'side', so the shop steward would become involved with such bargaining with his or her members.

These four sets of bargaining can give a wider dimension to the process than traditional aspects of 'negotiation' and can be used as a mechanism of change. Please refer to Activity LR6.7.

ACTIVITY LR6.7

CHANGE AT THE *FREE PRESS*

Activity code
✓ Self-development
✓ Teamwork
✓ Communications
☐ Numeracy/IT
✓ Decisions

The new production facility at the newspaper company had provoked quite a stir amongst the staff – particularly in the editorial and production departments. Computerization was seen to be identified with deskilling and redundancy. The joint committee of the Fathers of the Chapel (FOC) accepted, alongside management, the inevitability of the whole technological drive as the Free Press would not be competitive in a very demanding market unless it changed technology. They were not Luddites and they sought a 'new technology agreement on change'. As one FOC said, 'We make use of the chip or we face the chop'.

Given the history of the labour relations of the place, the managers were taken aback by this 'progressive' attitude. The managers had a clear view. They wished to introduce the new technology without individual 'disruption'. Job loss would occur but natural wastage would be used and enhanced severance monies would be paid if compulsory redundancies occurred. Retraining and flexible skill working would be required and these initiatives might eliminate the need for compulsory redundancy. The senior management agreed that they should let the unions 'run with the thing' as they had been reasonable to date. Further, if they could get an agreement on joint terms it would secure not only the deal itself but the longer-term profitability of the firm. They wished to avoid any disruption to their newspapers with lost revenue from circulation and advertising. The joint unions were asked to submit their views on the proposed agreement.

The unions claimed the following:

1 Adequate information to monitor all new changes in work method and the working information. This should be given (and not just requested by the unions) on an ongoing basis.
2 No deskilling.
3 No downgrading.
4 Agreement on staffing levels and job loss.
5 No compulsory redundancy.
6 No additional jobs/tasks for their members.
7 No contracting or subcontracting of work.
8 No change of work patterns.
9 No work measurement.
10 Redeployment.
11 Job security.
12 No pay 'incentives' which would cut jobs and mean longer/harder work.
13 Health and safety factors to be taken into account.
14 Full training and retraining.

Tasks
1 Assume you are part of the managerial team. Go through these claims and determine which would be acceptable as part of the agreement and which should be rejected. Some may require negotiation, of course, so classify the claim into 'accept', 'reject' and 'negotiate'. Give the rationale for each response.
2 How would you classify the potential types of negotiation in this scenario?

Other positive methods of change include:

■ *Training/education/communication* The need for change is explained in a logical manner and persuasion is employed through the communication channels of the organization.

■ *Participation* We have covered this subject and so it suffices to say that discussion prior to decisions being made can only cement the actual changes being made.

■ *Support* Retraining and facilitation of change strategies can act as a supportive mechanism to negotiation.

So manipulation and coercion may work at least in the short term – but participation and negotiation with the positive supporting functions noted above are being advocated. Much of the change strategy relates to the style of management and to the quality of labour relations.

The 'traditionalist' type of management, in the words of Purcell and Sisson,[31] with an autocratic and more participative approach may force change but the human cost will be high. The 'sophisticated paternalists' may 'sell' change and the human cost will be mollified. The 'standard moderns' with their reactive and pragmatic approach would do well to follow the example of the 'sophisticated moderns' with their belief in bargaining and communication with trade unions and employees. A negotiated agreement has more chance of acceptance in the long term than some diktat from above.

We conclude this unit and the book by looking at quality, which goes to the heart of effective labour relations.

Quality and Labour Relations

We started this book by looking at predictive models of labour relations and by suggesting a framework for coming to terms with the subject. We have used this framework throughout the book. It is fitting to conclude by looking at the concept of quality in labour relations from the perspectives of the main parties to the system.

Briefly, the State could define a 'quality' labour relations system as one that contributed meaningfully to the economic well-being of the country, was not conflict-prone and allowed for differences within the body politic without actually challenging the State and its apparatus. As we have seen there are many philosophies and potentially contradictory roles of the State in labour relations so these would impact on the issue of quality. Measures of potential quality would include:

- contributions to the economic well-being of the country either through increased productivity or peace and harmony at the workplace;
- labour relations being politically correct with a focus on terms and conditions of work rather than a vehicle of revolutionary change;
- collective bargaining being seen as a useful mechanism of social control;
- a flexible workforce facilitating the competitive advantage of firms – if not the nation at large.

The primary parties' concept of quality in labour relations is probably more significant for our purposes.

From a managerial perspective we could adopt the '7S' approach:[32]

- Style – actors' approach
- Staff – employees (staff and manual workers)
- Structure – structure of bargaining
- Skills – interaction (includes skills/knowledge)

- Systems – processes of the labour relations systems
- Strategy – policy as it is *one* function of management
- Shared values – belief systems as they may be different

Although not intended for this use, the adaptation could give us some 'quality indicators'. Please see Box LR6.7.

BOX LR6.7

Indicators of managerial quality in labour relations

Actors' approach	The approach of the actors; the degree of openness, consultation or autocracy and diktat, etc.
Employees	How the staff feel about 'what goes on around here' in labour relations from promotion policies to manning levels.
Interaction	How the parties conduct themselves, e.g. in negotiations, at meetings from disciplinary sessions to everyday consultations.
Processes	The make-up of the negotiation process and the various levels/types of subject matter being discussed by whom can give a 'feel' to the overall labour relations system.
Policy	The coherence and consistency of strategies employed by the parties can give a good insight into the quality of the relationship.
Belief systems	Without accepting the unitarist vision, there is some need for coexistence, so the type/nature of conflicts may have some relevance from a manager's point of view.
Structure	The structure of bargaining, for example, must relate to and reflect the objectives of the actors.

At the end of the day, though, managers will see the organization as an economic being. Any labour relations system will be subordinate to this economic being. So managers will look to profitability, potential investment, cost reduction, utilization of other raw materials, consistent output, a quality service, and maximizing the use of labour. Perhaps they will be conscious of their media image in labour relations but this is way down the scale of priorities, for economics predominate.

The absence of conflict or at least its minimization would be the first base on quality labour relations for most managers. Efficiency, productivity, flexibility, cost reduction, etc. would follow. Perhaps a satisfied and motivated (not necessarily the same things) labour force would appear under this quality vision of some managers as well. The real crux is control, the ability of making events go to plan.

From the employees' perspective we could look to a range of satisfiers[33] from achievement to job restructuring. Yet control of their working lives should also figure large in any debate on quality in labour relations or the satisfaction of the parties with their lot in the system of labour relations. We now turn to the key aspect of control as so much of the quality of labour relations revolves around this issue.

Braverman[34] has had a considerable impact on discussions concerning the nature of contemporary work and the quality of work. This impacts on the quality of labour relations as well.

His core thesis is that there has been a continuous and inevitable deskilling of jobs in the twentieth century. Jobs are becoming more routinized and mechanical and all levels of work are becoming degraded.

Labour by definition according to Braverman is alienated and degraded by working within the current mode of production. The issues are wage slavery and the abolition of private property, for changes here will alter this inevitable alienation.

The market relationship is based on a calculation that encourages rationalism. Employers have the ultimate decision over what employees do at the place of work in the pursuit of profit. Consequently the role of management in labour relations is to maintain control. To Braverman there is an inevitable and ongoing decline in the worker's command over the labour process with an increasing command on the part of management. Labour power must not only be curbed but harnessed.

The basic method of control is a ruthless division of labour and task specialization. 'Scientific Management' is the epitome of this control as it is not a 'science of work' but a 'science of the management of others' work'. The aim is the control of alienated labour by the application of science. Management 'masquerading in the trappings of science' should dictate to the worker the precise manner in which work is to be performed. 'Systematic soldiering' has to be overcome by management. Workers, to Taylor,[35] are guilty of 'natural soldiering', taking it easy; and 'systematic soldiering', keeping employers ignorant of how fast the work could be done. Management has to gain knowledge over the job. Managers do not possess that knowledge so they must gain greater control over the workers who possess the knowledge. Please refer to Box LR6.8.

Taylor may be dead but Taylorism lives. Deskilling of craft-based work and the reduction of worker dignity are now immediate with longer lasting effects, according to Braverman. Now conception and execution are separated for 'the production units operate like a hand, watched, corrected and controlled by a distant brain'.

BOX LR6.8

Management control strategies

The principles include the following:

- A gathering of knowledge and reducing that workers' knowledge to rules, laws and formulae – hence less 'systematic soldiering' and more management control.
- A separation of 'conception' from 'execution' – hence deskilling, as all possible 'brain work' has to be removed from the shop and centred in the 'planning department'.
- Work should be allocated on the basis of task specialization. Hence a worker skilled in a specific area is being deskilled as he or she will be unskilled elsewhere.
- People are an appendage to machinery and any job challenges and initiative are to be removed.
- Work study should be used to facilitate tighter management control.
- Implicit is the hierarchy of responsibility with a co-ordination of activities and an integration of production.
- Incentive schemes, e.g. payments by results and performance-related pay(?).

Braverman adds that a paper replication of the production process occurs at HQ. So the conceptualization and control passes outside the workplace of the manual workers to the managers' offices and HQ. Inside the factory (and the office within the service sector), jobs are simplified beyond recognition. This lowering of the working class, according to Braverman, is even more marked as the base was essentially a higher, more dignified, total craft job.

To Braverman, Taylorism becomes the basis of future work organization for

> its fundamental teachings have become the bedrock of all work design.

Indeed, he argues that Taylorism has been the mainline management school shaping the modern corporation and other institutions. It has not been superseded by the human relations school or whatever and it has been consolidated as time has passed.

As for the employer, manipulation seems to predominate according to Braverman. The manipulation by labour relations experts and by business school sociologists and consultants is backed by powerful economic forces. If manipulation fails, coercion still remains.

If we take Braverman's full thesis on board, there is little room for quality in labour relations from the perspective of the worker.

Of course, many would dispute the thesis in whole or in part. We shall develop some of this important critique before we look at the implications on quality. (See Box LR6.9.)

BOX LR6.9

Critique of Braverman

Philosophy

The debate on skill involves a fundamental division over the nature of society. To one group the capitalist economy contains the seeds of its own destruction; to another there is a tradition of democracy which must be upheld.

If the latter view is taken, Braverman's premises are questioned.

Class and control

The class divisions are very rigid – perhaps too rigid, for the capitalist is to be treated as a class 'for itself' conscious of its economic interests and developed enough to conspire to develop these class interests. The working class is treated 'in itself' and not as a class 'for itself'.

These class definitions are over-rigid and inadequate. On one level a united management hating labour with a fetish for control over the work process is inadequate. Certainly control is there, but so is profit maximization and shrewd management will trade control for profit maximization. Having said this, control or degrees of control will assist profit maximization. Other managerial functions are given short change but control is certainly the dominant function.

Labour

This view of labour is quite static, reactive to forces and the pawns of capitalist fate. The trade union movement would indicate otherwise. Even if the organization were designed purely for return on capital employed, management does not always get its own way.

Friedman[1] has argued for the existence of opposition to management initiatives. Indeed, key industrial groups, according to Sayles,[2] can frustrate managerial initiatives and stimulate conflicts of interest. Trade unions are not adequately covered by Braverman.

Job content

Braverman tends to romanticize the origins of the craftsman. Clawson's[3] painstaking treatise on the rise of pre-capitalist work patterns in the USA from 1860 to 1920 shows a more complex picture. The 'inside contracting' is also picked by Hobsbawm.[4]

Taylorism

Braverman bases much of his thesis on the work of Taylor but he is less solid on the impact of Taylorism. Littler's[5] critique is that Taylorism involves the bureaucratization of the structure of control but not of the employment relationship *per se*. However, to a great extent Taylorism is a frame of reference, an ideology of management which may not be implemented in full. Perhaps Braverman is guilty of seeing capitalism and Taylorism as one.

Other managerial control methods

There are other managerial control methods which Braverman fails to take fully into account. Edwards,[6] for example, makes much of 'company unions' as rival power bases which could be manipulated. More importantly, welfarism coexists with Taylorism and arguably it was and is a 'softer' way of obtaining control. It has the benefit to management of not provoking opposition and of binding some unitarist vision of the workplace. This has been pursued by human resource management strategies as well in a later context.

Workers' control

Workers have their controls as well. Dubois[7] notes a range of informal control activities which he terms 'sabotage': machine smashing, arson, sabotaging the product, working to rule, labour turnover, working without enthusiasm, strikes, go slows and absence. This direct action which bypasses negotiation can be quite an effective method of revolt and a 'making out', or coping mechanism under this deskilled/dehumanized work.

Other forces

The other actors in the system, the State and trade unions, would also have to be added to the melting pot.

Sources:

1 Friedman, *Industry and Labour*
2 Sayles, *Behaviour of Industrial Work Groups*
3 Clawson, *Bureaucracy and the Labor Process*
4 Hobsbawm, *Labouring Men*
5 See Littler, 'Deskilling and changing structures of control'
6 Edwards, *Contested Terrain*
7 Dubois, *Sabotage in Industry*

This whole debate stimulated by Braverman goes to the heart of work and to the nature of quality within labour relations. As an ideology of work and as an attitude towards relations at work, Taylorism is still very much alive and kicking. Variants appear in the 1990s under different guises. So Braverman's analysis can be criticized, but the overall thesis looks to be particularly relevant to factory/process/clerical workers and perhaps less applicable – at least in their own minds – to professional/technical/managerial employees. From a managerial point of view, such Taylorite principles cannot lend themselves to a high quality environment of labour relations.

From a worker's perspective, as a minimum position, an end to this degradation of work and almost inevitable deskilling must be the first port of call for a quality environment. Informal workgroup controls, enhanced job skills, transferable knowledge and strong trade unions determined to push the 'frontier of control' are all strong elements of this 'quality'.

Please tackle Activity LR6.8.

ACTIVITY LR6.8

QUALITY, TECHNOLOGY AND LABOUR RELATIONS

Activity code

✓ Self-development
✓ Teamwork
✓ Communications
☐ Numeracy/IT
✓ Decisions

The gist of the lecture on quality, technology and labour relations went as follows.

The pace of industrial change goes on unabated. Forced by technological pressures, the impact on labour is immense. Some workers face redundancy, others are deskilled while only some have enhanced status. ... The evidence from the research seems to be divided into two schools – the optimists and the pessimists. Let us look at their views in a little detail.

I'm not going to give you a whole list of researchers and their studies. I will give you some of their findings though . . .

- In a steel-rolling mill, the rollerman had been highly skilled but the new automated process required little intervention.
- Others note that the operator becomes a fault finder and the job becomes more complex and interesting as a result. Yet control often goes to the instrumentation rather than the worker.
- A view has been presented stating that irrespective of the machine-paced technology we will still need technical experts, so jobs become enhanced not deskilled.
- Loss of autonomy through work variation and error tolerance levels was reported in white-collar jobs – alongside a greater opportunity for learning.
- Perceptual skills were heightened when manual jobs became automated in a factory power plant.
- 'Programmable' activities are taken over in another study while human decisions are still required to augment these activities.
- In British and French oil refineries, automation reduced the monotony, danger and dirt but it did not impact on the significance of the worker's life.
- A study of Canadian government employees estimated great job loss and jobs devoid of skill and personal initiative.
- In Germany a study of robots showed that the use of one robot eliminated two to three jobs.
- In the USA by the year 2000 terminals will probably be as commonplace on office desks as telephones are today.
- At a machine tool plant in Japan the entire operation of the factory from replacing worn tools to preparing financial statements is done automatically.

> So before we go into discussion groups, we as groups need to analyse the following:
>
> 1 whether we accept a pessimistic/optimistic view and why;
> 2 the implications for labour relations;
> 3 and the implications for the quality of labour relations ...
>
> **Task**
> Your task is to carry out the analysis outlined in points 1–3 above.

Workers cannot depend upon the existence of a liberal managerial regime to enhance this quality of labour relations. Trade unions exist by definition to protect and advance the interests of their members. A terminal decline in the trade union movement would leave workers open to the mercy of management. We have been here before and such a move, human resources management and paternalism apart, would lead us to the fruition of Braverman's thesis.

The neutrality of the State in labour relations cannot be taken as a 'given', while the media in the main has a clear and not very objective stance on the whole subject. So quality must be gauged by the two primary parties themselves.

We could look to their policies and respective views on the labour relations system. This gives us a Jack Barbash[36] type of approach, seeing the subject through the eyes of the actors.

Perhaps we need to stand back and attempt to take an objective stance as well concerning quality. It seems that there has to be some degree of even-handedness. The 'frontier' is always tilted towards the side of management, so curbs on pure managerial prerogative may be one test of quality.

A quality approach to labour relations must involve some redrawing of this 'frontier' which is being seriously tipped in favour of management in this period of the early 1990s throughout most of the Western world. The border has been drawn up by management and, at the time of writing, invasions seem to be a daily occurrence, while wholesale annexation seems to be happening in some cases.

If these invasions and annexations continue unabated and without real resistance, in the long term we shall have a quality of labour relations akin to a scenario between the abuses of a Dickens novel and the degradation inherent in Braverman's work.

So quality in labour relations must be gauged from the perspective of the primary parties. The management of effective labour relations has a key role in establishing and maintaining a system which not only institutionalizes conflict but enhances equity and fair-mindedness at the place of work. Of course, given management's role in the economic stewardship of the organization, it would be naive to suggest that managers abandon controls over labour. However, control over labour should not degenerate into some fetish, and the shrewd manager of labour will realize that motivation may look like the polar extreme of control, but in effect is a more productive form of managing people and is also on the same continuum as control. To reiterate, organized labour has also a key role to play, for workers cannot and should not depend upon finding a liberal managerial style in labour relations.

Notes

1. Tony Benn, Labour Party Politician in the UK. Quote not published.
2. Flanders, *Collective Bargaining: prescription for change.*
3. Towers et al., *Bargaining for Change.*
4. RCTUEA 'Productivity bargaining/restrictive labour practices'.
5. NBPI, 'Productivity and pay during the period of severe restraint'.
6. Ibid.
7. See Anderson and Barker who develop this argument in *Effective Business Policy.*
8. Fleeman and Thompson, *Productivity Bargaining: a practical guide.*
9. Curson, *Flexible Patterns of Work.*
10. Walker, 'Workers' participation in management: concepts and reality'.
11. Blumberg, *Industrial Democracy, the Sociology of Participation.*
12. Walker, 'Workers' participation in management: concepts and reality'.
13. Guest and Fatchett, *Worker Participation: individual control and performance.*
14. Poole, *Industrial Relations – Origins and Patterns of National Diversity.*
15. Marchington, 'Employee participation' and 'The four faces of employee consultation'.
16. Walker, 'Workers' participation in management: concepts and reality'.
17. Tannenbaum and Schmidt, 'How to choose a leadership pattern'.
18. Anderson, *Effective Personnel Management.*
19. See, for example, Anderson and Kyprianou, *Effective Organizational Behaviour.*
20. The work of Husband is very good on the relationships between the factors making up the payment scheme – see 'Payment structures made to measure'.
21. See Armstrong, *Handbook of Personnel Management.*
22. Murlis argues that 'the key to PRP is fair and consistent assessment'. See *Personnel Management Plus.*
23. Association of University and College Lecturers, *AUCL Bulletin.*
24. Institute of Personnel Management, *The IPM Equal Opportunities Code.*
25. Paddison, quoted in *Personnel Management Plus*, October 1992.
26. The TUC in the UK is particularly active in attempting to stamp out this unacceptable behaviour at work, and this view is indicative of the TUC's perspective.
27. Kessler and Bayliss, *Contemporary British Industrial Relations.*
28. Bennis, *Organisational Development: its nature, origins and prospects.*
29. Kotter and Schlesinger, 'Choosing strategies for change'.
30. Walton and McKersie, *A Behavioral Theory of Labor Negotiations.*
31. Purcell and Sisson, 'Strategies and practice in the management of industrial relations'.
32. The '7S' approach belongs to the McKinsey consultancy firm.
33. Herzberg et al., *The Motivation to Work*, epitomize this 'satisfier' thesis.
34. Braverman, *Labor and Monopoly Capital.*
35. Taylor, *Scientific Management.*
36. Barbash, *The Elements of Industrial Relations.*

Conclusion

To conclude, we started by examining the nature of labour relations and tried to demonstrate its importance to the various 'actors'. A system was put forward as a mechanism of understanding and analysing, if not predicting, the subject matter. It was argued that rules and conflict coexist in this dynamic 'frontier of control'.

The parties to the system were then studied in the next two units. The role of a pro-active management taking a pluralistic vision or a sophisticated modern approach was advocated. Trade unions were seen as a fundamental right of working people to form associations in a democratic state. The lack of value neutrality by the State and the mass media was noted.

Conflict is the dynamic of the process – if not of the wider society – so considerable time was spent examining the concept and its causation and a wider system was put forward. Accommodation and conflict resolution through institutions and processes followed in the next unit.

The final section dealt with some topical issues confronting the actors in this system of labour relations. It was argued that the 'frontier' has moved more in the direction of management, particularly when backed by the State and by the media whether unwittingly or not. But this is only a moment in time and the 'frontiers' are very fluid indeed. So far as the effective management of labour relations is concerned, the need for control must be tempered by the needs and wants of the employees. We do not need or want a demotivated cowed labour force responding grudgingly to an authoritarian anti-union management. In the interests of democracy at the workplace and of wider democracy, we must have active trade unions with active labour relations managers. In this book we have advocated this from the outset; at the end of the day the parties will have to live with one another but it should not be in some latter-day resurrection of the master–servant relationship.

To come full cycle, it is worth reiterating the shrewd words of the *Industrial Relations Code of Practice*[1] on effective labour relations from a manager's point of view:

1. *The principal aim of management is to conduct the business of the undertaking successfully. Good industrial relations need to be developed within the framework of an efficient organisation and they will in turn help management to achieve this aim.*

2. *One of management's major objectives should therefore be to develop effective industrial relations policies which command the confidence of employees. Managers at the highest level should*

give, and show that they give, just as much attention to industrial relations as to such functions as finance, marketing, production or administration.

3. *Good industrial relations are the joint responsibility of management and of employees and trade unions representing them. But the primary responsibility for their promotion rests with management. It should therefore take the initiative in creating and developing them.*

This book has attempted to take these principles on board. It has also focused not only on efficiency but on effectiveness in one of the most critical areas of management of the whole series.

Note

1   HMSO, *Industrial Relations Code of Practice.*

Bibliography and Further Reading

ACAS, 'Labour flexibility in Britain', *Occasional Paper 41* (ACAS, London, 1988).

Adams, A. and Bray, F., 'Holding out against workplace, harassment and bullying', *Personnel Management* (October 1992).

Adams, R.J., *Comparative Industrial Relations* (Harper Collins Academic, New York, 1991).

Addison, J.T., 'Whatever happened to productivity bargaining?', *Management Decision*, 13, 5 (1975).

Albrow, M., 'The study of organisations – objectivity or bias?', in *Social Sciences*, ed. J. Gould (Penguin, Harmondsworth, 1968).

Allen, V.L., 'Marxism and the personnel manager', *Personnel Management* (December 1976).

Allen, V.L., *The Sociology of Industrial Relations: studies in method* (Longman, London, 1971).

Allen, V.L., 'Trade unionism, an analytical framework', in *Industrial Relations and the Wider Society*, eds B. Arret, E.D. Rhodes and J. Beishan (Collier Macmillan for Oxford University Press, London, 1975).

Anderson, A.H., 'A study into the managerial control of labour disputes – the roles of negotiation, sanctions, overt threats and procedure in the process of disputes accommodation', Unpublished thesis (*The Management College*, Henley, 1983).

Anderson, A.H., *Effective General Management* (Blackwell, Oxford, 1994).

Anderson, A.H., *Effective Personnel Management* (Blackwell, Oxford, 1994).

Anderson, A.H. and Barker, D., *Effective Business Policy* (Blackwell, Oxford, 1994).

Anderson, A.H. and Barker, D., *Effective Enterprise Management* (Blackwell, Oxford, 1994).

Anderson, A.H. and Ciechan, R., *Effective Financial Management* (Blackwell, Oxford, 1994).

Anderson, A.H. and Dobson, T., *Effective Marketing* (Blackwell, Oxford, 1994).

Anderson, A.H., Dobson, T. and Patterson, J., *Effective International Marketing* (Blackwell, Oxford, 1994).

Anderson, A.H. and Kleiner, D., *Effective Marketing Communications* (Blackwell, Oxford, 1994).

Anderson, A.H. and Kyprianou, A., *Effective Organizational Behaviour* (Blackwell, Oxford, 1994).

Anderson, A.H. and Nix, E., *Effective Accounting Management* (Blackwell, Oxford, 1994).

Anderson, A.H. and Woodcock, P., *Effective Entrepreneurship* (Blackwell, Oxford, 1994).

Anthony, P., *The Conduct of Industrial Relations* (IPM, London, 1977).

Anthony, P., *The Ideology of Work* (Tavistock, London, 1977).

Argyris, C., *Personality and Organisation: the conflict between system and the individual* (Harper and Row, New York, 1965).

Armstrong, M., *Handbook of Personnel Management* (Kogan Page, London, 1991).

Armstrong, M., 'HRM: a case of the emperor's new clothes?', *Personnel Management* (August 1987).

Armstrong, M. and Murlis, H., *Reward Management* (Kogan Page, London, 1991, 2nd edn).

Ash, P., 'The parties to the grievance', *Personnel Psychology*, 23 (1970).

Association of University and College Lecturers, *AUCL Bulletin*, Special Issue on PRP, Spring 1993.

Atkinson, G.M., 'Bargaining: the rules of the game', *Personnel Management* (February 1976).

Atkinson, G.M., *The Effective Negotiator* (Quest Research Publications, London, 1977).

Atkinson, J. and Meager, J., 'Is flexibility just a flash in the pan?', *Personnel Management* (September 1986).

Bain, G.S. and Price, R.J., 'Union growth: dimensions, determinants and destiny', in *Industrial Relations in Britain*, ed. G.S. Bain (Blackwell, Oxford, 1983).

Bain, G.S. and Price, R.J., 'Who is a white collar employee?', *British Journal of Industrial Relations*, 10 (1972).

Baldamus, W., *Efficiency and Effort* (Tavistock, London, 1961).

Barbash, J., *The Elements of Industrial Relations* (University of Wisconsin Press, Madison, Wis., 1984).

Batstone, E., Boraston, J. and Frenkel, S., *Shop Stewards in Action, the Organisation of Workplace Conflict and Accommodation* (Blackwell, Oxford, 1977).

Beal, E.F. and Begin, J.P., *The Practice of Collective Bargaining* (Irwin, Homewood, Ill., 1982, 6th edn).

Beharrell, P. and Philo, G., *Trade Unions and the Media* (Macmillan, London, 1977).

Behrend, H., 'Why so much fuss about industrial relations?', *Industrial Relations Journal*, 8, 4 (1977–8).

Bendix, R., *Work and Authority in Industry – ideologies of management in the course of industrialisation* (Harper and Row, New York, 1963).

Bennis, W.G., *Organisational Development: its nature, origins and prospects* (Addison Wesley, Reading, Mass., 1969).

Bierstedt, R., 'An analysis of social power', *American Sociological Review*, 15 (1950), pp. 730–8.

Blackburn, A.M., *Union Character and Social Class* (Batsford, London, 1967).

Blackburn, R. and Prandy, K., 'White collar unionisation: a conceptual framework', *British Journal of Sociology* (June 1965).

Blain, A.N.J. and Gennard, J., 'IR theory – a critical review', *British Journal of Industrial Relations* (November 1974).

Blake, R.R., Shepherd, H.A. and Mouton, J.S., *Managing Intergroup Conflict in Industry* (Gulf Publishing, Houston, Tex., 1964).

Blaumer, R., *Alienation and Freedom* (University of Chicago, Chicago, Ill., 1964).

Blum, A.A., *International Handbook of Industrial Relations: contemporary developments and research* (Greenwood Press, Westpoint, Conn., 1981).

Blumberg, P., *Industrial Democracy, the Sociology of Participation* (Constable, London, 1968).

Bramham, J., *Human Resource Planning* (IPM, London, 1990).

Bramham, J., *Practical Manpower Planning* (IPM, London, 1982).

Braverman, H., *Labor and Monopoly Capital* (Monthly Review Press, New York, 1974).

Brown, R.K., *Understanding Industrial Organisations – theoretical perspectives in industrial sociology* (Routledge, London, 1992).

Burnham, J., *The Managerial Revolution, What is Happening in the World* (John Day, New York, 1941).

Business Technician and Education Council (BTEC), 'Common skills and experience of BTEC programmes' (BTEC, London, n.d.).

Cadbury, A., 'The 1980's: a watershed for British industrial relations', Annual Hitachi Lecture, IMS, University of Sussex, Brighton, March 1986.

Cameron, G.C., 'Post-war strikes in the North East shipbuilding and ship repairing industry', *British Journal of Industrial Relations*, 2, 1 (1964).

Chamberlain, N.W., *Collective Bargaining* (McGraw-Hill, New York, 1951).

Chamberlain, N.W. and Kuhn, J.W., *Collective Bargaining* (McGraw-Hill, New York, 1965).

CIR, 'Facilities afforded to shop stewards', *CIR 17* (CIR, London, 1971).

Clawson, D., *Bureaucracy and the Labor Process* (Monthly Review Press, New York, 1980).

Clegg, H.A., *How to Run an Incomes Policy and Why We Made Such a Mess of the Last One* (Heinemann, London, 1971).

Clegg, H.A., *The Changing System of Industrial Relations in Great Britain* (Blackwell, Oxford, 1979).

Coser, L.A., 'Social aspects of conflict', in *International Encyclopedia of the Social Sciences* (Macmillan, New York, 1968).

Coser, L.A., *The Functions of Social Conflict* (Routledge and Kegan Paul, London, 1956).

Cowan, L.D., 'A pay policy for all time', *Personnel Management* (June 1978).

Croner Employer's Briefing, 'Employee benefits', 21 January 1992.

Croner Employer's Briefing, 'Performance management', 20 October 1992.

Crouch, C., *The Politics of Industrial Relations* (Fontana, London, 1979).

Curson, C. (ed.), *Flexible Patterns of Work* (IPM, London, 1986).

Dahl, R., 'The concept of power', *Behavioural Science*, 2 (1957).

Dahrendorf, R., *Class and Class Conflict in Industrial Society* (Routledge and Kegan Paul, London, 1959).

Department of Employment, 'Distribution and concentration of industrial stoppages in Great Britain', *Department of Employment Gazette* (HMSO, London, November 1976).

Department of Employment, *Industrial Relations Code of Practice* (HMSO, London, 1972).

Department of Employment, 'Large industrial stoppages, 1960–1979', *Department of Employment Gazette* (HMSO, London, September 1980).

Department of Employment, *Sexual Harassment in the Workplace: a guide for employers* (HMSO, London, 1992).

Department of Employment, 'Tables on strike incidence, British strike statistics and patterns of strike activity', *Department of Employment Gazette* (HMSO, London, July 1989).

Department of Employment, 'The incidence of industrial stoppages in the UK', *Department of Employment Gazette* (HMSO, London, February 1976).

Dubin, R., 'Constructive aspects of conflict', in *Collective Bargaining*, ed. A. Flanders (Penguin, Harmondsworth, 1969).

Dubin, R., 'Power and union management relations', *Administration Science Quarterly*, 2 (June 1957).

Dubois, P., *Sabotage in Industry* (Calmann-Levy, Paris, 1976) (translation).

Dunlop, J.T., *Industrial Relations Systems* (Holt, New York, 1958).

Dyar, D.A., 'Analysis of negotiation, interaction, and behaviour', *Industrial Relations Journal*, 8, 4 (Winter 1977–8).

Edwards, R., *Contested Terrain* (Heinemann, London, 1979).

Eldridge, J.E.T., *Industrial Disputes* (Routledge and Kegan Paul, London, 1968).

Equal Opportunities Review, 'Sexual harassment: an organisational challenge', *Equal Opportunities Review*, 36 (March–April 1991).

Farnham, D. and Pimlott, J., *Understanding Industrial Relations* (Cassell, London, 1990, 4th edn).

Flanders, A., 'Collective bargaining: a theoretical approach', *British Journal of Industrial Relations* (March 1968).

Flanders, A., *Collective Bargaining: prescription for change* (Faber and Faber, London, 1967).

Flanders, A., *Industrial Relations: what is wrong with the system* (Faber and Faber, London, 1965).

Flanders, A., *Management and Unions* (Faber and Faber, London, 1970).

Flanders, A., *Trade Unions* (Hutchison, London, 1968, 7th revised edn).

Fleeman, R.K. and Thompson, A.G., *Productivity Bargaining: a practical guide* (Butterworth, London, 1970).

Fossum, J.A., *Labor Relations: development, structure, process* (Business Publications, Dallas, Tex., 1982).

Fowler, A., 'When Chief Executives discover HRM', *Personnel Management* (January 1987).

Fox, A., *Beyond Contract: work, power and trust relations* (Faber and Faber, London, 1974).

Fox, A., 'Coming to terms with conflict', *Personnel Management* (June 1972).

Fox, A., 'Industrial sociology and industrial relations', RCTUEA Research Paper 3 (HMSO, London, 1966).

French, J.R.P. and Raven, B.H., 'The bases of social power', in *Studies in Social Power*, ed. D. Cartwright (University of Michigan, Ann Arbor, Mich., 1959).

Friedman, A., *Industry and Labour* (Macmillan, London, 1977).

Friedmann, C., *The Anatomy of Work* (Heinemann, London, 1961).

Glasgow University Media Group, *Bad News* (Routledge and Kegan Paul, London, 1976).

Glasgow University Media Group, *More Bad News* (Routledge and Kegan Paul, London, 1977).

Glasgow University Media Group, *More Bad News Vol. 2* (Routledge and Kegan Paul, London, 1980).

Goodman, J.F.B. and Whittingham, T.G., *Shop Stewards in British Industry* (McGraw-Hill, Maidenhead, 1969).

Goodrich, C., *The Frontier of Control* (Bell, London, 1920; Pluto Press, London, 1975).

Gouldner, A.W., *Wildcat Strike – a study in worker–management relationships* (Harper and Row, New York, 1954).

Greenhill, R.T., *Performance Related Pay for the 1990's* (Director Books, Cambridge, 1990, 2nd edn).

Greiner, L.E., 'Evolution and revolution as organisations grow', *Harvard Business Review* (July–August 1972).

Guardian, quotation on unions derived from *The London Evening Standard*, 16 April 1993.

Guest, D. and Fatchett, D., *Worker Participation: individual control and performance* (IPM, London, 1974).

Hanson, C., Jackson, S. and Miller, D., *The Closed Shop: a comparative study in public policy and trade union security in Britain, the USA and W. Germany* (Gower, Aldershot, 1982).

Hawkins, K., *Conflict and Change – aspects of industrial relations* (Holt, Rinehart and Winston, London, 1972).

Hawkins, K., *The Managers of Industrial Relations* (Penguin, Harmondsworth, 1978).

Herzberg, F., Mausner, B. and Snyderman, B., *The Motivation to Work* (Wiley, New York, 1959).

Hobsbawm, E.J., *Labouring Men: studies in the history of labour* (Weidenfeld and Nicolson, London, 1964).

Human Resources, 'Benefit matches', *Human Resources* (December 1991).

Husband, T., 'Payment structures made to measure', *Personnel Management* (April 1975).

Hyman, R., *Dispute Procedures in Action – a study of the engineering industry disputes procedure in Coventry* (Heinemann, London, 1972).

Hyman, R., *Industrial Relations: a Marxist introduction* (Macmillan, London, 1975).

Hyman, R., *Strikes* (Fontana, Glasgow, 1975).

Hyman, R., 'Trade unions, control and resistance', Open University, DE 351 Unit 14 (Open University Press, Milton Keynes, 1976).

IDS, 'A study of annual hours', Study 486, July 1991.

IDS, 'Company councils', Study 437, July 1989.

IDS, 'Flexibility in the 1990's', Study 454, March 1990.

IDS, 'Profit sharing and share options', Study 468, October 1990.

IDS, 'Sharing productivity gains', Study 443, October 1989.

IDS, 'The background to teamworking', Study 419, October 1988.

ILO, 'Examination of grievances and communications within the undertaking', *Labour Conference Report*, 7, 1 (ILO, Geneva, 1965).

IMS, 'Introducing flexible benefits: the other side of the coin', IMS Report 231 (IMS, Brighton, 1992).

Industrial Relations Briefing, 'Combating sexual harassment and protecting the dignity of women and men at work: a code of practice', *Industrial Relations Briefing*, 17 (January 1992).

Institute of Personnel Management, *Practical Participation and Involvement* (IPM, London, in five volumes: *Communication in practice*, 1981; *Representative Structures*, 1981; *The Individual and The Job*, 1982; *Meeting Educating and Training Needs*, 1982; *Pay and Benefits*, 1982).

Institute of Personnel Management, *the IPM Equal Opportunities Code* (IPM, London, 1986).

IRRR, 'Nissan: a catalyst for change', *IRRR 379*, 4 November 1986.

IRS Employment Trends, 'Restructuring terms and conditions for British Gas', Study 503, January 1992.

IRS Employment Trends, 'Unions and productivity under scrutiny', Study 468, July 1990.

Jackson, M. and Leopold, J., 'Casting off from national negotiations', *Personnel Management* (April 1990).

Jacques, E., *Equitable Payment* (Heinemann, London, 1961).

Jennings, S. and Undy, R., 'Auditing managers' IR training needs', *Personnel Management* (February 1984).

Jennings, S., McCarthy, W.E.J. and Undy, R., *Managers and Industrial Relations: the identification of training needs* (Manpower Services Commission, Sheffield, 1983).

Jones, J.A.G., 'Training intervention strategies', ITS Monograph no. 2 (Industrial Training Service Ltd., London, 1983).

Kamata, S., 'Diary of a human robot', *The Sunday Times*, 17 April 1983.

Karrass, C.C., *The Negotiating Game* (World Publishing, New York and Cleveland, Ohio, 1970).

Kerr, C. and Siegal, A., 'The inter-industry propensity to strike – an international comparison', in *Industrial Conflict*, eds A. Kornhauser, R. Dubin and A.M. Ross (McGraw-Hill, New York, 1954).

Kessler, S., MBA Seminar, 'Incomes policies', City University Business School, 1983.

Kessler, S., 'The prevention and settlement of collective labour disputes in the UK', *Industrial Relations Journal*, 2, 1 (1980).

Kessler, S. and Bayliss, F., *Contemporary British Industrial Relations* (Macmillan, London, 1992).

Knowles, K.G.J.C., *Strikes: a study in industrial conflict* (Blackwell, Oxford, 1952).

Koontz, H. and O'Donnell, C., *Principles of Management: an analysis of managerial functions* (McGraw-Hill, Maidenhead, 1968).

Koontz, H., O'Donnell, C., and Weihrich, H., *Management* (McGraw-Hill, Maidenhead, 1980, 7th edn).

Kornhauser, A., Dubin, R. and Ross, A., *Industrial Conflict* (McGraw-Hill, New York, 1954).

Kotter, J.P. and Schlesinger, L.A., 'Choosing strategies for change', *Harvard Business Review* (March–April 1979).

Kuhn, J.W., *Bargaining in Grievance Settlement* (Columbia University Press, New York, 1961).

Labour Relations Agency, *The Consultative Draft Code of Practice in Northern Ireland* (*Labour Relations Agency*, Belfast, n.d.).

Labour Research Department, 'HRM – human resource manipulation', *Labour Research*, London (August 1989).

Laffer, K., 'Is industrial relations an academic discipline', *Journal of Industrial Relations* 16, 1 (1974).

Lawshe, C.H. and Guion, R.M., 'A comparison of management labor attitudes towards grievance procedures', *Personnel Psychology*, 4 (1951).

Lewis, P., 'Employee participation in a Japanese owned British electronics factory: reality or symbolism', *Employee Relations*, 11, 1 (1989).

Lewis, R., 'The historical development of labour law', *British Journal of Industrial Relations*, 14, 1 (March 1976).

Likert, R., *New Patterns of Management* (McGraw-Hill, New York, 1961).

Littler, C.R., 'Deskilling and changing structures of control', in *The Degradation of Work*, ed. S. Wood (Hutchison, London, 1982).

Littler, C.R., *The Development of the Labour Process in Capitalist Societies* (Heinemann, London, 1982).

Livy, B., *Job Evaluation, A Critical Review* (Allen and Unwin, London, 1975).

Lloyd, J., 'Can the unions survive?', *Personnel Management* (September 1987).

Lovell, J. and Roberts, B.C., *A Short History of the TUC* (Macmillan, London, 1968).

MacGregor, I. and Tyler, R., *The Enemies Within: the story of the miner's strike 1984–5* (Collins, London, 1986).

Management Charter Initiative (MCI), *Diploma Level Guidelines* (MCI, London, n.d.).

Mann, M., *Consciousness and Action Among the Western Working Class* (Macmillan, London, 1973).

March, J.G. and Simon, H.A., *Organisations* (Wiley, New York, 1958).

Marchington, M., 'Employee participation', in *Handbook of Industrial Relations Practice: practice and the law in the employee relationship*, ed. B. Towers (Kogan Page, Maidenhead, 1981).

Marchington, M., *Managing Industrial Relations* (McGraw-Hill, Maidenhead, 1982).

Marchington, M., 'The four faces of employee consultation', *Personnel Management* (May 1988).

Margerison, C.J., 'What do we mean by industrial relations? A behavioural science approach', *British Journal of Industrial Relations*, 7, 2 (1969).

Marsden, R., 'Industrial relations: a critique of empiricism', *Sociology, The Journal of the British Sociological Association*, 16, 2 (May 1982).

Marsh, A.I., 'Disputes procedures in British industry', RCTUEA Research Paper 2, Part 1 (HMSO, London, 1966).

Marsh, A.I., 'Engineering procedure and central conference at York in 1959', *British Journal of Industrial Relations* (July 1964).

Marsh, A.I. and McCarthy, W.E.J., 'Disputes procedures in Britain', RCTUEA Research Paper 2, Part 3 (HMSO, London, 1968).

Marx, K. and Engels, F., *Manifesto of the Communist Party* (Progress Publishers, Moscow, 1967; translation of 1888 edn).

McCarthy, W.E.J., 'The nature of Britain's strike problem', *British Journal of Industrial Relations* (July 1964).

McCarthy, W.E.J., *Trade Unions* (Penguin, Harmondsworth, 1972).

McCarthy, W.E.J. and Parker, S.R., *Shop Stewards and Workshop Relations – results of a study of the Government Social Study on the RCTUEA* (HMSO, London, 1968).

McKersie, R.B. and Hunter, L.C., *Pay, Productivity and Collective Bargaining* (Macmillan, London, 1973).

Megginson, L.C. and Gullett, C.R., 'A predictive model of union–management conflict', *Personnel Journal* (June 1970).

Metcalf, D., 'Can the closed shop ban open new doors for unions?', *Personnel Management* (September 1989).

Mills, D.Q., *Labour–Management Relations* (McGraw-Hill, New York, 1982, 2nd edn).

Ministry of Labour, *Handbook of Industrial Relations* (HMSO, London, 1961).

Murlis, H. and Wright, V., 'Decentralising pay decisions: empowerment or abdication', *Personnel Management* (March 1993).

Nagel, J.H., 'Some questions about the concept of power', *Behavioural Science*, 13 (1968).

NALGO, *Benefit of Union Membership – a discussion document* (NALGO, London, January 1985).

NATFHE, *Performance Related Pay* (NATFHE, London, October 1992).

NBPI (National Board for Prices and Incomes), 'Productivity and pay during the period of severe restraint', Report 23 (HMSO, London, 1966).

NEDO (National Economic Development Office), *Changing Working Patterns: how companies achieve flexibility to meet new needs* (NEDO/Department of Employment, London, 1986).

NEDO/MSC (Manpower Services Commission), *Competence and Competition, Training and Education in the Federal Republic of Germany, the United States and Japan* (NEDO/MSC, London, 1984).

O'Brien, R., 'Points of procedure', *Personnel Management* (August 1972).

Oldfield, F.E., *New Look Industrial Relations* (Mason Reed, London, 1966).

O'Toole, B.J., *Private Gain and Public Service – the Association of First Division Civil Servants* (Routledge, London, 1989).

Panitch, C., 'Recent theorisations on corporatism: reflections of a growth industry', *British Journal of Sociology*, 31, 2 (1980).

Parker, S.R. and Scott, M.H., 'Developing models of workplace industrial relations', *British Journal of Industrial Relations* (July 1971).

Parsons, T., *Essays in Sociological Theory* (Collier Macmillan, London, 1960).

Parsons, T., *The Social System* (Routledge and Kegan Paul, London, 1951).

Parsons, T., *Structure and Process in Modern Societies* (Free Press, Chicago, Ill., 1960).

Pascale, R.T. and Athos, A.G., *The Art of Japanese Management* (Penguin, Harmondsworth, 1986).

Peach, D. and Livernash, E.R., *Grievance Initiation and Resolution: a study in basic steel* (Harvard University Press, Cambridge, Mass., 1974).

Pelling, H., *A History of British Trade Unionism* (Penguin, Harmondsworth, 1963).

Perlman, S., *A Theory of the Labor Movement* (Kelley, New York, 1949).

Personnel Management, 'Report on PRP' (IPM, London, October 1991).

Personnel Management Plus, article on harassment citing L. Paddison (IPM, London, October 1992).

Personnel Management Plus, 'Hidden inflation in skills based pay' (IPM, London, February 1993).

Personnel Management Plus, 'Key to PRP is "fair and consistent assessment"' (IPM, London, April 1993).

Personnel Management Plus, 'Merit scheme does not work' (IPM, London, October, 1991).

Personnel Management Plus, 'New report underlines need for careful planning in introducing skills-based pay' (IPM, London, December 1992).

Personnel Management Plus, quoting J. Foulds, Director of Employment Affairs, Chemical Industries Association (IPM, London, January 1993).

Personnel Today, 'Serious approach to those unwelcome advances at work', 5 April 1988.

Pollert, A. (ed.), *Farewell to Flexibility* (Blackwell, Oxford, 1991).

Poole, M., *Industrial Relations – origins and patterns of national diversity* (Routledge and Kegan Paul, London, 1986).

Poole, M., *Workers' Participation in Industry* (Routledge and Kegan Paul, London, 1978).

Price, R. and Bain, G.S., 'Union growth in Britain: retrospect and prospect', *British Journal of Industrial Relations*, 21, 1 (1983).

Purcell, J., 'The management of industrial relations in the modern corporation: agenda for research', *Journal of Industrial Relations*, 25, 2 (June 1983).

Purcell, J. and Earle, M.J., 'Control systems and industrial relations', *Industrial Relations Journal*, 8, 2 (1977).

Purcell, J. and Sisson, K., 'Strategies and practice in the management of industrial relations', in *Industrial Relations in Britain*, ed. G.S. Bain (Blackwell, Oxford, 1983).

Rackham, N. and Carlisle, J., 'The effective negotiator, the behaviour of successful negotiators', parts I and II, *Journal of European Industrial Training*, 2, 6–7 (1978).

Rackham, N. and Morgan, T., *Behavioural Analysis in Training* (McGraw-Hill, London, 1977).

RCTUEA (Royal Commission in Trade Unions and Employer Associations), 'Productivity bargaining/restrictive labour practices', Research paper 4 (HMSO, London, 1967).

RCTUEA, *Report 1965–1968*, Cmnd 3623 (HMSO, London, 1968).

Read, S., *Sexual Harassment at Work: is it just 'fun and games'?* (Hamlyn, Middlesex, 1992).

Reeves, T.K., 'Constrained and facilitated behaviour – a typology of behaviour in economic organizations', *British Journal of Industrial Relations*, 5, 2 (1967).

Rhys, D., 'Employment, efficiency and labour relations in the British motor industry', *Industrial Relations Journal*, 5, 2 (1974).

Roberts, B.C. (ed.), *Industrial Relations: Contemporary Problems and Perspectives* (Methuen, London, 1962).

Rose, E., 'Work control in industrial society', *Industrial Relations Journal*, 7, 3 (1976).

Ross, A., *Distressed Grievance Procedures and Their Rehabilitation*, reprint (Institute of Industrial Relations, University of California, Berkeley, 1963).

Roy, D.R., 'Banana time – job satisfaction and informal interaction', *Human Organisation*, 18 (1960).

Roy, D.R., 'Quota restriction and goldbricking in a machine shop', *American Journal of Sociology*, 57, 5 (1952).

Rubenstein, M., 'Devising a sexual harassment policy', *Personnel Management* (February 1991).

Salaman, M., *Industrial Relations – theory and practice* (Prentice Hall, Hemel Hempstead, 1992).

Samuelson, P., *Economics* (McGraw-Hill, New York, 1967).

Sayles, L.B., *Behaviour of Industrial Work Groups* (Wiley, New York, 1958).

Schelling, T.C., *The Strategy of Conflict* (Harvard University Press, Cambridge, Mass., 1960).

Seaton, J., 'Trade unions and the media', in *Trade Unions in British Politics*, eds B. Pimlott and C. Cook (Longman, Harlow, 1982).

Sherman, B., 'The role of procedure agreements', *Industrial Relations Review and Report*, 54 (April 1973).

Shils, E., 'Center and periphery', *Essays in Macrosociology* (University of Chicago Press, Chicago, Ill., 1975).

Singleton, N., *Industrial Relations Procedures*, Department of Education Manpower Papers 14 (HMSO, London, 1975).

Somers, G.G. (ed.), *Collective Bargaining: contemporary American experience* (IR Research Association, Madison, Wis., 1980).

Somers, G.G., *Essays in Industrial Relations Theory* (University of Iowa, Iowa City, Iowa, 1969).

Spoor, A., *White Collar Union: 60 years of NALGO* (Heinemann, London, 1967).

Stagner, H. and Rosen, H., *Psychology and Union Management Relations* (Tavistock, London, 1965).

Stieber, J., 'Grievance arbitration in the United States', RCTUEA Research Paper 8 (HMSO, London, 1967).

Stoner, J.A.F. and Wankel, C., *Management* (Prentice Hall, Englewood Cliffs, N.J. 1986).

Storey, J., 'Developments in the management of human resources: an interim report', *Warwick Papers in Industrial Relations*, 17 (November 1987).

Storey, J., *Managerial Prerogative and the Question of Control* (Routledge and Kegan Paul, London, 1983).

Storey, J., 'Workplace collective bargaining and managerial prerogatives', *Industrial Relations Journal*, 7, 3 (1976–7).

Sulkin, H. and Pranis, R., 'Comparison of grievants and non-grievants in a heavy machinery company', *Personnel Psychology*, 20 (1967).

Swingle, P., *The Structure of Conflict* (Academic Press, New York, 1970).

Training Commission/Council for Management Education (CMED), 'Classifying the components of management competencies' (Training Commission, London, 1988).

Tannenbaum, A.S., *Control in Organisations* (McGraw-Hill, New York, 1968).

Tannenbaum, R. and Schmidt, H.W., 'How to choose a leadership pattern', *Harvard Business Review* (March–April 1958).

Taylor, F.W., *Scientific Management* (Harper, New York, 1947).

Taylor, R., *The Fifth Estate* (Pan, London, 1978).

Teasdale, A., 'The paradoxes of Japanese success', *Personnel Management* (November 1981).

Tedeschi, J.T., 'Threats and promises', in *The Structure of Conflict*, ed. P. Swingle (Academic Press, New York, 1970).

Thomson, A. and Murray, V., *Grievance Procedures* (Heath, Farnborough, 1976).

Thompson, E.P., 'Time, work discipline and industrial capitalism', *Past and Present*, 38 (1967).

Timperley, S.R., 'Organisation strategies and industrial relations', *Industrial Relations Journal*, 2, 5 (1980).

Torrington, D. and Hall, L., *Personnel Management: a new approach* (Prentice Hall, Hemel Hempstead, 1987).

Towers, B. (ed.), *A Handbook of Industrial Relations Practice: practice and the law in employment relationship* (Kogan Page, London, 1989).

Towers, B., 'British incomes policy', *Occasional Papers in Industrial Relations* (Universities of Leeds and Nottingham and IPM, 1978).

Towers, B., Whittingham, T.G. and Gottschalk, A. (eds). *Bargaining for Change* (Allen and Unwin, London, 1972).

TUC (Trades Union Congress) 'Evidence to the Royal Commission on Trade Unions and Employer Associations' (HMSO, London, Reported 1968).

Turner, H., *Labour Relations in the Motor Industry* (Allen and Unwin, London, 1967).

Turner, H., *Trade Union Growth, Structure and Policy. A comparative study of certain unions* (Allen and Unwin, London, 1962).

Tweedie, D.P., 'Management's changing attitudes towards inflation 1968–1975', *Industrial Relations Journal*, 7, 1 (Spring 1976).

Viteles, M.S., *Motivation and Morale in Industry* (Steeple Press, London, 1954).

Walker, K.F., 'Workers' participation in management: concepts and reality', in *Industrial Relations and the Wider Society*, eds B. Barrett, E. Rhodes and J. Beishen (Open University, Milton Keynes, 1975).

Walton, R.E. and McKersie, R.B., *A Behavioral Theory of Labor Negotiations* (McGraw-Hill, New York, 1965).

Warner, M., 'Workplace participation and employee influence: a study of managers and shop stewards', *Industrial Relations Journal*, 13, 4 (1982).

Warren, A., 'The challenge from below: an analysis of the role of the shop steward in industrial relations', *Industrial Relations Journal* (Autumn 1971).

Webb, S. and Webb, B., *History of Trade Unionism* (Longman, London, 1896).

Webb, S. and Webb, B., *Industrial Democracy* (published by the authors, 1898).

Weber, M., *The Theory of Social and Economic Organisation* (Oxford University Press, Oxford, 1947).

Wickens, P., *The Road to Nissan, Flexibility, Quality, Teamwork* (Macmillan, London, 1987).

Winkler, J.T., 'The ghost at the bargaining table: directors and industrial relations', 12, 2 (1974).

Wood, J., 'The case for arbitration', *Personnel Management* (October 1980).

Wood, S., 'Ideology in I.R. theory', *Industrial Relations Journal*, 9, 4 (1978–9).

Woodward, J., *Industrial organisation – theory and practice* (Oxford University Press, Oxford, 1965).

Zimmerman, C., 'The practicalities of rule use', in *Understanding Everyday Life: towards the reconstruction of sociological knowledge*, ed. J. Douglas (Routledge and Kegan Paul, London, 1971).

Index